AVALON
WITHIN

About the Author

Jhenah Telyndru, who has been called "the mother of the Avalonian revival" by *PanGaia*'s Elizabeth Barrette, developed the Avalonian Tradition and has been teaching it for more than two decades. She is the founder and Morgen of the Sisterhood of Avalon, an international Celtic women's mysteries organization that has served thousands of women since 1995. Jhenah also serves as Director of the Avalonian Thealogical Seminary, teaches Avalonian intensive workshops around North America, and facilitates pilgrimages to sacred sites in the British Isles. Visit her online at www.ynysafallon.com.

To Write to the Author

If you wish to contact the author or would like more information about this book, please write to the author in care of Llewellyn Worldwide and we will forward your request. Both the author and publisher appreciate hearing from you and learning of your enjoyment of this book and how it has helped you. Llewellyn Worldwide cannot guarantee that every letter written to the author can be answered, but all will be forwarded. Please write to:

Jhenah Telyndru
^c/o Llewellyn Worldwide
2143 Wooddale Drive
Woodbury, MN 55125-2989

Please enclose a self-addressed stamped envelope for reply, or $1.00 to cover costs. If outside the U.S.A., enclose an international postal reply coupon.

Many of Llewellyn's authors have websites with additional information and resources. For more information, please visit our website at

www.llewellyn.com

AVALON
WITHIN

A SACRED JOURNEY
OF MYTH, MYSTERY, AND INNER WISDOM

JHENAH TELYNDRU

Llewellyn Publications
Woodbury, Minnesota

First Edition, 2005
BookSurge Publishing

Second Edition
First Printing, 2010

Cover design by Kevin R. Brown
Cover painting from Tate Gallery, London/ET Archive, London/SuperStock;
    Celtic designs from iStockphoto.com/Michael Platt, Ronald Carlucci, Trudy Karl
Celtic knotwork design on pages 7, 21, 37, 67, 87, 107, 129, 149, 171, 195, 215, 231, and
    251 from *159 Celtic Designs* by Amy Lusebrink (Dover Publications).
Editing by Laura Graves
Interior illustrations on pages 10, 61, 113, 122, 124, 237, and 274 by Llewellyn art
    department
Classical Labyrinth Seed Pattern: ("How to Draw a Seven Circuit Labyrinth" on page
    124) from *Labyrinths—Ancient Myths & Modern Uses*, Sig Lonegren, 1991: © Jeff
    Saward/Labyrinthos, adapted by the Llewellyn art department
Plan of Glastonbury Tor Labyrinth (page 113) from *In the Nature of Avalon* by Kathy
    Jones, Ariadne Publications, adapted by the Llewellyn art department
Photos on pages 204–210 by Jocelyn A.E. Russell
Photo of Glastonbury Abbey on page 7 of the color insert appears courtesy of the
    Glastonbury Abbey Trustees

Llewellyn is a registered trademark of Llewellyn Worldwide Ltd.

Library of Congress Cataloging-in-Publication Data
Telyndru, Jhenah, 1970–
   Avalon within: a sacred journey of myth, mystery, and inner wisdom /
Jhenah Telyndru.—2nd ed.
      p. cm.
   Includes bibliographical references and index.
   ISBN 978-0-7387-1997-9
   1. Women—Religious life. 2. Spiritual life—Sisterhood of Avalon.
3. Sisterhood of Avalon—Doctrines. I. Title.
   BP605.N46T46 2010
   299'.94082--dc22
                                        2010014382

Llewellyn Worldwide Ltd. does not participate in, endorse, or have any authority or responsibility concerning private business transactions between our authors and the public.
   All mail addressed to the author is forwarded, but the publisher cannot, unless specifically instructed by the author, give out an address or phone number.
   Any Internet references contained in this work are current at publication time, but the publisher cannot guarantee that a specific location will continue to be maintained. Please refer to the publisher's website for links to authors' websites and other sources.

Llewellyn Publications
A Division of Llewellyn Worldwide Ltd.
2143 Wooddale Drive
Woodbury, MN 55125-2989
www.llewellyn.com

Printed in the United States of America

To my Sisters in Avalon and in the love of the Lady
Past, Present, and Future

In memory of those who have made the Journey to the Other Shore,
especially Tammi Boudreau, Suzanne Yelton, and Gina Gambidilla

For my Mom

TO PART THE MISTS ...

The path to the top of the Tor
Is also the spiraled way to the woman within
A journey of growth, empowerment,
And self understanding
Voyage to the Source ... the Center ... the Goddess ...
She whose Name can only be found in the silence of the soul
Delve into your darkness ... enter your pain
Conquer your fears ...
Call the Barge to take you
To the Holy Island of Healing which resides within ...
And emerge renewed

The Mysteries of Avalon are alive
Her Apples are red and sweet ...
Do you dare take a bite?

Become the Woman you were born to be ...
Remember ...

—JHENAH TELYNDRU, 1995

CONTENTS

ACKNOWLEDGEMENTS

I would like to give my thanks for the blessings I received from so many in the course of birthing this book. Foremost, I would like to thank the Sisterhood of Avalon for their gracious assistance and loving support of this project; it simply would not have been possible without my Sisters.

There are so many beautiful women who have assisted and sustained me in both my inner and outer processes during the writing of this book; heartfelt thanks to Debra Schneider, Vyviane Armstrong, Alicia Grosso, Kim Davis, Andrea Smith, Sharone Farrar, Jackie-Kopp Accurso, Lizabeth Doty, and Lisa Siano. I have been truly gifted by your presence in my life!

I would like to express my sincere appreciation for my incredible editors Elysia Gallo and Laura Graves, whose professionalism and expertise are second only to their commitment to midwifing this book in a way that both honored and honed its vision. I am very grateful to them and to everyone at Llewellyn who worked to make this book a reality. I am deeply indebted to all who have shared the beautiful photos and images that have made this book so magickal, especially Bettina Auerbach, Diana Byron, Alicia Grosso, Jackie Hewitt, Kathy Jones, Danna Kline, Dawn Kline, Elisa Maistrellis-Ryng, Jocelyn Russell, Jeff

Saward, and Robin Wallace. I am also grateful for the generosity of Chalice Well Trust, the National Trust, the White Spring Companions, and Glastonbury Abbey for permitting us to include photos of the sacred sites entrusted to their care.

Deepest thanks to the Lady for the blessing of my family and their unconditional love and support of me and my need to write this book. Loving thanks to my husband Matthew for all his encouragement and for the sacrifices that opened the space that allowed this book to happen; to my family for the priceless gift of time; and to my beloved children for being my life's inspiration and the greatest teachers I have ever had.

Above all, I thank the Goddesses of Avalon for Their abundant blessings, limitless love, and for the divine grace of Awen.

Introduction

SEEKING THE HOLY ISLE

S HE STANDS IN THE PROW, her form cloaked by dark robes and
clinging mists. Her voluminous hood conceals her age—she could
be anyone's daughter, sister, or mother. Her foothold is sure, her body
steady. Through the thickening mists and fitful waters, she stands firmly in her place and ever-certain of the way; she has conquered this lake
and parted these mists to find her way to Avalon. Now, in service, she
guides others through what appears to be the impenetrable, until they
too can arrive at the Holy Shore unaided.

She is a Priestess of Avalon.

It has been long since the chord of Avalon has sung out in the hearts
of women. In the centuries since her end, we find scattered notes of
Avalon's song still playing to us down through the stream of time in
art, literature, music, and legend. The last one hundred years have especially heralded her re-emergence. The Pre-Raphaelite movement and
the writings of Yeats and Tennyson beautifully illustrate the Victorian romance with the Arthurian mythos. The magickal traditions that
emerged at beginning of the twentieth century also began to tie into
the energy of Avalon, most especially as seen in the work of author and
mystic Dion Fortune.

The power of Avalon, and indeed, the entire Arthurian legend, is not a fancy of bygone days; we need only look around us to find ample proof of its relevance. Tales of Arthur, Morgan le Fay, and Merlin can be found on every bookshelf. Psychologists, fantasy writers, Celtic scholars, and personal growth proponents have all gained insight from the Arthurian mythic cycle. There are many Pagan and Wiccan groups that draw heavily from the realm of Arthur, finding a path of spiritual growth symbolized by the quest for the Grail and the code of Chivalry.

Yet from all of these, we gain but glimpses of Avalon's entirety. At the end of his life, Arthur was borne on the barge to her shores to await Britain's need. In the same way, Avalon's memory has been kept alive through the tales of that once and future king. Hidden in shadow, the barest glimmer of all that was once Avalon whispers to us from the traditions of Arthurian legend. And, like Arthur, her re-emergence comes at a time of great need.

We live in an era when opportunities for women stand almost unrivaled in Western culture since the dawn of patriarchy. The societal support of a woman's worth, however gradual and hard won, has encouraged many women to seek a spiritual path of female empowerment. No longer are these women contented with religious forms that do not allow them to participate in the ecclesiastic realms, or which teach them they are flawed beings by virtue of their "misfortune" of having been born female. The renewed concept of woman as sacred has truly transformed mindsets, dissolved outdated paradigms of a woman's place, reset our search for human purpose, and redefined our concept of the nature of the Divine.

For many women seeking a spiritual home, the legend of Avalon has called to them from across the ages. It is an island of women's mysteries, a sanctuary of service to the Goddess, an honored haven of learning and healing, a place of solitude, and a center for women to come into their personal power through inner wisdom. These images have resonated with innumerable women, and the resulting quest for her shores has served to pull Avalon even further from the mists.

In all this seeking, we are faced with the question: What is Avalon? Is she an allegory for women's empowerment? A myth whose legend serves to inspire us so that we may draw wisdom from her symbolism? There are many traditions that connect her with the Fortunate Isles, the Gateway to Annwn, and the Apple Island Paradise. Is Avalon another guise of the Celtic Otherworld? Is she, as some have posited, a feminist's pipe dream—a romanticization of a matriarchal ideal spun out of a need to believe that such places did indeed once exist? Was Avalon a physical place where priestesses trained to keep the sacred mysteries and manifested a place of growth and healing?

In truth, definitively "proving" Avalon existed in the earthly realm may not matter much. The varying perspectives and the scholarly cases for or against her existence pale in comparison to Avalon's greater purpose. Whatever she may once have been, she serves today as a resource for women seeking to come into their power. She holds the keys of women's wisdom, once honored and sought after, now returning to the consciousness of those with the courage to seek it. She is a focus for all the Mother's daughters—a goal, a template, and an endless source of inspiration. Avalon is a beacon, shining out from the maternal waters, promising connections between the women of today, continuing the forgotten knowledge of the women of yesterday, and serving as a promise of constancy for the women of tomorrow.

Through the legends of Avalon, we are called to be self-sufficient and empowered women, gifted with the blessings of Sight. Improving our vision and exploring the landscape with discernment is but the first step into the greater mysteries. Clear Seeing comes through first turning the eye within—the deeper we can peer into our own recesses, making conscious those things which reside in the shadow, the further we can cast out our eye to glimpse the far horizon. This Sight is not a trick of the psyche, but rather is the developed ability to read the greater pattern and understand the nature of the flow of energy. Understanding these cosmic tides need not come from a classroom—it lies within. A component of that greater rhythm, we cycle the same as all things—somewhere between the tiniest subatomic particle and the vastness of the universe can we find our own essence. Knowing the one brings knowledge of the All.

Avalon's allegory is profound in its simplicity; the path to reaching her shores is well marked. We are called to cross the lake—to embark upon the journey through the unconscious—the watery realm of memory and emotion. From here we must part the mists—rending the veil of illusion that obscures our clarity of sight. This artifice is the greatest barrier keeping us from obtaining our true goal: reaching the Island of Avalon. The Holy Isle represents the truth of our sacred nature—the paradisial existence of the actualized self.

Once we arrive on the shore, there is much to explore—sacred sites and places of power dot Avalon's landscape. As we map this unknown country, we must also appraise our inner landscapes with eyes clear of mist. We must come to truly know ourselves and make sacred the space within us. Inhabited by powerful, holy women working together to create and support a self-sufficient community with the Goddess at its center, Avalon itself serves as a model for the fully integrated and individualized self: all parts are conscious of purpose, acknowledge strengths and weaknesses, and work to keep the core intact—a sacred center fully aware of its Divinity.

It is no accident that Avalon's ancient name is *Ynys Afallon*, the Island of Apples, for the fruit of wisdom grew abundantly in her orchards. We must seek this fruit within ourselves and cultivate the seeds of wisdom already within us—this is our birthright as daughters of the Lady. The Avalonian Tradition provides a pathway by which each woman can seek, discover and acknowledge her innate wise woman—the priestess within. The teachings of Avalon aim to awaken the seeker to the direct experience of the inner mysteries, for they will only reveal themselves to those who have earned their gifts. As the Hermetic axiom states, "the lips of wisdom are closed, except to the ears of Understanding." The mysteries guard themselves. The path of Avalon is one of active and dedicated seeking; our rewards are proportional to our efforts.

What does it mean to be a priestess of the Holy Island? It is a vocation that has changed greatly in the centuries since the last woman of Avalon wove the ritual way to the top of the Tor. We are orphans in a sense, for the ancient place of training and learning the ways of a priestess of Avalon no longer exists on this plane. How can we, who have heard the Voice of the Lady of the Apple Isle, fulfill this calling?

Becoming a priestess in the old sense is not a process anyone can confer upon you. It is an honor earned, a potential realized, and a birthright claimed—and only by Her hand can it be made so. She alone chooses who will serve. Reading this or any other book will not make one a priestess of Avalon. Attending workshops, completing study courses, going on pilgrimage—none of these will initiate us into the mysteries. We can only walk the priestess' path through hard work, inner seeking, issue resolution, effecting positive change in our lives, and nurturing the ability to manifest the women we were born to be. When we have finally come to acknowledge and actualize the true self, we will finally know the truth of the Goddess within. The closer we draw to manifesting our genuine natures, the greater our ability to touch the essence of the Lady. The brighter our souls shine in wholeness, the more of Her light is reflected through us into the world.

The greatest challenge in becoming a priestess is becoming the authentic self—the best we can be. When we touch that part of ourselves not frozen in fear or bled anemic by soul wounds, we touch the Divine within us. The more whole we are and the more empowered we allow ourselves to be, the more we are examples to our sisters walking their own paths to the Lady. Although no two women will come into their power in the same way, all women can touch the Goddess.

With each step towards authenticity, the spirit of Sovereignty awakens. With each inspired soul, the Voice of the Goddess sings louder, enflaming the hearts of all who seek Her. Always awaiting our need, Avalon is re-emerging, once more answering the ancient call of her daughters.

THE FRUIT OF WISDOM

The Island of Apples which men call "The Fortunate Isle" gets its name from the fact that it produces all things of itself; the fields there have no need of the ploughs of the farmers and all cultivation is lacking except what nature provides. Of its own accord it produces grain and grapes, and apple trees grow in its woods from the close-clipped grass. The ground of its own accord produces everything instead of merely grass, and people live there a hundred years or more.

VITA MERLINI, GEOFFREY OF MONMOUTH

THE WAY OF AVALON AND the spiritual path known as the Avalonian Tradition is a complex interweaving of history, myth, legend, folklore, symbolic language, geomancy, Druidry, Western Esoteric philosophy, and Goddess Spirituality. There is no unbroken lineage of Avalonian priestesses stretching back to ancient Britain, and no written records of Avalonian beliefs or practices exist—indeed, there is no direct proof that the Island of Avalon and her attendant priestess existed at all outside of the realms of legend and folk belief.

What we do have are brief but powerful images of Avalon that have survived the passing centuries, igniting the imagination of many generations. Layer upon layer of mythos and meaning have been built around the idea of Avalon over the millennia. It has been ascribed physical locations, given both Pagan and Christian significance, and taken its place in one of the greatest mythic cycles of Western culture. Yet, to truly understand Avalon, we must first allow the various glamours surrounding it to fall away in order to see what lies at its most fundamental core. In order to understand the very heart of its existence, we must explore the power of its very name.

Avalon. Ynys Afallon. The Island of Apples.

Etymologically, the name Avalon can be traced back to the Proto-Indo-European root word *abel* (meaning "apple"), which passed into the Celtic languages as *afal* in Welsh, *aval* in Cornish and Breton, and *ubhal* in Irish Gaelic. Throughout time and across many cultures, apples appear in mythology and folklore as a sacred and honored fruit. We see them featured as the objects of quests, as the catalysts of personal trials and tests, and as the custodians of wisdom and immortality. We will discuss the importance and symbolism of the apple as found in Celtic mythos throughout the course of this book, especially as it relates to the Otherworld and the inner pilgrimage of the Celtic Wonder Journey known as the Immram. In Druidic lore, the apple was one of the seven Chieftain trees of the ogham system, and a Celtic triad underscores its importance, saying:

> *Three unbreathing things paid for only with breathing things:*
> *An apple tree, a hazel bush, a sacred grove*

The apple is a symbol of fertility and sexuality, and is especially representative of women's Mysteries. Archetypally, the apple embodies the essence of the Divine Feminine, who is revealed through Her three sacred colors—the red of the Mother in her skin, the white of the Maiden in her flesh and the black of the Crone in her seeds. These are also the colors of the alchemical process—the stages of transformation whereby dross is changed to gold; both sets of correspondences are appropriate for this powerful symbol of Avalon.

Just as the blossoms of the apple tree are its sexual organs, drawing bees and other flying insects to drink its sweet nectar and pollinate its fragile white flowers, so are the fruits themselves the red and fertile wombs of the tree, each bearing the black seeds that will birth the next generation. It is no accident this prominent symbol of Otherworldly paradise is related to the Feminine in Celtic (and other) cultures, for like the cauldron—another one of the great symbols of the Avalonian Tradition—it bears a strong association with wisdom and the womb, a powerful call to women to seek the source within.

The Five Seeds of Wisdom

When we slice an apple horizontally, we reveal the five-pointed star that lies at its very heart—recalling both the pentacle and the homunculus, and which preserves a map of the Fivefold Mysteries of Avalon. Five seeds lie in the center of the Apple of Wisdom, each holding the potential for growth and the transformation needed to obtain knowledge of the true self.

This fivefold construct holds many correspondences central to the Avalonian Tradition, and the immersion into this pentad of energy is what makes up the primary focus of this book. It represents the five goddesses in the Avalonian pantheon; it aligns with the five major power places in the ancient Avalonian landscape; it holds resonance with the five inner energy centers worked with by the women of Avalon today; it informs the path to wholeness represented by the Avalonian Cycle of Healing (which we will be examining in great depth); and ultimately instructs us on how to embark upon the Path of the Priestess.

In Celtic myth and Arthurian legend, the voyage to the islands of the Otherworld and the journey to Avalon involves a trip over water. Making this crossing requires a magical ship, a fantastic bridge between two islands, or some kind of mediator who knows how to traverse the distance between this world and the Otherworld—between what is

The Apple of Wisdom

known and what is unknown. It was under Merlin's guidance that Arthur took a boat into the water to receive the sword from the Lady of the Lake that marked him as king and guardian of Avalon. Later, it was a barge of three queens, including his sister Morgan, that bore the wounded King Arthur to the Holy Island. It is here we who seek the Isle of Apples must begin.

Overlaying the fivefold energetic construct found in the Apple of Wisdom on the prominent components of what is described in myth as the journey to Avalon, we are presented with a metaphorical process that can guide us in our quest for the Holy Isle. This quest is an inner one, for if Avalon once existed on the physical plane—and indeed there are places that hold pieces of its energies enough to serve as portals—it no longer does so, requiring us to journey in a more subtle manner. We no longer need board a vessel and sail to a distant shore; instead, we must journey within through the eddies and tides of the unconscious to arrive at the archetypal realm of Avalon—a powerful island of wholeness and healing, very much intact on the astral plane.

Seed One: Calling the Barge

Somewhere deep in the soul of every Daughter of Avalon, the song of ancient memory sparks a longing for the home of our spiritual Mothers. Called to the quest, we stand at the shore of our becoming, daring to speak our need into the moonlit night. We embark upon the journey over the lake to Avalon, navigate the inner waters, and seek the reflection of our inner truths.

Seed Two: Parting the Mists

Confronted by the mists of illusion, we must find the word that will cause them to part—naming that vital element that is the root of our illusion. In naming this, we set ourselves free and lift the veil of the shadow so that our journey to wholeness may continue.

Seed Three: Retrieving the Sword

The veil parts, and through the water's glassy surface we see the Lady of the Lake holding aloft the sword of truth. We have earned this tool against the darkness of illusion, and taking it in hand, we are empowered to establish inner queendom and step into a place of personal Sovereignty illuminated by the light of right action.

Seed Four: Reaching the Shore

At last, we find ourselves on solid ground—setting our feet on the sacred shores of Avalon. Our journey culminates in this moment of attainment; we have obtained our desire and overcome the obstacles preventing us from realizing our goal. Touching the core of our Sacred Nature, we rejoice in the knowledge that we have the power to transform our lives and draw closer to manifesting our authentic self.

Seed Five: Reclaiming the Isle

Bringing the energies of the landscape with us, we embark upon the labyrinthine path leading us to the top of the Tor, that place of ultimate connection with the Divine. At this sacred center, we pull in the threads of all aspects of the soul's landscape—light and shadow, descending and emerging—to create the full tapestry of the self. Spinning ever higher, we gain the perspective that brings clear sight and the ability to read the great pattern. With the arch of the heavens above us, and the cauldron of the valley below, we bridge the realms of being and stand fully in the Sacred Essence of Avalon.

The Avalonian Cycle of Healing

A further reflection of the fivefold pathway to wisdom and wholeness is the Avalonian Cycle of Healing, a core paradigm of the Avalonian Tradition. Informed by the energies of the Apple of Wisdom and reflecting the cyclic course of transformation found in the myth of Ceridwen, one of the five goddesses of the Avalonian pantheon, the Avalonian Cycle of Healing combines several key energetics of the Avalonian Tradition to form a tool that has the power to transform the lives of all who seek the Holy Island. We will explore the energetic correspondences and allegorical symbolisms encoded in the Cycle of Healing, and will learn accessible ways to embrace this powerful process of soul growth and put it to work in our lives. For now, an overview will provide us with a foundational context from which we can proceed in our studies.

The Avalonian Cycle of Healing is a symbolic distillation of the soul's journey from woundedness to wholeness, from inauthenticity to sovereignty, and from disconnection to connection with the Divine. It provides a loom with which we can weave the tapestry of our fully actualized selves; in the Avalonian Tradition, this is the priestess self—she who is self-sufficent, connected with Goddess, and who lives in egoless service to the Holy Island within.

As with any cycle, the Cycle of Healing describes a circuit of energy that is whole and without any true beginning or end. However, for our purposes, we will artificially break down the Cycle into its five primary components, called Stations, in order to better understand the functioning of the whole. Each Station represents a corpus of energetic correspondences, some of which will be explored in depth as our work unfolds. These correspondences are crucial due to the fundamental power of cyclic thought: if you understand how one manifestation of cycle works, you gain an understanding of how *all* manifestations of cycle work. This concept is important and will be explored more as we proceed.

The Station of Descent

This Station of the Avalonian Cycle of Healing is concerned with turning the eye within in order to take spiritual inventory and identify the areas where we manifest disharmony and imbalance. We work to recognize outmoded patterns of behavior that play out in our lives and acknowledge destructive beliefs we hold about ourselves, our abilities, and our ultimate worth. This Station's task is to consciously descend into the realms of the personal shadow, so that we may understand the ways our unconscious fears and pain control and direct our lives.

The Station of Confrontation

This Station of the Avalonian Cycle of Healing is concerned with ferreting out the root cause of the wounds and imbalances identified through the work of the Station of Descent. There is a saying: that which is unconscious, controls us. Naming something relinquishes its power over us, although this is only the first step to creating true and lasting change. Once we have revealed that which dwells in the darkness of the shadow, we must work to reclaim the energies that have been tied up in generating the negative patterns that are the outgrowth of our unconscious pain. The task of this Station is to see shadow aspects of the self for what they truly are, and to confront the old specters of fear and hurt—often wounds of the past which are still active and working through us in our present—and to choose, with consciousness, to walk a different energetic path.

The Station of Emergence

This Station of the Avalonian Cycle of Healing is concerned with redirecting energies freed from the unconscious motivations of the shadow self and using them to support the actualized essence of the priestess self. Just as we took inventory of energetic patterns that do not serve us during the Station of Descent, at Emergence we work on mapping the path we need to walk in order to unlock the potential of our inner gifts, to manifest our life's goals and long-standing dreams, and to live from a center that is clear and connected to Goddess. This Station's task is to plant the seeds of outer change and work toward keeping the vision of the priestess self foremost in our lives so that we may work to become the women we were born to be.

The Station of Resolution

This Station of the Avalonian Cycle of Healing is concerned with bringing aspects of the priestess self to fruition, as well as acknowledging and celebrating the growth and change we have been able to manifest in our lives. While there is still work to be done, it is important for us to recognize our triumphs and honor the progress we have made down the path towards our inner Sovereignty—a self that makes fully conscious life decisions based in wholeness and right action, rather than from a reactionary place of unconscious motivations. The task of this Station is not only to see closure (*resolution*) of a particular issue or situation, but also to harness the will—the *resolve*—to build upon our accomplishments and continue down the road of growth as the Cycle turns back down into the Station of Decent. This time, however, we look into the shadow from a different perspective and with a trust in the process of the Cycle of Healing. We have learned that our inner sight is sharpened when piercing through the illusions we hold about ourselves, and that by daring to see ourselves in a new light, we change the world by changing ourselves.

The Station of Integration

This Station of the Avalonian Cycle of Healing is concerned with bringing together all of the insights, lessons, and changes experienced as we journey through the Cycle, weaving them into the pattern of our soul. This Station lies at the Cycle's center, as well as between each Station, reminding us that each step we take is but a stitch in the tapestry of our life's big picture. To shift our perspective to see this big picture, we need but take a moment to breathe and connect with our center, where all aspects of the self are united, and aim to live from the clarity that comes from understanding the whole. While this may seem ethereal and abstract, at its heart, this Station's task is to learn to experience life with consciousness and to see the gift in each challenge as well as the challenge in each gift. The Goddess is found in these connections; our purpose unfolds.

The Sacred Landscape of Avalon

A third major repetition of the fivefold energy of the Apple of Wisdom can be found in ancient Avalon's landscape. Of the several places in the British Isles that scholars and theorists believe may have been the real location of the Island of Avalon, history and tradition has for centuries associated the final resting place of Arthur with the Somerset market town of Glastonbury. Somerset is renowned for its abundant apple orchards, and for its cider production especially. Local folk belief birthed the winter tradition of the Apple Wassail—a ritual where people enter apple orchards, sing songs to the trees, hang wheat cakes in the tree boughs, and pour libations of cider over their roots, in hopes of driving away evil spirits and ensuring bounty in the next harvest. The area's strong association with apples makes it an attractive choice for Avalon's real-world location, as does the similarity of the name Somerset, believed to reflect the area's ancient Britons naming it the Summer Country (the Summerlands being one name for the Celtic Otherworldly paradise).

Once almost completely surrounded by water save for a small land bridge in an area today called Pointer's Ball, Glastonbury was one of a series of moorland islands resulting from an egress of the Bristol Channel into southwest Britain. The platforms and artificial islands built over the marshes to support the round houses of the ancient Glastonbury Lake Village were a wonder of Iron Age engineering; a network of wooden tracks constructed to connect the water-bound settlements with each other date back to the pre-Celtic Neolithic period. Although the area around Glastonbury has been drained to reveal its rich farmland (the first attempts at drainage beginning in the Roman period), the area periodically floods in winter and reveals some of the island's boundaries once more.

Since ancient times, Glastonbury has been a place of spiritual power for Pagans and Christians alike. The distinctive geologic features of its landscape may have been a compelling draw for the stone age-era Britons who first settled in the area, but there is something about Glastonbury that has continued to attract people even into the present day. Perhaps the power of the myths and legends associated with the Island of Avalon and Glastonbury itself have made this town a pilgrim's destination for more than a thousand years. Or perhaps these legends came to reside in this area because of the landscape's unique energies.

There is an area of Glastonbury that, from a geomantic perspective holds incredible transformative powers and which will be referred to throughout this book as the Tor Valley Complex. Geomancers believe that two major ley lines (rivers of planetary energy that criss-cross the globe much like terrestrial acupuncture meridians) intersect on the Glastonbury Tor, a strange spiraled hill unlike anything else in the surrounding Somerset Levels. These two ley lines, one masculine and one feminine, are most often called the Michael and Mary lines (although some Pagans favor naming them Merlin and Morgan), and it is believed they correspond with the white and red dragons of Arthurian Tradition. Red and white are the colors of the Otherworld in Celtic myth, and British folklore has long held the Tor to be a portal to the Otherworld and, for many, the location of the Blessed Isle itself.

Perhaps it is the confluence of these energetic streams which has shaped the physical form of Glastonbury, and in turn generated a spiritual essence whose effects would be felt by many throughout time. Perhaps it was these energies that generated awe in the souls of the firstcomers, and inspired them to settle in the area. Later, these energies may have supported the existence of a druidic college and temple of holy women at the site of ancient Avalon. Perhaps again this spiritual essence motivated the British Isles' first Christian community to be built in Glastonbury and evolve to hold, for the modern seeker, a center for progressive spirituality in myriad forms and manifestations. Whichever may have come first—a powerful place that generated myths and legends, or the myths and legends which themselves built up the place's power—there is no question for anyone who has been to Glastonbury that the land itself is sacred and that through its very nature, stimulates the spirit to grow.

From the Avalonian Tradition perspective, the Tor Valley Complex is a geologic manifestation of the Apple of Wisdom and its five-stage journey to wholeness. This area of the ancient Priestess Isle features two prominent hills (the Tor and Modron's Mound/Chalice Hill) and two sacred springs (the Red Spring and the White Spring)—each comprised of a pair of energetic polarities. The fifth point, holding the essence of the fully integrated Center, lies between these in the heart of this small valley, and acts as a proxy to represent the whole of the Island of Avalon itself.

Each of these five sites corresponds to a Station in the Avalonian Cycle of Healing, and connecting with each area of the sacred landscape—either literally, as by undertaking pilgrimage, or energetically, as through Immrama or trance journeying—will bring insight to the sister energy dwelling within us. As we come to understand archetypal patterns encoded in the essence of each geographic area, we begin to activate the corresponding energies in our inner spiritual landscapes, allowing us to harness the catalytic energies of these power spots in our own transformations. For example, connecting with the energies of the Red Spring can assist us in the work of the Station of Descent as well as lead us to a greater understanding of this area of the ancient

Avalonian landscape. As we progress through the Avalonian Cycle of Healing, we will find that harnessing the Hermetic Principle of Correspondence, best distilled in the axiom "as above, so below; as below, so above," leads us down the path to revealing Avalon Within.

Five Seeds Correspondence Chart

Station	Journey	Element	Goddess	Area
Descent	Calling the Barge	Water	Rhiannon	Red Spring
Confrontation	Parting the Mists	Earth	Ceridwen	The Tor
Emergence	Retrieving the Sword	Air	Blodeuwedd	White Spring
Resolution	Reaching the Shore	Fire/Awen	Arianrhod	Modron's Mound
Integration	Reclaiming the Isle	Spirit	Branwen	Isle of Avalon

While there may never be definitive proof that Glastonbury was once indeed the Island of Avalon, it has held the energies of Avalon for centuries, and has done so for spiritual seekers of the Holy Isle into the modern day. Fabricated or authentic, there is an energetic connection to Avalon that overlays the town of Glastonbury like an ancient mist, constructed over time and through the workings of the collective unconscious. It is through this overlay that a real and transformational connection to Avalon may be made.

And so we begin our quest for the Holy Isle with an act as simple as it is symbolic. Standing at the doorway to the inner realms, we affirm our dedication to the rarifying Cycle of Healing and to our commitment to the revelation of true wisdom by lifting a glorious, red apple to our lips, and taking a deep and conscious bite. It is not accidental this potent symbol is intended to be devoured; knowledge becomes wisdom only when integrated into our essences. Now the journey can begin.

2

ENTERING THE CAULDRON

Thither after the battle of Camlan we took the wounded Arthur, guided by Barinthus to whom the waters and the stars of heaven were well known. With him steering the ship we arrived there with the prince, and Morgen received us with fitting honour, and in her chamber she placed the king on a golden bed and with her own hand she uncovered his honourable wound and gazed at it for a long time. At length she said that health could be restored to him if he stayed with her for a long time and made use of her healing art. Rejoicing, therefore, we entrusted the king to her and returning spread our sails to the favouring winds.

VITA MERLINI, GEOFFREY OF MONMOUTH

ONE OF AVALON'S MOST ENDURING legacies is its renown as a wondrous Island of Healing. Like Morgan of Avalon who gave refuge to the wounded King Arthur and promised to restore his vitality with her healing arts, the cornerstone of the Avalonian Tradition today is the restoration of personal Sovereignty—the authentic core of the self which is our strongest and deepest connection to the Divine. In Arthurian legend, the Holy Grail healed the Fisher King of his grievous wound so that he might once again be sovereign over his land—a land that suffered as he suffered. In Welsh mythology, Bran the Blessed possessed a wondrous Cauldron of Healing that could resurrect the dead. These vessels—the cup and the cauldron—are powerful symbols of the Divine Feminine, and so women of Avalon today look to the goddesses of the ancient Britons to guide us on the path to wholeness. The goddess Ceridwen especially has much to teach us about the transformational power of the cauldron to assist us in our soul healing through the process of coming into our true wisdom.

The Lady of the Cauldron

Our primary source of information about the goddess Ceridwen is the Welsh *Tale of Gwion Bach*. Living in the center of Llyn Tegid, a lake in the Penllyn area of northern Wales, Ceridwen is married to the giant Tegid Foel, and has two children: a daughter named Creirwy, one of the most beautiful women in the world, and a son, Afagddu, hideous beyond description, and whose very name means "utter darkness."

In order to help Afagddu overcome his physical deformity and take his place in the world, Ceridwen brought to bear her knowledge of magic and herb craft to create a brew that would bestow the gifts of wisdom and prophecy to whoever drank it. Creating such an elixir was an enormous undertaking, requiring the liquid to brew for a year and a day. During this period, Ceridwen gathered the required herbs and put them in a water-filled cauldron, each at their proper times according to the cycles of the moon, sun, and stars.

She set a blind man named Morda before the cauldron, charging him to keep the fire beneath it burning, while a young boy called Gwion Bach was tasked with continuously stirring the steaming potion as it simmered. At the close of the year and a day, Ceridwen positioned Afagddu in front of the cauldron to await the brew's completion. She sat down to rest, weary from her mystical exertions, and had barely closed her eyes when the elixir was done at last. Three shining drops emerged from the depths of the cauldron, and before anyone knew what was happening Gwion pushed the waiting Afagddu aside and received the streams of wisdom for himself. At that moment, the poisonous dregs of the brew shattered the cauldron into pieces, and spilled its foul liquid over the hearth.

The terrible sound caused Ceridwen to awaken, and Gwion—now possessing the gifts of wisdom and prophesy—knew she would stop at nothing to destroy him for what he had done. He set off running, transforming himself into a swift hare, but Ceridwen pursued him in the form of a greyhound. Narrowly escaping her sharp teeth, Gwion jumped into the lake, turning himself into a salmon. Ceridwen was right behind, however, in the form of quick-swimming otter.

Gwion launched himself into the air at the last moment, flying above the water in the shape of a wren. Escape was not to be, however, for Ceridwen soared after him in the form of a mighty hawk. The chase continued, and sharp flashing talons raked across Gwion's borrowed shape. He quickly turned himself into a grain of wheat and fell onto the threshing floor of a farm below. Hiding among thousands of other grains, Gwion believed himself safe, but Ceridwen found him, and as a hungry black hen, scratched and pecked her way through the wheat until she finally devoured him.

Nine months later, a son was born of Ceridwen's swollen belly—Gwion's final and greatest transformation. Although her anger at him had not subsided, Ceridwen could not bring herself to destroy the beautiful infant. Instead, she swaddled him in a leather bag and set him adrift on the sea in a little coracle. On Calan Gaeaf, he was discovered in a salmon weir by the Welsh prince Elphin. Upon unwrapping the baby, the prince was amazed by his illuminated countenance and named the boy Taliesin—"Shining Brow." This twice-born son of Ceridwen grew to be renowned for his poetry and prophecy and became the greatest bard Britain had ever known.

The Path to Wisdom

There are many layers of meaning encoded in the myth of Ceridwen. It is a metaphorical encryption of a Druidic rite of passage; Druidic lore speaks of a dedicant having to undergo a symbolic three-fold death through the Three Realms of Land, Sea, and Sky. This is echoed in a Celtic triad, which proclaims:

The three foundations of learning:
Seeing much; studying much; and suffering much.

It is believed her myth can also be used as a key to unlock the bardic art of obtaining Awen—the Divine spark of inspiration. While some account Cerdiwen's name to mean "white sow" reflecting Her aspect as the Devouring Mother (the Crone of death and rebirth), She is most primarily the patroness and muse of bards, bestowing Awen or inspiration from Her Cauldron of Wisdom. As such, there is an etymological school of thought that believes Her name derives from the words *cyrdd*—meaning "song"—and *wen*—meaning "white/shining/holy." Having attained enlightenment in rebirth from the Cauldron, Taliesin becomes the greatest of all bards—the paragon to which all bards aspired. Hoping to obtain a degree of his wisdom and art, the ancient bards honored their source and called themselves "Cerddorion," the Children of Ceridwen.

Women of Avalon see Ceridwen's story as an allegorical system brimming with wisdom, applicable and relevant to the spiritual seeker's life. Entering the Cauldron of Transformation is an initiatory process, rarifying the essence of the seeker and distilling her down into her most fundamental components. The cyclic dance through the elements is revealed as a means to acquire wisdom. The pathway to wisdom is the pathway to the Godhead—the pathway to wholeness. The spiritual path is nothing more than moving one's self from a place of disconnection to connection…from woundedness to wholeness…from darkness into light.

Ceridwen is a Divine Healer as well as the Mistress of Awen. True healing is a function of the soul, and it is significant that one of Avalon's greatest heritages is the healing gifts of its priestesses. Like Ceridwen, the Nine Morgens or High Priestesses of Avalon were known to be powerful shape-shifters, taking the form of ravens to fly wherever they willed. There is a profound connection between self-change and healing, and both figure strongly as fundamental elements of the Avalonian Tradition.

Women of Avalon embrace the female energetic power—the inward turning spiral that leads to the sacred, sovereign, fully actualized center within us all. It is a path that reclaims inner darkness and births the inner priestess into being—transforming fear into love, and pain into power. At the center of the labyrinth of our soul's journey is the Divine weaver, spinning the matrix of our lives and the very fabric of the universe. Consciously turning the eye within allows us to see the greater tapestry and our place within it—past illusion, expectation, and all unconsciously embraced limitation. The more we come to recognize our inherent Divinity, the more we activate the Goddess in Her role as Lady of Sovereignty—She Who Empowers—in our lives. The veil becomes lifted, and the Island of Avalon—whole and holy—is revealed within us.

The archetypal image of a priestess of Avalon is a powerful one; she is a complete and centered woman, fully aware, and at one with herself and the Goddess. How she came to be that way, however, is through the path that lies within—the inner journey that begins with the descent into the shadow, and ends with the ultimate manifestation of the true self in the light. As women, this descent is a critical element of our passage into fullness. We are at home in the night, in the darkness of the cosmos, in the blackness of the womb. It is here where we must go to seek out our healing. Immersing ourselves into the hidden energies by delving into our shadow or lower self is the first step in the healing process.

The descent is never easy; it demands great courage of us. Hidden in the shadow are those aspects of ourselves we would rather not acknowledge, seeking to rule us by remaining in the unconscious realm. Many of our patterns of behavior are dictated by the hidden hurts, unmet needs, and unfulfilled dreams dwelling in the darkness. If we never root out the insidious energies that cast their pallor over how we view ourselves and the circumstances of our lives, never clearing the false filter through which we view the world, we will forever be victims of our wounded perspective.

A dog that has been regularly beaten by its owner will come to react with fear or aggression toward any person it meets; even when greeted with kindness, the dog expects to be beaten. We too tend to become fixed in our past, and learn to *react* to our environments based on what *was* rather than what *is*. Until the dog comes to realize that not every human is cruel, until we come to acknowledge that we exhibit coping mechanisms and defenses based upon past experiences to which we need no longer cling, the present will always be interpreted through the pain of our wounds rather than with the clarity of our wholeness.

We must fight to bring these aspects of self into the light—transforming them through illumination. Reclaiming energies engaged in order to maintain self-destructive patterns provides us with renewed resources with which to manifest the potential of our higher selves. Descent into the shadow brings with it a commitment: it signals a willingness to examine damaging patterns of our lives with honest, self-appraising eyes.

Self-examination is a crucial part of growth. It demands that we become clear enough to hear and see ourselves with brutal honesty. Great courage is needed in this quest for inner understanding. Once we have seen the mechanisms that bring pain and unhappiness to our lives, preventing us from being who we truly are and keeping us from attaining our full potential, the universe will demand that we make the choice to change. With knowledge comes responsibility. This is the path to wisdom: the choice to enter the Cauldron and be remade.

The Cycle of Initiation

Unlike most cultures, no clear creation myth from any Celtic culture is known to have endured the passage of time. Yet here, in the story of Ceridwen and Taliesin, we have a myth of self-creation, rich in symbolism and powerful in application. It is from this Divine template, in resonance with the mysteries of the apple, that the Avalonian Cycle of Healing was birthed.

The pattern of archetypes present in Ceridwen's myth has its counterpart in the microcosm of our souls. We can take the myth's universal lesson and the many layers encoded in its symbolism, and apply them to the individual. When analyzing myths in this way, each character represents an aspect of the self, and each action is a metaphor for the steps the soul needs to take on its journey to inner understanding.

In Ceridwen's story, the Goddess Herself represents the higher self of the seeker, our innate Divinity. She knows the soul's potential and seeks to bring it into fullness. Guiding us through our lessons and trials, the higher self helps us recognize the illusion of the shadow, so that we may choose to walk the path of wholeness into the wisdom of our inner truth.

Afagddu ("utter darkness") represents the unconscious, where the shadow dwells. The shadow possesses the dark or "ugly" parts of our selves that are repressed from the conscious mind; it is the abyss that holds our wounds, feeds our fears, and triggers our pain. Ceridwen seeks to help Afagddu become accepted into the ranks of nobility by brewing the draught of wisdom for him. In the same way, our higher selves encourage us to seek the hidden wisdom in the darkness of the shadow. Through this, we may enter into the "noble company" of the Divine. Great are the gifts that dwell deep in our shadow. Jungian psychology teaches that it is through the personal unconscious that we can access the collective unconscious and the powerful energies of the archetypal realms. The path to transformation, therefore, lies within.

Ceridwen's daughter Creirwy is hailed in a Welsh Triad as one of the three fairest women of Britain. Creirwy symbolizes the conscious self, those aspects of the self that already dwell in the light; the tools, gifts, and potentials already realized and activated in our lives. They are beautiful because they are outwardly manifested facets of our authenticity, reflecting the Divine light that dwells within us. Even so, we must be vigilant for signs of ego, the conscious counterpoint to the unconscious shadow. Ego expands while shadow represses, here metaphorically expressed as a female representation of active consciousness and a male representation of passive unconsciousness. Like the yin-yang symbol, each polarity contains the seed of the other.

Morda, the blind old man who kindles the fires that fuel the transformational power of the cauldron, represents the inner impulse to seek illumination, even from a place of darkness—even when immersed in shadow. Morda is the essence of hope that supports our quest for wisdom, granting us the tenacity and will to follow the process to its completion, even if we cannot see where the journey will take us—trusting that change will come is enough.

The small child, Gwion Bach, represents our inner potential seeking self-knowledge. He is the impulse that sets us down the path of personal growth, knowing what we want—or at least, thinking we do—but unsure of how to obtain it. He is the energy of evolution in our lives, bringing us closer to our genuine selves. The quest for transformation is activated through the receiving of the three drops of the draught of wisdom, or the Graal. Like the Kabalistic lightning bolt down the Tree of Life, the Three Rays of Awen illuminate the pathway to reconnection with the Divine through the act of re-creation.

The breaking of the Cauldron echoes the death of the old self that is the consequence of the illumination of wisdom. Limitations that once restrained potential and constrained the ability to see clearly are dissolved, their poisons leeched from our souls and laid bare once and for all. We have outgrown the vessel that once contained us, and have liberated the gifts of wisdom that dwell within the shadow. This burst of energy catalyzes great change in our lives, and we are never the same once we have undergone this alchemy of the soul.

The Five Cauldron Transformations

The shape-shifting dance of Ceridwen and Gwion, known in the Avalonian Tradition as the Five Cauldron Transformations, symbolize the transmutation of each part of the self from unconsciousness into consciousness. As we ride the cycle of inner exploration, we are challenged to effect change in all five realms of our beings—each change determining and stimulating the next. Representing the tension between the higher self and the shadow—one part seeking consciousness, the other wishing to remain hidden in the unconscious—the chase teaches us that we cannot escape responsibility for our growth and our lives—true wisdom *must* be earned.

When we break down this cycle into its five key elements, we find yet another repetition of the fivefold pattern found in the Apple of Wisdom, and we can better understand the energetic correspondences, transformational symbolism, and spiritual challenges each represent. If we follow the flow of energy in the order presented in the story of Ceridwen, we find ourselves guided through a process that moves us through the five elements of Western Tradition—Earth, Water, Fire, Air, and Spirit—in ascending vibration. Mirroring the Druidic initiatory rite through the Three Realms of Land, Sea, and Sky, we are called to gather threads of being in all aspects of our lives to achieve true and positive change.

Hare and Greyhound

ELEMENT: Earth

LEVEL OF BEING: Physical

ENERGY CENTER: Root

ASPECT OF THE SELF: Shadow self

THE CALL: To identify the manifestations of shadow in our lives in order to redirect its energy to soul growth and self-actualization

THE QUEST: Seeking balanced abundance and personal mastery, and embracing self-worth

THE CHALLENGE: In what ways have our unconscious illusions of shadow taken root in our lives?

AVALONIAN CYCLE OF HEALING: The Station of Confrontation

Salmon and Otter

ELEMENT: Water

LEVEL OF BEING: Emotional

ENERGY CENTER: Womb

ASPECT OF THE SELF: Unconscious self

THE CALL: To obtain discernment between intuitive insights and the fear-based defenses generated by attachment to shadow

THE QUEST: Seeking compassionate empathy and soul healing, and coming to trust inner wisdoms

THE CHALLENGE: What patterns of destructive behavior have their source in inner woundings?

AVALONIAN CYCLE OF HEALING: The Station of Descent

Wren and Hawk

ELEMENT: Air

LEVEL OF BEING: Mental

ENERGY CENTER: Throat

ASPECT OF THE SELF: Conscious self

THE CALL: To overcome the shadow-generated filter of illusion defining our personal limitations and choices

THE QUEST: Seeking new perspectives and clear communication, and living the truth of the authentic self

THE CHALLENGE: How can we reclaim the energies tied up in maintaining false perceptions of our selves and the world?

AVALONIAN CYCLE OF HEALING: The Station of Emergence

Grain and Hen

ELEMENT: Fire

LEVEL OF BEING: Spiritual

ENERGY CENTER: Heart

ASPECT OF THE SELF: Higher self

THE CALL: To manifest the higher self potential realized by disempowering the hold of shadow on the self

THE QUEST: Seeking a center of right action and Divine inspiration, and effecting personal transformation

THE CHALLENGE: How can we move ourselves from a place of unconscious reaction to one of conscious action?

AVALONIAN CYCLE OF HEALING: The Station of Resolution

Gwion and Taliesin

ELEMENT: Spirit

LEVEL OF BEING: Divine

ENERGY CENTER: Third Eye

ASPECT OF THE SELF: Inner Divine

THE CALL: To consciously recognize and fully embrace the unity of the Divine and the self

THE QUEST: Seeking the complete actualization of the truth of the Goddess within

THE CHALLENGE: How can we live consciously in the material world while embracing the truth of our Divine nature?

AVALONIAN CYCLE OF HEALING: The Station of Integration

The result of our transformations—the death of the old self—is represented in Ceridwen's story by the devoured seed. This piece of grain is the potential that lies in the darkness, awaiting rebirth. The nine months spent in Ceridwen's womb symbolizes our need to enter into the mysteries of the Divine Feminine, where we can find wisdom through this immersion in the unconscious. Outwardly, there is no action, but deep within we must experience a period of gestation; a reconfiguration of internal energies and how they are used.

Metaphorically, the radiant brow of the reborn Gwion—now Taliesin—demonstrates enlightenment obtained through Cycle work. Passing through our challenges and effecting positive change, wisdoms earned and gained are manifested aspects of the actualized self. Yet, for all he had attained, Ceridwen cast the infant Taliesin out into the water to be found in a salmon weir (the salmon being a powerful Celtic symbol of wisdom) by the Welsh prince Elphin. Although changed,

Taliesin was still incomplete, and had to return to the watery realm of the unconscious to turn the wheel of Cycle once more.

Like Taliesin, we too must re-enter the Cauldron to begin our work anew. We bring our lessons and wisdoms with us, but we are not made complete in just one revolution. Our lessons permit us to see more of the "light"; our sight, perception, and understanding have expanded but there is still a long road of growth ahead of us. The beauty of this work is that each time we enter into the mystery of Cycle, we come to it with our new perspectives, easing our process and accelerating the quest for wholeness. But where is this Vessel of Transformation to be found? Therein lies the heart of the quest.

Seeking the Cauldron

In Caer Pedryvan, four its revolutions;
In the first word from the cauldron when spoken,
From the breath of nine maidens it was gently warmed.
Is it not the cauldron of the chief of Annwn?
What is its intention?
A ridge about its edge and pearls.

—PREIDDEU ANNWN—THE SPOILS OF ANNWN

Powerful symbols of the Feminine, cauldrons feature prominently in Celtic myth and legend as objects sought in quest and pilgrimage. In Welsh mythos, we see it manifest in several guises—the Cauldron of Plenty, the Cauldron of Regeneration, and the Cauldron of Inspiration and Wisdom. Pre-cursors to the Grail quest, these stories reflect Pagan Britain's beliefs, transmitted through a timeless oral tradition. Stories tell of the sacred Otherworld and the journey to claim the cauldron, a task undertaken by brave warriors facing challenges of the Fortress of the Old Ones.

The fourteenth-century Welsh poem *Preiddeu Annwn—The Spoils of Annwn* is an early contribution to Arthurian mythos. *Preiddeu Annwn* spins the tale of Arthur's journey in his boat, Prydwen, into the

Otherworld in search of the Cauldron of Inspiration. This theme is echoed again in the Welsh story of *Culhwch and Olwen*, where Arthur sets sail for Ireland in order to retrieve a magical Cauldron of Plenty. In *Branwen, Daughter of Llyr*, one of the Four Branches of *The Mabinogi*, we see another cauldron brought back from Ireland. The sacred item in this tale is the Cauldron of Regeneration which possesses the power to bring the dead back to life. We see a pattern revealed in these stories—the need to travel over water to seek a vessel of transformation, wisdom, and rebirth. This theme survives in the quest for the Holy Grail where the cup of Christ is sought to heal the Wounded King and bring renewal to the land.

The original quest is for the draught of wisdom brewed in the Cauldron of Ceridwen. Bards sought this vessel in their pursuit of Divine illumination, believing that true Awen could be incubated in the time spent in Ceridwen's womb; their subsequent rebirth and stream of inspiration heralded their initiation into Her mysteries. We too can partake of this mystery by riding the Cycle of Healing and consciously participating in the process of our inner distillation. Separating the three drops of wisdom from the poisoned remainder of the brew is an important part of liberating the energies of Sovereignty tied up in the unconscious impulses of the shadow. Here is the quest for the touch of the Goddess and the bounty of Her Cauldron.

With the coming of Christianity, the vessel of the Goddess is transformed into the cup of the Last Supper, the Holy Grail. Raising the cauldron up off the earth, the grail becomes a cup on a stem, thus distancing it from the more Pagan sexual aspects of the cauldron and moving it from chthonic root energy into the realm of allegory and intellect. Yet, the transpersonal symbolism of the quest remains, be it for cup or cauldron. Just as the knight seeks the grail, so the higher mind function seeks the primal unconsciousness, and the patriarchy seeks the lost Divine Feminine.

For women, the quest takes on a different meaning, for in myth and essence and biology, we have always been the keepers of the sacred vessel. As women seeking the grail, therefore, we are on a quest to restore our inner Sovereignty—that essence of fully conscious self-determination—and to acknowledge the Goddess within. We must activate and maintain our personal power instead of giving it up to someone or something else. To accomplish this, we must begin to fill our own cup so we may drink of the healing draught therein.

This work towards inner unfolding is the true nature of the grail quest. Whom does the grail serve? Each step taken towards wholeness is another drop of precious liquid in our own personal grail … and when it overflows, the Inner Sovereign is revealed and the land—our souls—are healed. The grail quest is a personal pilgrimage on the unknown pathway. The journey into the self is the microcosm of the journey into the All. Magick is soul healing…"the ability to change consciousness at will." Women of Avalon are bearers of the grail and the daughters of Ceridwen. As such, we act as spiritual midwives, birthing ourselves and attending the births of each other into the Sovereignty of womanhood. We each must find and heal our inner queen. Just as King Arthur was brought to the holy island for healing and left in the safekeeping of her priestesses, the gift of spiritual abundance is found by voyaging to the Otherworld in search of the vessel of Sovereignty.

Entering the Cauldron of Ceridwen allows us to connect with our priestess self—that fully conscious and empowered essence held by the ladies of Avalon. As we embark upon this quest for wholeness we gather the scattered parts of ourselves; at different times and in different seasons, we add them to the brew. Through this alchemical process, we reveal the three drops of Awen—the illumination within the shadow. Freeing these drops causes the vessel to break—the unneeded elements of the brew are our outmoded patterns, and the image of the person we thought we were is shattered by the truth's revelation of the light.

It is an endless process, for the gifts of wisdom must be earned. Submitting to the trials of the Cauldron requires us to effect change in all aspects of the self. We must move through the Cauldron Transformations, returning at last to the inner Cauldron—the womb of the devouring mother who gathers us inside of Herself so that we may integrate all that we have seen, experienced and suffered, and we may be reborn—connected and whole. We become the Radiant Brow—our changes and energetic shifts visible for all to see.

Yet, this victory is not the last, for with each turn of the Cycle, and with each phase of our learning, we must return again to the mysteries of the Cauldron and immerse ourselves once more into the waters of our unconscious to seek the next level of wisdom. We are constantly rarified in the Cauldron of Ceridwen, each revisit bringing us closer to our true essence. As we go, our vision becomes clearer and more of our path to wholeness is revealed. Then, with increased clarity and discernment, we can use the Avalonian Cycle of Healing to part the mists of illusion and find the essence of Avalon Within.

3

THE OTHERWORLDLY JOURNEY

There are many different roads leading to our English Jerusa-lem, 'the holiest erthe in Englande'. We can approach it by the high road of history ... Or we can come to Glastonbury by the upland path of legend ... And there is a third way to Glaston-bury, one of the secret Green Roads of the soul—the Mystic Way that leads through the Hidden Door into a land known only to the Eye of Vision. This is Avalon of the Heart for those who love her ... Legend and history and the vision of the heart blend in the building of the Mystical Avalon.

GLASTONBURY: AVALON OF THE HEART, DION FORTUNE

THERE IS GREAT WISDOM AND deep insight in the preceding words, penned by perhaps one of Glastonbury's most famous residents in modern times. An accomplished occultist and founder of an esoteric order called the Society of the Inner Light, Dion Fortune understood the mechanism for opening the doors of learning and understanding beyond what is assessable through more "orthodox" methods of inquiry. Wisely, she calls for the journey to be undertaken from a place of balance—three roads interwoven, bringing us at last to our destination—Avalon of the Heart.

Very little can be stated authoritatively about Avalon's history, and legend leaves us with but a taste of the full course of the sacred island's surrounding tradition. To spread our focus, Druidism and other Celtic Pagan practices are still much obscured by the passage of time; while theories and reconstructions abound, we may never fully know what was. We who seek Avalon's shores are both challenged and gifted by the few glimpses we find of her existence that have survived the ages.

One note in the vast song of Celtic spirituality, Avalon has become enshrouded in the mist of distant memory. How then can we seek to reconstruct the entire tapestry from a few salvaged threads? What value is there in following a path with so much of its length obscured by time and overgrown from disuse? How can we hope to find the way when the destination itself appears to be uncertain? There are many tools at the disposal of she who would part the mists. Material culture in the form of artifacts, classical accounts, medieval manuscripts, and tomes of historical information gathered about the Celts are very important in our quest, and should be well studied and consulted—but these are only the beginning. We must treat these sources as a springboard and a mirror of truth.

In each object, verse, and description we find remnants of a symbolic language—the language of the collective unconscious, the language of the Gods, the language of our souls. A great deal of information is encoded in these symbols, and anyone seeking to work within the Celtic archetype would do well to immerse themselves in understanding this language. Symbols are the keys that open the door to consciousness. One need only look at a deck of Tarot cards, the Kabalistic Tree of Life glyph, Druidic ogham, or any pictorial alphabet to see how very powerful symbols can be. Their meanings transcend time and language; they are not limited by speech or the written word. They are both fluid and enduring, and beyond them lies an understanding of the Divine.

Symbols are a medium between flesh and spirit, thought and emotion, this world and the Otherworld. Understanding how symbols work is a powerful way to tie into otherwise hidden or occult knowledge. We are empowered because we are not limited to what is written; we can gain direct access into the archetypal realms. When we reach these realms, we can connect with the Divine source. The Gods were not meant to be worshiped and adored from afar; direct experience of Them is an attainable reality. They *want* us to reach towards Them and ask for direction. They will readily provide us with the information we need to progress on our path to wholeness, for what is the goal of spirituality, if not evolution and growth?

It is important to begin in study—to learn, experience, and understand as much as possible relating to what is known about Avalon through history and literature, art and archaeology, myth and folklore. We can seek out the patterns, uncover the symbols, and learn to reveal the way toward a place of true understanding. Only the path of the inner quest will reveal the whereabouts of the grail, and once found, we can drink deeply of the same draught our foremothers tasted. And oh—what changes will occur in our lives and beings!

We will have come to know the nature of Avalon, for we have studied her and have understood her for what she is. We will have unveiled the pattern that has resulted in Avalon's existence as well as the reasons for her re-emergence. Most importantly, as we act in the world from our changed heart, having returned to Avalon at last, we will see how the knowledge of her will ripple from our individual ponds to cause lasting change in the Earth and our sisters' lives everywhere.

The Path of History

Arthur himself, our renowned King, was mortally
wounded and was carried off to the Isle of Avalon,
so that his wounds might be attended to. He handed
the crown of Britain over to his cousin Constantine, the
son of Cador, Duke of Cornwall: this in the year 542
after our Lord's incarnation.

—GEOFFREY OF MONMOUTH,
THE HISTORY OF THE KINGS OF BRITAIN

There are many theories about the real-world location of the Holy Isle, almost all of them centering on Avalon as the final resting place of King Arthur. According to the research presented in their book *Journey to Avalon* (1997), Barber and Pykitt place Avalon on Bardsey Island, off the coast of Wales. In *The Keys to Avalon* (2000), Blake and Lloyd contend that many Arthurian locales known to us from legend and regional lore were in fact transplanted from Wales to Britain and Cornwall. Both works cite religious and political gain as the motivation for the cooption of the Arthurian landscape by English royalty and the Church. As we will see, there is precedent for this sort of enterprise.

The most compelling connection between Glastonbury and Avalon—and the most highly debated—is the discovery of the burial place of Arthur and Guinevere in 1191 by the monks at Glastonbury Abbey. A lead cross, documented in *Britannia* by William Camden in 1607, bore the words *"Hic Jacet Sepultus Inclitus Rex Arturius In Insula Avalo-*

nia" (Here lies buried the famous King Arthur in the Island of Avalon). The cross has since been lost to time, but it lies at the center of great controversy. Today's historians believe this grave marker to be a forgery created by the Glastonbury monks seeking financial gain for the ailing Abbey. Indeed, excavation of this grave brought renewed fame and fortune to Glastonbury, and it became a place of pilgrimage and tribute for royalty and commoners alike. The alleged remains of the legendary King and Queen were reburied in a marble tomb in front of the high altar of the Abbey Church in the thirteenth century, and later lost in the destruction of the Abbey during Henry VIII's Dissolution in 1539. Today, all that remains of this tomb is a plaque marking its location on the Abbey grounds.

A strong link exists between Avalon and Glastonbury, despite other evidence indicating Arthur's final resting place may have been elsewhere. To this day, that small Somerset town is the destination of spiritual pilgrims from all over the world. There is some compelling archaeological evidence that the Vale of Avalon, at the very least, was once a sacred Pagan site. From a geomantic perspective, Glastonbury's landscape lends itself to the alchemical mysteries that are at the heart of Avalon's work. The cyclic transmutation of energies is visible in the most prominent features of this hallowed land, making Glastonbury a fitting vessel to hold the energies of Avalon, and it is this perspective—that ancient Avalon once existed as an inland island on what is today Glastonbury— that this book has embraced.

While there may never be definitive proof that Glastonbury was once indeed the Island of Avalon, it has held the energies of Avalon for centuries, and has done so for spiritual seekers of the Holy Isle into the modern day. Fabricated or authentic, there is an energetic connection to Avalon that overlays the town of Glastonbury like an ancient mist, accumulated over time and through the workings of the collective unconscious; it is through this overlay that real and transformational connection to Avalon may be made.

The Path of Legend

"… To the island–valley of Avilion;
Where falls not hail, or rain, or any snow,
Nor ever wind blows loudly; but it lies
Deep–meadow'd, happy, fair with orchard lawns
And bowery hollows crown'd with summer sea,
Where I will heal me of my grievous wound."

—ALFRED LORD TENNYSON,
IDYLLS OF THE KING (427–432)

Just as the search for the physical location of Avalon is anchored in the lore of the mighty Dark Age King, the majority of what we know about the Holy Island of Avalon comes to us through Arthurian legend. Indeed, some of the earliest stories of Arthur show him voyaging to the Celtic Otherworld in search of the Sacred Cauldron, paving the way for his later connections both with the Holy Grail and with Avalon. Just as when he sought the cauldrons in *Culhwch and Olwen* and in *The Spoils of Annwn*, Arthurian mythos depicts him traveling by boat to receive the sword of kingship from the hand of the Lady of the Lake, an archetypal echo of the Goddess of Sovereignty. Later, we see the mortally wounded king being borne over the Western Sea to Avalon by three queens to receive healing so that he could return once more to champion the Island of the Mighty. Clearly, then, the journey to the Otherworld is strongly associated with a voyage over water towards an island to the west. This paradisiacal island is also the providence of women, a motif seen both in Welsh and Irish mythology. Examples of sacred islands of women abound in Celtic lore, oftentimes found inhabited by a ninefold sisterhood, ostensibly Pagan priestesses in service to the Goddess.

As we have seen in Welsh legend, the Otherworld Cauldron of Inspiration and Plenty is warmed by the breath of nine maidens. These priestesses appear to play an oracular role as well, as the poem indicates that the cauldron speaks poetry in the form of divinely inspired verses.

Inspiration is related to the act of breathing, the taking in of spirit, and it is this breath that warms the cauldron and ignites the "Fire in the Head" that comes with acquiring Awen. As Ceridwen is considered the bardic muse, and the bubbling forth of Awen from Her Cauldron is the source of all poetry, an argument can be made that the cauldrons in *The Spoils of Annwn* and the myth of Ceridwen is one and the same.

The Île de Sein, or the Island of Sena, off the coast of Brittany in northwestern France is also known as the Isle of Druidesses. There, nine priestesses known as the *Gallicenae* served as oracles and healers. Renowned for their ability to shape-shift, they were said to hold power over the wind and waves. According to Breton legend, no man was ever allowed on Sena; the priestesses themselves took a boat to the mainland whenever their services were needed. Said to live in perpetual virginity (meant in the old sense of being tied to no man), they nevertheless took lovers on the mainland, always returning to dwell alone on their island. Classical accounts paint these priestesses as Bacchantes, recounting how during the annual re-thatching of their temple, the first woman to drop her bundle would be set upon by the others and torn to pieces in sacrifice.

Breton legend also speaks of the Korrigan and her nine sisters, a group of women with magical powers associated with springs and water. These women, sometimes collectively called the Korrigan, are said to be shape-shifters, talented singers, and potent healers with the ability to travel wherever they willed using the power of thought. Captivatingly beautiful by night, the Korrigan are revealed to have white hair and red eyes by day—colors giving a powerful indication of their Otherworldly origin and connection to the mysteries of the Goddess. Although reduced to the status of fairy folk in Breton lore, this sisterhood could well reflect the memory of an order of priestesses that dwelt in the local forest; they have been linked to stories of the Gallicenae.

The Korrigan is sometimes seen as an individual personage, possessing a wand used to turn the forest into a wondrous castle. There, by night, she and her impossibly beautiful sisters work seductive spells on hapless men, lulled into a state of forgetfulness. When daylight comes, the woods return to their natural state; the women are transformed into hideous hags and the men become their victims. This theme may be a later demonization of the ancient rites of Sovereignty, whereby the Goddess chose the man most fit to be king, while the old king died in sacrifice. The enchanted castle and the forgetfulness of mortal visitors are common motifs in Celtic legends dealing with the Otherworld. Scholars see a strong relationship between the Korrigan and Ceridwen, as both possess similar powers and embody the primal power of the Great Goddess—the polarity of life and death.

Another goddess of inspiration and healing is Brigit of Ireland. Her shrine at Cill Dara—the Church of the Oak, that most venerated of Celtic trees—was centered on an eternal flame kept alight by nineteen priestesses. This tradition survived into Christian times, safeguarded by nuns dedicated to Saint Brigid. Objecting to its Pagan origin, the flame was extinguished by the Archbishop of Dublin in 1220 CE. The sacred fire was revived after his death, only to pass into darkness once more during the Reformation. Joyfully, in 1993 the Brigidine Sisters kindled the perpetual flame anew at the site of the original shrine in Kildare, Ireland. It remains today as a place of pilgrimage and devotion to those dedicated to Brigit in all of Her guises.

Perhaps in resonance with the healing powers attributed both to the Island of Avalon and the goddess-made-saint, Brigit became associated with Glastonbury during the later Christian period in the guise of the much-loved Saint Brigid. The tower of Saint Michael on Glastonbury Tor bears a carving of Her image, and tradition holds that She left relics behind in Glastonbury during Her pilgrimage there in 488 CE. Near Wearyall Hill in an area known as Beckery—which means "Little Ireland"—is a small hill called Bride's Mound, presently being reclaimed for the Goddess in modern-day Glastonbury. Bride is another name for Brigit.

The Shrine of Brigit at Cill Dara is but one example of a community of holy women from Irish tradition. There is a genre of early Irish writing known as *Immrama*—the Wonder Voyage. In one such tale, the Voyage of Bran Mac Febal, a mysterious woman appears before a gathering, encouraging Bran to begin his journey across the sea into the Otherworld. She holds in her hand a branch from the orchards of *Emhain Abhlach*—the Plain of Apples. After embarking on their journey and finding one fantastic island after another, Bran and his crew encounter the Land of Women. Here, each of his men finds companionship with one of the beautiful female inhabitants of the land. Their plates are never emptied of food and they are given anything they desire. Time passed differently in this land; one year in the Land of Women was equal to several years in the rest of the world. This kind of temporal dissonance is a common feature of the Otherworld in Celtic traditions.

Another Immram, the Voyage of Maldun, speaks of the Island of Women, describing it as possessing a mound and a fortress filled with people, where maidens tended to a fountain or bath, and whose mother greeted the travelers on the back of a swift horse. The men of Maldun's ship were welcomed to the island, and told that all who dwelt therein would never die. In both stories, it is exceedingly difficult for the sailors to leave the company of these Otherworldly women, and their departure is marked by great sorrow.

Maldun and his crew also encountered an Island of Apples, and although they sailed around the island for three days and nights, could find no way to land upon its shores. Maldun broke a twig off of one of the overhanging apple trees which later produced three apples, each providing enough food for the crew to last for forty days. As with Avalon, which was said to produce abundant food of its own accord, these holy places of apples and women mirror the functions of the Sacred Cauldron—providing healing, abundance, and inspiration.

The Ninefold Sisterhood of Avalon

There nine sisters rule by a pleasing set of laws those
who come to them from our country. She who is first of
them is more skilled in the healing art, and excels her
sisters in the beauty of her person. Morgen is her name,
and she has learned what useful properties all the herbs
contain, so that she can cure sick bodies. She also knows an
art by which to change her shape, and to cleave the air on
new wings like Daedalus; when she wishes she is at Brest,
Chartres, or Pavia, and when she will she slips down
from the air onto your shores.

—VITA MERLINI, GEOFFREY OF MONMOUTH

Legend tells of another group of priestesses dwelling upon a sacred island renowned for its healing arts—a place of tranquility for departed
souls. Its keepers were the Ninefold Sisterhood of Avalon. These wom-
en were learned in language, science, mathematics, music, and healing.
The Island of Avalon, or *Ynys Afallon*, appears to have been a religious
center for women's study in the mode of the Druidic Colleges established all over the British Isles. The Island of Anglesey, or *Ynys Mon*, is
a prominent example of these communities, perhaps serving as inspiration for, or evolving into, later monastic Christian settlements like on
the Island of Iona.

Like the Korrigan, the Priestesses of Sena, and Ceridwen Herself, the
Women of Avalon were shape-shifters. Able to transform themselves
into ravens (a bird associated with the Otherworld and the totemic ani-
mal of the goddess Branwen), the Ladies of Avalon were able to transport
themselves anywhere they wished. This shape-changing ability suggests
facility with shamanic techniques, and may refer to the initiatory rites
that were a part of the Avalonian Mysteries—resulting in the transformation of the self. This may also serve as evidence that the name Morgan
did not refer to an individual, but rather was used as a title by the high
priestesses of Avalon, known as the Nine Morgens. Different women
bearing the same name could contribute to the notion of shape-changing

and would explain how "Morgan" could be in more than one place at a time or travel over great distances in the span of a heartbeat.

According to Malory, Morgan is one of the veiled women in black, riding the barge that comes to take Arthur to Avalon. The dark cloaks of these sisters, like those reported in descriptions of the siege of Anglesey—where women dressed in black clothing aided the Druids of Ynys Mon against Roman invasion—could also account for their association with ravens.

In his *Le Morte D'Arthur*, Malory tells us Morgan le Fay was sent to study at a nunnery, where she became a "great clerk of necromancy." While the early Christian settlement in Glastonbury is said to have had a monastic building for women on Wearyall Hill near a shrine to Mary Magdalene, this nunnery could also refer to the memory of Glastonbury as a pre-Christian women's religious center. It is not a far stretch to consider that the nunnery grew out of the priestess center since the historic record indicates this often happened in the British Isles as part of the transition from Paganism to Christianity. Geoffrey of Monmouth gives the names of Morgan and her sisters in the *Vita Merlini*: Moronoe, Moroe, Gliorn, Glitonea, Gliten, Tythonoe, Tythen, and Tithen. The names of these women are of obscure origin though scholar Stuart McHardy has traced them linguistically to water deities and water nymphs from Celtic and Classical sources. The name Morgan itself comes from the Welsh, meaning "shore of the sea."

Again, we return to the realm of water—associated with the Otherworld in Celtic myth and the medium through which we can obtain access to the domain of the unconscious. The Island of Avalon is the soul's destination—the Wonder Journey into the heart of the self. It holds the key to unlocking the treasure of women's wisdom, thus providing the map to seeing our life's patterns, granting us the power to change our course if we so choose. The more conscious we become of our inner landscape, the greater will be our ability to steer the ship of our soul to a place of empowered Sovereignty.

The Path of Spirit

A branch of the apple–tree from Emain
I bring, like those one knows;
Twigs of white silver are on it,
Crystal brows with blossoms.
There is a distant isle,
Around which sea–horses glisten:
A fair course against the white–swelling surge,
Four feet uphold it.

—THE VOYAGE OF BRAN, SON OF FEBAL

Considered to be the parent culture of modern European and Indian languages and society, the mysterious Indo-Europeans were a nomadic people living in the area between the Black and Caspian Seas in eastern Europe around 3000 BCE. Beginning approximately in 2500 BCE these people spread out, migrating in many different directions. They moved east to northern India, Afghanistan, Iran, and Russia; south to Armenia; and west to Greece, Germany, Italy, Spain, France, Britain, Ireland, and Scandinavia. Wherever they settled, the Indo-Europeans appeared to overcome existing populations and imposed their language and customs upon them. The peoples we today recognize as the Celts evolved from the Indo-European "mother culture," therefore sharing an ancestral bond with peoples and civilizations seemingly as far removed from the Celtic homelands as Greece and Persia.

Recognizing this ancestry is important when considering the commonalties of the various cultures we consider part of Western civilization. Of specific note, it paints a picture of interconnectedness that belies the view that ancient peoples were isolated in time and space from each other. This is often erroneously assumed through the non–holistic study of history that examines each culture and people separately and out of context. In truth, there was much more communication than we may give the ancients credit for. For example, Cornwall was part of a thriving tin trade route with the Middle East, while Greek *ampho-*

rae were highly prized and seen in royal burial mounds of continental Celts. We see, therefore, that not only was there a common Western origin, but the peoples of the West and the ancient Near East also enjoyed continued connection through trade and exchange—of goods as well as ideas.

From a Jungian perspective, we can infer that these peoples drew, at the onset, from a common and well-established collective unconscious. This would explain how the many cultures share so many similar manifestations of belief system and philosophy, giving them a Western "feel." In contrast, the peoples of the East seem to draw from a different set of patterns and symbols, thus shaping a distinctly Asian family of belief and philosophy.

As the Indo-Europeans migrated and settled, they developed cultural differences dictated by their adaptation to different environments, assimilation of indigenous populations, and different cultural needs. These needs helped create pieces of the collective unconscious, and became distinctively part of the culture that birthed it, forming what can be described as a specific archetypal realm. These archetypal realms exist within the greater collective, and yet carry a specific cultural signature. This signature is what energetically allows us to differentiate between what is Greek or Norse or Celtic in form and energy. Every archetypal realm possesses a specific set of rules, symbolic language, set of tools, belief system, and philosophical perspective. These reflect the spiritual, material, and emotional needs of the culture that spun the archetype. For this reason, it is important to become familiar with the culture from which spiritual inspiration is drawn, otherwise a complete understanding of the archetypal realm can never be obtained—indeed, its deeper levels will remain closed.

The Avalonian archetype is a thread in the Celtic archetypal realm, which in turn is a patch in the quilt of the Western collective unconscious. Because of this energetic family tree, it is appropriate to say the Avalonian Tradition is part of the Western Mystery Tradition, and therefore shares commonalties with other Western esoteric paths. These commonalties are what allow us to use Western esoteric tools and techniques in our quest for Avalon. As there are no complete and authentically ancient Celtic religious traditions in existence today, we can use general Western techniques to unlock lost wisdoms—the Mystic Way extolled by Dion Fortune.

From an archetypal perspective, whether Avalon as reflected in myth, legend, and literature actually existed in a distant Celtic past is irrelevant. Over the past two millennia, and especially in the last 150 years, enough psychic energy has been invested in the symbol of Avalon as the Blessed Isle of Women—the resting place of Arthur, the nunnery of magick, the Druidic College and Priestess Temple dedicated to the Goddess—that the essence of Avalon firmly resides as an archetypal realm on the astral as part of the Otherworld. As such, the Holy Isle is accessible through the collective unconscious.

While there are advantages to working directly on the site of what was once ancient Avalon, there are alternative ways of connecting to the Sacred Landscape. It is powerful to visit the physical location of ancient Avalon as it exists today in the small Somerset town of Glastonbury, for the energetic resonance there is very strong and can facilitate our connection to the Avalonian archetypal realm. Yet, such a journey may not be possible for everyone, or if made, permits only a temporary connection unless one permanently moves to Glastonbury. Happily, there are other options at our disposal, for, as part of their legacy, the Celts have provided us with a powerful tool with which to access the realm of the Otherworld—the Immram. While the word itself is of Irish origin and refers to a classification of Irish tales, there are similar stories in Welsh mythos depicting journeys to the Otherworld over water. As research has yet to uncover a specific Welsh word to describe these types of tales, the Avalonian Tradition has adopted the use of the term to describe this powerful meditative tool.

The Immram is a deeply effective spiritual technique, analogous to Shamanic journeying and Kabalistic pathworking. What makes this Journey different from a guided meditation is that it is specifically keyed to allow the seeker to gain access to an established archetypal realm. As a spiritual mechanism, the Immram can be used as a means to reclaim and reactivate the spiritual essence of ancient Avalon, as well as a method of understanding the inner terrain in order to bring ourselves to wholeness.

The Immram takes us in journey across the waters of the personal unconscious until we pass over the last vestige of what is conscious—analogous to the Celtic concept of the Ninth Wave that marks the boundary between what is known and what is unknown. Only then can we enter into the transpersonal realm of the collective unconscious.

Undertaking the wonder voyage provides access to several categories of information about the archetypal realm to which we are journeying. These are:

OUTER KNOWLEDGE: A generalized corpus of information about the archetypal realm that any seeker may obtain. This is universal knowledge and can include the physical description of the place, its history, and traditional lore, as well as its cultural and spiritual importance.

OUTER WISDOM: Through the Immram, moving from mental comprehension to actualized implementation of insights we have received about a place. If the space to which we are voyaging was used for divination, for example, obtaining mastery of this skill will allow us to use this area of the archetypal landscape for its original purpose.

INNER KNOWLEDGE: Using the vibratory energetic of the realm to stimulate personal issues of like energy is a powerful tool for the Great Work. As like attracts like, voyaging to a space of predominantly earth-aligned energies, for example, will bring up issue work relating to the same element.

INNER WISDOM: Accomplishing the activation of a space in order
to utilize it in obtaining one's fullest potential. For example,
harnessing the divinatory power of the Red Spring to illuminate
situations in your own life that need expanded Sight. Not only
can the Immram bring personal issues to light, it can also be
a tool for soul growth by acting to effect lasting change in the
whole person.

One of the islands in the Western Sea, the Isle of Avalon still exists
as part of the collective unconscious, as it was in its height a Women's
Mystery school and temple to the Goddess. Even here, there are many
archetypal layers that have been built into Avalon's essence over millennia; these include Christian mythic overlays, the Arthurian legends,
and the present-day New Age movement. We need to be sure, therefore, that we set our course for the Avalon to which we wish to arrive.

The Immrama presented in this book and the information given for
each of the main sacred sites on Avalon are keyed to access a particular
aspect of the Avalonian archetypal realm and to help ground you in
the time period when Avalon was at its height as a temple and training
center. As you journey, should you find yourself in a different time period, make note of what you see; the information will still be pertinent
and will reconnect with the work presented here. It is not wrong to see
any aspect of Avalon from different time periods, especially if you have
been to Glastonbury physically in this life, or have a personal incarnational history with the site. Over time and with practice, you will become disciplined enough to consistently visit the Avalonian archetype
with which you are most interested in working.

With all of these things in mind, what follows is the basic format for
this Otherworld journey to Avalon. Initially, you will travel to the Holy
Island to meet a priestess who has agreed to act as your guide in your
growth and in all things Avalonian. She will be an important resource

as you walk this path, and it is essential that you put in the time and effort necessary to build a good relationship with her.

The more you walk the archetypal landscape of Avalon, the better worn the energy channel you create and the more readily the door to the hidden realms will be opened to you. When you have done so, you can begin to explore the island further. As you journey, take note of the paths you have been shown, and upon your return, be sure to plot out a map of where your travels have taken you.

Exploring the archetypal landscape of Avalon should not dissuade you from making an actual pilgrimage to the physical plane vessel of the energies of the Holy Island. Rather, connecting with the essence of ancient Avalon through Immrama is sure to augment your experience of the sacred sites of Glastonbury should you choose to journey to her shores. If you have already made the voyage in the realm of the physical, the tools presented in this book will help you to maintain your connection with these places of power, no matter how distant you may be in space and through time.

The Immram will work best when you have firmly laid down the journey in the pathways of your inner self. Until such time, it is helpful to memorize or create a recording of the Immram. Do at least ten minutes of breathing, as described below, before beginning the journey, becoming calm, focused, and centered. Be sure you are in a comfortable position, with all of your limbs uncrossed to facilitate the free flow of energy. It is never a good idea to do your work in bed at the end of the night, as you will probably find yourself asleep before you can get any inner work done. Surrounding yourself with Avalonian energies and influences will be helpful for the Immram. See the Solitary Avalonian Ritual on p. 255 for more information on how to set up your space for inner work.

The Power Breath

The foundation of any energy work or spiritual discipline is breath. Rhythmic breathing especially acts to bring us in line with the cosmic tides, and opens the channels of our bodies to receive from the universe. Observing someone in deep sleep will reveal the way we are programmed by nature to breathe rhythmically automatically. This is part of our bodies' cleansing process and the way we realign and reactivate our energy centers. Rhythmic breathing with intention during waking time ties us to that unconscious wisdom that takes over when we sleep. Opening our breath rocks our sacrum and our occiput—bones at the base of our spine and the base of our skull, respectively. This rocking helps circulate cerebrospinal fluid, keeping neural function at optimum and energy channels clear.

To find your breath, sit and clear your mind. Bring your attention to your breathing and keep it natural. Don't get caught up in any stray thoughts that may come; acknowledge and release them. Return your focus to your breath. There are many perspectives about rhythmic breathing. Some sources recommend adapting a universal breathing pattern of a set number of counts in, a set count held, and a set count out, but it is equally empowering to find that rhythm specific to your own body. You may find a repetition of inhalation and exhalation to a count of three feels right to you, while someone else prefers a count of seven. You may prefer to breathe in through your nose and out through your mouth, while another sister only breathes through her mouth. It may take some experimentation and time to listen to what your body wants to do, but it is worth it to find this inherent pattern, called the Power Breath. When you have found it, keep with it and incorporate it into a daily practice, paying attention to how it makes your body feel and how it shifts your energy. Don't be surprised if this process turns out to be difficult at first; persistence is key. In time, it will be easy to reach that Power Breath, and you will begin to feel its effects in your life.

Do your best to be as conscious of your breathing as you can throughout the day. At work, while driving, walking, or performing any activity, be mindful of your breath. Note how making the shift to rhythmic breath changes your perspective on any activity. Keep tuning yourself in to your rhythm. This will cleanse your energy centers all day long, keep you connected to your body, and keep your energy circulating. When you sit down to do your breathing work then, much of the struggle to overcome blockages will be lessened, and you will find it easier to "snap" to that space. As you integrate Power Breath into a daily discipline of meditation and journeying, you will find that the more adept you become at breathing, the easier the other work will be, because your breath has become a trigger for that empowered and clear space.

It is essential to come to any ritual or meditation work with as clear an energy field as possible. This fosters a strong connection to our higher self while opening us to be as receptive as possible to the wisdoms and insights we hope to obtain. This inner clarity helps us in our daily lives as well, allowing us to see things for what they are rather than through a screen of lower-self-generated illusion. Living from a clear center is a way to greater consciousness—the illuminated path that leads to self-actualization.

The Immram to Avalon

The Journey Begins

Find yourself in an ancient forest. It is night and the moon is full, though you can barely make out her outline through the thick overhang of the trees above you. There is enough ambient light for you to see that you stand on a once well-used path leading through the woods. Experience the feel of the space, the sounds of the night, and the desire to travel up the path through the dense trees. You feel very safe and supported. With each sure step on the path, feel your mundane worries and cares fall away and become absorbed into the earth. With every footfall, know that many women have walked this path before you, many now walk beside you, and many will come to walk it after you. Connect with this feeling of timelessness, and continue forward through the woods, noting everything you can about your surroundings.

As you continue, notice the woods are becoming thinner. There is moisture in the air and springiness underfoot. The path curves left. The trees give way to brush. The brush gives way to a clearing. Find yourself on the marshy shore of a dark, still lake. The moon is high and bright in the sky. Notice her reflection on the glassy surface of the water. Listen to the sounds of the lake and all the creatures that live in and around it. Cast your eyes over the water to the far shore. A wall of mist descends, hiding it from your sight before rolling in to surround you. Feel the moisture on your face; experience what it is like to be enveloped in the mist.

You become aware of something shining through the grayness, a glint of metal condensing the now–diffused moonlight. Hanging by a crimson ribbon from the overhanging limb of a gnarled and ancient tree, a branch bedecked with nine silver apples glows invitingly through the surrounding brume. Inspired, you remove the Silver Branch and discover that each of the hanging apples is a cleverly wrought bell of silver. Grasping what appears to be a handle, well polished and smoothed by the hands of many pilgrims, you succumb to the inexplicable urge to shake the branch. Three times you shake it, and three times the tinkling laughter of the bells echoes across the lake, becoming absorbed into dense mists. Returning the branch to its resting place, you note that the only reply to the bells is a deep and expectant silence.

After a time, you sense rather than hear the movement of a vessel across the water. Almost instantly, the prow of a small watercraft is visible to you as it comes to a halt on the shore in front of you. It is the Barge of Avalon. Three dark robed and hooded figures stand in the prow; one of them extends her hand to you. You take it and she helps you on board. You take the place that has been prepared for you as the hooded figures move to the far end of the Barge, the thick mists obscuring them from your sight. The boat begins to move, gliding effortlessly across the water. Again, you sense, rather than see, movement in the front of the Barge, barely detecting a hint of muted sound. As if by magic, the veil of mists is rent in two and the far and shining shore is clear and close before you. Breathe in all that is this wonder—the blessed Island of Avalon.

As quickly as this journey across the water began, it comes to an end, and the Barge scrapes lightly upon the hallowed shore. Looking to the hooded figures, they seem to nod assent, and you disembark, stepping for the first time on this sacred ground. Plant your feet firmly here, and feel the energy of place course through your feet and up your limbs, infusing your very being with its vitality.

You have come home, Sister.

Note: This is the point from which the other Immrama in this book proceed. When doing this working for the purpose of meeting your Avalonian guide for the first time, please continue below. Otherwise, continue with the journey to the landscape area as described in their corresponding chapters.

Meeting Your Guide

After a time, you feel drawn to move forward and walk away from the marshy shoreline in the direction of the slumbering rise of the distant Tor. You are engulfed by a sweet, heady scent and find yourself in a vast apple orchard in full springtime bloom. The white blossoms glow silver in the moonlight. They burst forth from each limb and litter the dark ground like stars in the night. Ancient trees surround you, wonderfully gnarled and twisted. Walk among them, feeling compelled to move forward, at last finding yourself in the center of the orchard, standing in front of the largest and most ancient tree on the whole of the island.

This is the Mother Tree of Avalon, whose roots are firmly anchored in the distant past of Avalon's beginnings, and whose curving limbs reach out towards the unknowable future—some bearing delicate blossoms, others burgeoning with ripened fruit, and still others grasping for the sky with skeletal fingers, bare as bones. Her powerful trunk is thick and twisted with age yet more solidly strong than the most well-tempered steel. She is the vital heart of this most sacred grove—the Guardian of the Orchard and Keeper of Wisdom.

Approach the venerable being and extend your consciousness to honor the tree and introduce yourself. Give your name and speak your intention to learn the ways of the Goddess and Avalon. Explain that you are a student and seeker of wisdom, and ask in all humility for a guide to these shores … those within and without. When you are done, wait quietly and respectfully for a response. The Mother Tree begins to glow brightly, and a soft breeze rustles through her branches like a contented sigh. On the wake of the wind, one green leaf drifts down and lands on the ground in front of you. The moment it makes contact with the earth, it is engulfed in a blinding flash of light, and when your vision clears, you see a figure standing before you—your guide to the realms of Avalon.

Introduce yourself to your guide, and once more explain why you have come and what you wish to learn from walking the Avalonian path. Take as much time as you need to fill yourself with every detail you can about her appearance and her energy. Ask her for a name you can use to call her and for a symbol you can use to connect with her. Listen to her words. Receive the gift she holds for you. Ask how and where you can connect with her again.

This is the beginning of an important relationship, so take as much time as you need to make this first contact. Extend your hand to her and hold hers in your own. When you are done speaking with her, give her a gift in return and be sure to thank her graciously. Do not make this connection lightly. You are announcing your commitment to Avalon and to your growth. With knowledge comes responsibility.

After the Connection to Your Guide Has Been Made

When you are ready, bid your guide farewell. Thank the orchard and the Mother Tree for receiving you and facilitating your connection with your guide. Return the way you came, back to the lake's marshy shores where the Barge awaits you. Turn towards the island one last time. Take in three deliberate breaths of its essence to take back with you. Bow in reverence and deep gratitude. When ready, take your place on the Barge.

Effortlessly again, you glide across the water. With magickal swiftness, you find yourself on the far shore once more. Again, disembark from the vessel. Thank the priestesses in the prow for seeing you safely to Avalon and back. As one, they incline their head to you, and the Barge departs, the curtain of mist again enshrouding it and the sacred lake. Find the path that led you here, and enter the woods once more, reaching at last the place where this journey began. Making this inner pilgrimage changes you, and each time it is undertaken, the pathway becomes clearer. Take three deep calming and centering breaths, and return to your space, remembering all you have seen and experienced.

As we can see, the Immram is a powerful tool. It is a means to reclaim and reactivate the spiritual essence of ancient Avalon and also a potent method of understanding our inner terrain in order to bring our selves to wholeness. In all of our travels, we must not lose sight of the purpose of our strivings. On the one hand, we must adapt a discipline and commit ourselves to clearing the landscape so that we may travel less encumbered by our own issues, illusions, and expectations. On the other hand, while we seek to remember what is on ancient Avalon and to reclaim her wisdom as a legacy for the women of tomorrow, we must also renew the lessons of Avalon in our own lives.

Personal Alchemy and the Avalonian Cycle of Healing

There is much to explore in the Avalonian landscape—many power places with which to work and sacred sites to see and reclaim. When we call to these ancient sites, kindred energies within us rise to meet them. When we sing the song of the sacred landscape, our inner notes peal forth in harmony, allowing us knowledge both of what is within and what is without.

Each sacred site is a portal into the shining realms of Avalon. Through them, we can access specific information about their ritual usage, their symbolic place in Avalonian cosmology, and their importance in the training and initiation of a priestess. Once this information is reclaimed, their wisdoms can be put to practical use, and we can step through the mists to walk the holy landscape of Avalon once more. We need not stand directly on the ground which once held the energies of these sacred sites; these are but contact points which anchor the essence of place to the physical plane.

This akashic, or mystical, resonance is accessible through the path that lies within. Once we can approximate the energetic signature of a place, we can access its archetypal symbolism and the Otherworld becomes opened to us. By journeying to the archetypal landscape of ancient Avalon though Immrama, we awaken its corresponding energies within ourselves. These akashic power points can then be used as practical tools for self-understanding and personal transformation.

Each Immram presented in this book brings the seeker to a physical landscape area of the Holy Isle that is an energetic mirror of a Station in the Avalonian Cycle of Healing. Each of these unique natural phenomena cycles energy in a very particular way. We see these Stations mirrored in the Sacred Landscape of the Island of Avalon, specifically set in the natural phenomena embodied by the Tor Valley.

The Red Spring holds the energy of the first Station of the Avalonian Cycle of Healing—the Station of Descent. This is the journey undertaken at *Calan Gaeaf* (Samhain) and during the waning aspect

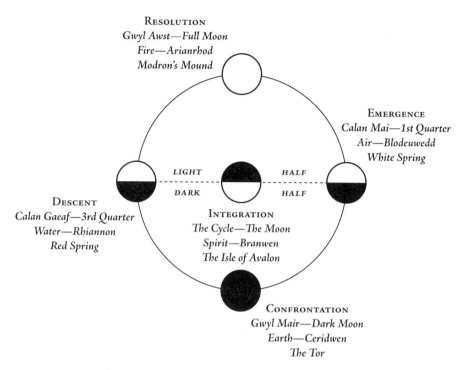

The Avalonian Cycle of Healing with Major Correspondences

of the lunar dance. Here is when the intention to uncover the shadow has been expressed to the universe; we begin the process of delving within—seeking out things that bring us pain, leave us unfulfilled, and which manifest repeatedly as destructive patterns in our lives. Journaling, meditation, and connection with the Source are invaluable tools for this archaeology of the soul.

Next, embodied in the energy of the Tor, comes the Station of Confrontation—the recognition and naming of the root of the issue first examined at Descent. Women of Avalon use the black void of the dark moon and *Gwyl Mair* (Imbolc), the nadir of the Wheel of the Year, as mirrors that reveal all truths—no matter how difficult or painful they may be to look upon.

With the knowledge gained through the ordeal within the darkness, the ascent begins, shedding the light of the waxing moon and the fires of *Calan Mai* (Beltane) upon the long-hidden pieces of the self. Aligned with the White Spring, Emergence into the world of illumination brings the wounds of the soul to the surface of understanding. This is the time to sow the seeds of abundance where there was once only limitation, cultivating wholeness where there was once only shadow.

Resolution occurs in the fullness of the moon, at the zenith of *Gwyl Awst* (Lughnasadh); this Station corresponds with Modron's Mound (Chalice Hill). Here, the fruits of our re-creation hang heavy in the orchards of our soul. We have successfully reclaimed energy bound in darkness, and re-channeled it into positive movement towards growth and self-realization.

At the center and between each of the other four Stations is a time of reflection and integration. Here, we synthesize lessons we have learned, assess the challenges that yet lie before us, and honor the Divinity within as our work takes us ever closer to the Source. With new tools at our disposal, we begin the Cycle again, seeing the journey with new eyes. The Station of Integration is symbolized by the whole of the Island of Avalon.

Entering the Cauldron for the first time is the most difficult for the woman who begins this cycle of Descent, Confrontation, Emergence, Resolution, and Integration. Change can be painful and is often shadowed by fear of the unknown. Like the Fool card of the Tarot, we must stride into the abyss with the faith that what lies beyond is a place of greater clarity, shifted perspective, and a step closer to wholeness. Once we have completed the first revolution and have seen progress made in our journeys toward actualization, that fear will be diminished for the next time through the Cycle. We have learned to trust the process and have come to know that the universe will support our own movement towards growth. We are never alone in our changes.

The great beauty of the Avalonian Tradition and the concept of sisterhood is that the seeker has access to other women, who also walk an inward (yet parallel) path, to use as resources and role models. Knowing that these women have faced their shadow and have emerged triumphant from the process is comforting and empowering. Every woman's passage to self-knowledge and healing is unique, but there is no better support system than those who are doing the work and living with a commitment to personal growth and wholeness. How very blessed are we who know such sisterhood in our lives!

In the end, however, no one can bring us to our healing but ourselves. As such, those who ride the Barge to Avalon as a solitary path are not at any disadvantage. Whether we are in community or follow Her ways in solitude, the work can only be done as an individual within our own selves. The Goddesses are our greatest advocates for empowerment. Honored and celebrated on Avalon, They were not supplicated in hopes of performing miracles, making everything instantly better. More than anything, the Goddesses want for Their daughters to be out of pain and attain true wholeness; however, They cannot—and will not—do the work for us. They are with us every step of the way, and every turn of the Cycle. Lovingly, They are always available to guide, counsel, console, encourage, and inspire we who seek to know Them. Yet, when all is said and done, only *we* can change ourselves; only *we* can choose the path of wisdom that lies within. The Avalonian Cycle of Healing is a powerful companion for our journey.

It is important then to meditate upon why one is drawn to this work. Know that the path of Avalon is a path of service, and it is only through clear and unconditional surrender to this service that true Sovereignty can be obtained. Three chains uphold the vessel of service; they are necessary to support the Cauldron from which the Elixir of Wisdom can be brewed. These foundations are:

SERVICE TO SELF: This service demands a commitment to personal
growth and obtaining inner authenticity. We must seek to heal
wounds preventing us from being all we truly are and we must

reclaim the gifts lying dormant in our shadow. This service frees us from the outmoded perspectives that bind us to endless iterations of reactive behavior, having nothing to do with the present. The first foundation of wholeness is the ability to love ourselves.

SERVICE TO SISTERS: This service demands a commitment to supporting other women in their personal process and building a strong, healthy community. We must seek the Goddess in our sisters, recognize the sacredness of the Feminine in all women and honor the lessons each of Her reflections brings to our lives. This service frees us from the competitiveness and mistrust for other women promoted by a society that seeks to keep us disconnected from our sisters and, therefore, from our power. The second foundation of wholeness is the ability to love others; true love can only come with the ability to first love oneself.

SERVICE TO GODDESS: This service demands a commitment to revealing the Divinity inherent in all things and actively working to recognize our connection to the All. We must seek the Goddess within ourselves and manifest the whole of our potential, for it is through us that the Lady works in the world. This service frees us from the limitations of our physicality and the illusion of our disconnection from the Source. Our gifts are the blessings of the Goddess and are meant to be given to the world. The third foundation of wholeness is the ability to love the Goddess—without fear and without shame. Only by loving the Goddess within the self and within others, can knowledge of Her complete and unconditional love be obtained.

To travel with clarity to the Island of Avalon is to commit to the healing found on her shores. We do not reclaim her ways for the sake of reclaiming—she is not a trophy to be hunted, hung on walls for admiration. What we discover about Avalon requires us to discover the corresponding energy within ourselves. Piece by piece, we heal the inner landscape, reclaiming our personal Sovereignty as we reactivate the archetypal realms of Avalon. It is this process of reactivation that has been poetically termed "drawing Avalon from beyond the mists."

In this process is an interesting duality: the more time, intent, and energy collectively invested in reactivating the archetypal realms of Avalon, the more accessible these realms become to any who seek her. And yet, the ways will never be completely open—it will still require much work and rarified discernment to fully part the veil and walk her sacred shores.

We who seek to be daughters of the island must acknowledge and honor our spiritual ancestors, those women of wisdom who have walked the path to the top of the Tor before us. We recognize the years of effort and standards of attainment upheld by these women and seek to integrate this into our own dedication to Avalon. This work is process-oriented—bringing forth the authentic self. A Daughter of Avalon is known by her sense of presence—a centered nature, a commitment to know herself and her connection with the All, a willingness to look into the waters of the soul and the courage to change what she sees. She is willing to facilitate the growth of others without interfering in their process: she holds up a mirror for them to see themselves, and is not unwilling to look into the mirror held up to her by others. There is never a time or a place where personal growth ends. No matter how long one walks the path of Avalon—four months or forty years—we must always return to look into the mirror pool—each time with increased sight and sharpened sense of clarity.

In the broadest sense of the word, a woman of Avalon is a midwife. She brings forth the priestess or wise woman within, sees and supports the emergence of the higher self potential in others, and knows that through her work and her life, the Lady of Avalon shines forth in all that she is and does. She has patience for herself and her process, and in the process of others. As the seamstress holds the shears, she must at times cut through entanglements of persons, perspectives, and situations in order to free herself from that which does not support her higher good. She does not passively accept the shadow face of others—a midwife empowers growth and does not enable destructive patterns.

Things must be cut away in order to move forward; a tree grows best when pruned of dead weight and diseased limbs. There is a delicate balance to be found: supporting others' growth and keeping open a space for their journeys while also recognizing that ultimately one is only responsible for oneself. The wise woman knows she cannot change others—she can only support change through word, deed, and example.

It is because of this that the foundation for the way of Avalon is found within. Through the dance of the Cycle that moves us through our healing, we gain clearer sight and improved discernment by way of issue resolution and the quest for self-knowledge. The clearer our sight becomes, the more we are able to recognize the truths of the greater pattern. We can see the stitches that have brought us to where we are and follow threads that lead us to our destination.

Expanding our sight to see the full spectrum from horizon to horizon empowers us with choice. At every moment, we have the power to change the course of our direction. We must first acknowledge that we have this power, and then foster the ability to see the nature of the changes we need to make. This often involves seeking out the origin of any misplaced stitches so that we have the ability to rip them out, and set the weaving right.

This work is meant to initiate the journey to wholeness. Each journey provides energetic clues and resonances that facilitate a tie-in to the energy signature of the Avalonian archetypal realm. These Immrama open the door to consciousness—it is up to seekers to step through the portal and do the work for themselves. Once grounded in the archetype and working through the tides of Cycle, the Cauldron of Transformation will begin to reveal itself and the Elixir of Wisdom will emerge from this process of self-distillation.

4

THE POWER OF CYCLE

Three things on which every person should reflect: whence they come, where they are, and whither they shall go.

CELTIC TRIAD

FROM THE WHIRLING OF GALAXIES to the Earth's revolution around the sun ... From the seed-bearing coils of a pinecone to the logarithmic spiral of a mollusk's shell ... From the intertwining double helix of the DNA molecule to the subatomic particles spinning around their nuclei—the power of Cycle is a fundamental expression of universal energy, revealing itself in many ways. It is constantly flowing around us, working through us and moving within us.

Consciously acknowledging and working with the wisdom of the Cycle as part of our inner process can be a powerful tool in our quest for wisdom and personal transformation. Aligning with the cycle of the universe permits greater insight into the rhythmic nature of our unfolding. Harnessing this never-ending, ever-turning cycle will synchronize our lives and our growth process with the ebb and flow, descent and emergence of the universe, allowing us to break though the barriers preventing us from being fully conscious and connected to the All.

The Whole

Understanding any manifestation of Cycle brings understanding of all the ways in which this cosmic force expresses itself; all cycles are one Cycle. The Cycle is a continuum, endless and indivisible. It is helpful to the human mind to break the Cycle down into disparate energetic components in order to understand the magnitude of the totality, but we must remember that these divisions are solely for the purpose of study. The Cycle can be divided in many different ways but the truth beyond all divisions is that by nature, the Cycle is a whole, encompassing all and endlessly turning—repeating the great pattern found in all things.

It is important to keep in mind the context of the division of cycle one is using in order to maintain consistency of perspective—that is, staying with the same divisional "lens" through which to consider the whole. At times, correspondences seem to change alignments depending upon the filter through which they are being considered. These are not inconsistencies, but rather a reflection of the indivisible nature of Cycle. In reality, the studied aspect is unchanged, only perception of it has shifted according to its assigned mental map.

As an example, think of a car and its driver. As the operator of the vehicle, the driver represents the active force, while the car is the passive force—taking direction from the driver. At the same time, the actively moving car passively carries the driver, seeming now to have switched energetic polarities. We can consider the car to be passive to its driver while at the same time it is active to the road as it moves upon it. The energetic essence of all things considered do not themselves change; the car, the driver and the road are what they are. What *has* changed is the perspective through which each aspect of the Whole is viewed. Context is the key, and is a very important part of Cycle study.

Dualities

The first major energetic differentiation of the Cycle is into halves. The Hermetic principle of polarities states that opposites are the same in nature, differing only in degree. In this way, we can best come to understand the Cycle's dual nature by contemplating the differences in the polar extremes, as well as the center at which they both resolve. One of the most visible dualities in Celtic thought is the concept of the Dark and Light Halves of the Year.

The Cycle in Halves

Active	Passive
Masculine	Feminine
Above	Below
God	Goddess
Mind	Body
Conscious	Unconscious
Force	Form
Linear	Cyclic
Outward	Inward
Light	Dark
Waxing	Waning
Expanding	Contracting
Differentiating	Consolidating

Triads

Numerologically, three is an unstable number, ever in motion and constantly evolving into the next phase; as such, it is an agent of change as well as the number of physical manifestation. The sacred triplicity is especially important in the Celtic worldview. Cosmologically, it is represented in the Three Realms of Land, Sea, and Sky. We see it again in the Three Illuminations of Awen—the three rays representing active, neutral, and passive energies streaming down to the physical plane from the unity of the Divine. Many Celtic gods and goddesses appear in threefold aspect, encompassing the full breadth of skill, existence, and experience. The Celtic triskele symbol beautifully embodies the nature of triadic energy. Dividing the Cycle into thirds, then, evokes the energies of creation.

The Cycle in Thirds

Masculine	Neutral	Feminine
Air	Earth	Water
Sky	Land	Sea
Maiden	Crone	Mother
Mind	Body	Soul
Future	Present	Past

Quarters

Dividing the Cycle into quarters resonates strongly with the physical plane and encapsulates the totality of the Middle World experience. We see it in the four elements of Western esoteric thought, the four lunar Holy Days of the Celtic traditions, and the four Cauldron Transformations necessary to gain entrance into the mysteries of Ceridwen which lie at the Center. The Equilateral Celtic Cross recalls the four directions, the four seasons, the four elements, and all aspects of the natural world existing in balanced and stable harmony.

The Cycle in Quarters

Active of Active	Passive of Active	Active of Passive	Passive of Passive
Air	Fire	Water	Earth
Maiden	Mother	Matriarch	Crone
Mind	Heart	Soul	Body
To Think	To Act	To Feel	To Be
Spring	Summer	Autumn	Winter

Fifths

Five is the number of the quest—that imbalance which propels us to expand beyond what is in order to pursue what can be. It is humankind's striving to rise above its physical nature in order to come to know itself and the Divine. We see this expressively visualized in the pentagram, depicting the four elemental qualities of the Earth plane forming the foundation, with the fifth element of Spirit rising above the rest. We see this image mirrored at the heart of the Apple—that powerful Avalonian symbol—representing the heart of women's wisdom. Each seed represents one of the five Goddesses in the Avalonian pantheon and corresponds to a Station in the Avalonian Cycle of Healing.

The Cycle in Fifths

Spirit	Air	Fire	Water	Earth
Third Eye	Throat	Heart	Womb	Root
Integration	Emergence	Resolution	Descent	Confrontation
Sight	Smell	Taste	Sound	Touch
Branwen	Blodeuwedd	Arianrhod	Rhiannon	Ceridwen

There are further significant divisions of the Whole relevant to the work of the Avalonian Tradition; these are beyond the scope of our present discussion and will be touched upon in later works. It is important to come away with the understanding that our intention influences the way we approach the Whole. Although our perception changes and we may focus on particular aspects of a cyclic division at different times, these are just mental constructs. The All is indivisible and constantly in motion—a continuum without limits.

All Cycles Are One Cycle

It is essential to recognize that all cycles are but manifestations of the Great Cycle. The Hermetic axiom of "as above, so below" is an integral part of this understanding. All things cycle, and all things holding the corresponding Station in the Cycle are related to each other. They are manifestations of the same vibration—the microcosmic echo of the macrocosmic template.

The pattern repeats over and over, as seen in this Cycle chart of correspondences. When reading horizontally across the chart, the cyclic progression from one Station to the next is illustrated using examples of several different manifestations of Cycle. When reading vertically, all of the Cycle aspects in each column hold the same Station in the Cycle, and can therefore be said to correspond with each other.

Cycle Chart of Correspondences

Elemental Cycle	Air	Fire	Water	Earth
Lunar Cycle	1st Quarter	Full Moon	3rd Quarter	Dark Moon
Seasonal Cycle	Spring	Summer	Autumn	Winter
Daily Cycle	Dawn	Noon	Dusk	Midnight
Directional Cycle	East	South	West	North
State of Matter Cycle	Gas	Plasma	Liquid	Solid
Agricultural Cycle	Sow	Fruit	Reap	Fallow
Plant Energy Cycle	Flower	Leaves	Fruit	Root
Life Cycle	Maiden	Mother/ Amazon	Matriarch	Crone
Fertility Cycle	Menarche	Fertility	Menopause	Wise Blood Runs Within
Menstrual Cycle	Uterine Lining Buildup	Ovulation	Uterine Lining Breakdown	Menstruation

Understanding the succession of energy in its myriad forms of revelation is but a portion of the work necessary to come into conscious partnership with the Cycle. Knowledge can only transform into wisdom through experience. Immersion into the Cycle is therefore of utmost importance.

The key feminine energetic tool—the way through which women come to understand both the inner and outer worlds—is through the act of merging. The path of mastery for the passive energetic is to seek power *with*. Becoming one with something: an emotion, energy, perspective, or area, to name examples—can bring us to full understanding of that thing. The path of understanding for the active energetic is through the conquering of a thing—exploring and analyzing it until power *over* it has been obtained. We see this interplay of perspective countless times in human history, society, and even biology. The net result of these actions is the same; what differs is simply the perspective.

Our goal, therefore, is to become fully immersed in the rhythm of the Cycle—that is, merging with its essence in order to identify with our own route to wholeness. With this understanding comes the wisdom to use this tool to effect lasting inner change, harnessing the Cycle's momentum. The Earth's seasonal changes are one of the most powerful and accessible manifestations of Cycle. Its divisions align beautifully with our inner process, triggering the corresponding aspects within ourselves as it unfolds around us. Vitally important to the agricultural Celtic Britons, we will use this Cycle as the focus for our study, revealing the Cycle's potential as a tool for personal empowerment and self-actualization.

The Sacred Year

It is easy to find a very clear example of the importance of Cycle to the Celtic people. As agriculturalists, their very existence depended upon the stable repetition of the solar year as manifested in the seasons. Allying themselves with the seasonal shifts, they worked with the changes of the Wheel of the Year and harnessed its power for optimal gain. Their lives revolved around the agricultural cycle, and their activities at any given time of the year were influenced by the point of cycle presently active. It is no accident that the economic, communal, and individual lives of the Celts harmoniously reflected the fundamental energies of the Great Cycle, conscious or not. We see this illustrated by examining the only known written Celtic calendar, the Gaullish Coligny calendar, which dates to the first century CE.

Months of the Coligny Calendar

Month	Period	Meaning
Samonios	October/November	Seed-fall
Dumannios	November/December	Darkest Depths
Ruiros	December/January	Cold-time
Anagantios	January/February	Stay-home time
Ogronios	February/March	Time of Ice
Cutios	March/April	Time of Winds
Giamonios	April/May	Shoots-show
Simivisonios	May/June	Time of Brightness
Equos	June/July	Horse-time
Elembiuos	July/August	Claim-time
Edrinios	August/September	Arbitration-time
Cantlos	September/October	Song-time
Mid Samonios	Extra thirteenth lunation being duplicated	

Matthews, Caitlin. *The Celtic Tradition.* 1996.

Some months' names refer directly to the agricultural cycle, such as Samonios and Giamonios, whereas others allude to social activities (Equos,

Anagantios) or administrative endeavors (Elembiuos and Edrinios). In contemplating these months, a pattern of seasonal activities comes to light.

The winter seemed mostly to be a period of inactivity when the Celts remained at their farmsteads, presumably using what small amounts of spelt cultivation were necessary. Springtime hallmarked the return of life to the land, and the sowing of new crops and appearance of new livestock dominated the activities of this time. Not many social activities could have taken place until the summer, when the crops were well on their way, and the herds needed less attention. The summer months appear to have been abounding with social intercourse of both administrative and recreational natures. Autumn marked the winding down of the year as everyone worked to harvest their crops and to prepare for the long winter months ahead. When examining the four great festivals of the Celtic tradition, we will see more clearly the way the agricultural cycle determined and mirrored religious and communal activities. There is a certain beauty in the way their spiritual lives came to reflect this pattern as well.

Cultural Context—The British Celts

Neolithic migrants arriving on southern British shores between 4600 and 2400 BCE were greeted by a landscape that shaped the society the Gaullish Coligny calendar agriculturalists developed. Ancient Britain's geography and environment presented many difficulties for the agricultural settlers from the European continent; indeed, the most pressing difficulty was that of available, arable land. The primeval British landscape was densely forested and far beyond the newcomers' Neolithic technology to clear. Clear land that did exist was widely dispersed throughout the countryside; the resulting settlements' isolation created problems of agricultural risk sharing, limited livestock pools, few perspective mates, and a lack of unified defense against raids.

Solitary farmsteads seemed to be the smallest economic unit in ancient Britain as a response to the environment's forced natural isolation. Settlements were located near or adjacent to the land inhabitants cultivated. Called "Celtic fields," the parcels of land ranged in size from .33 to 1.5 acres, and were square in shape. These types of fields were common on the chalk downs, presumably because there was less forest growth to clear. Hundreds of acres of these field systems are known thus far, telling a tale of massive and concentrated field allotment programs. In time, these field systems and their later linear earthworks (defining ownership and possibly providing protection) became associated with hillforts. Evidence suggests land distribution was initially in the hands of the clans, which would explain the fields' regional concentrations and relative uniformity of shape and size.

Entering the early Iron Age, farmsteads began to show signs of extended families and clan groups living together in nucleated hamlets with privately owned lands adjacent to their homesteads. Presumably, iron usage facilitated the ability to clear land, thus allowing use of larger land areas. A greater number of people were able to live and work at these Iron Age settlements, yet the difficulties of isolation remained. There needed to be meeting and mingling with other settlements to trade locally unavailable goods and resources, arrange risk-sharing relationships with farmers growing different crops in different areas, and strengthen livestock breeds.

Establishing social cohesion was imperative, and one way of accomplishing this was through using *foci*. A foci is a central area, where at certain times of the year, festivals were held for purposes of social, cultural, and economic exchange. During Neolithic times, these places of communal gatherings happened at causewayed camps—ditched hilltop enclosures constructed specifically to be the foci of tribal groupings. Even into the Iron Age, when many of the causewayed camps had hillforts constructed at their sites, they continued to be used as tribal centers. Of prime importance in these festivals was the religious element; surely without it, festivals may not have occurred at all.

These semi-religious gatherings were based on agricultural and seasonal cycles. Sacred festivities were supplemented by the more mundane activities of trading, matchmaking, and marketing, thereby creating a medium where the socio-economic needs resulting from isolation could be met. Assembly times at these central places was dictated by the Celtic calendrical system. This system's foundation was the turning of the seasons, agricultural activities associated with the different times of the year, and was inextricably tied in with Celtic religious belief; indeed, for the ancient Britons, it appears that the three were one.

The Great Festivals

Calan Gaeaf

SOLAR OBSERVANCE: November 1

LUNAR OBSERVANCE: First full moon when the sun is in Scorpio

The Celtic year began on the festival known as *Calan Gaeaf* (Welsh) or *Samhain* (Gaelic). This day marked the beginning of winter; the last of the harvest was collected and the livestock were gathered into winter barracks and stockades after any excess had been slaughtered and smoked for the winter's stores. All food, fodder, and fuel had to be stored away by this day. The buying and selling of livestock took place at the clan central places at Calan Gaeaf. Accounts were settled on this feast day; rents and debts were paid and servants and workmen received their wages.

The actual feast day of Calan Gaeaf was considered to be out of time; it was neither a part of the old year nor a part of the new, making it religiously significant. It was believed that on this day that was not a day, and at this time that was not a time, the Otherworld and its inhabitants could be easily accessed. Celts performed rites and ceremonies, contacted the dead, made divinations for the coming year, and recounted the tales of their Gods and great heroes. The main theme that ran through the socio-cultural and religious activities of this great Celtic Fire Festival was that of taking accounts, reflecting upon the deeds of the past, and preparation for the coming year.

Gwyl Mair

SOLAR OBSERVANCE: February 2

LUNAR OBSERVANCE: First full moon when the sun is in Aquarius

The next great religious festival was the point midway between Calan Gaeaf and Calan Mai (Beltane) was known as *Imbolc* ("In the Belly") to the Irish and as *Gwyl Mair* (the Feast of Mary) to the Welsh. The long dark winter was a time of inactivity for the Celtic Britons. Social and political activities came to a standstill during the winter months of merciless wind and driving rains—weather that further reinforced the isolation of their disparate homesteads. It is because of the imposition of the elements that Gwyl Mair celebrations often only occurred on a local basis—travel was almost impossible in the middle of winter.

Regardless of weather conditions, Gwyl Mair was considered a herald of the springtime season; the first welcome signs of spring began to stir after the grip of winter had finally relinquished. Ewes began to lactate following the birth of their lambs, supplying protein from milk, cheese, and whey, most welcome at this time of year. The spring work of plowing and tilling the soil began, and fishermen on the coastal areas began to repair their boats, anticipating the beginning of the fishing season and their sojourns out to sea. Divinations concerning weather and household prosperity were made at this time, while the farmers and householders checked their stores of food and hay, which would have been half gone by this time. Surviving the trials of winter depended on how well prepared the homestead had been. Any possible improvements were taken into account in planning for the next season as they looked ahead to spring's work.

Calan Mai

SOLAR OBSERVANCE: May 1
LUNAR OBSERVANCE: First full moon when the sun is in Taurus

In direct opposition to Calan Gaeaf in the yearly cycle, *Calan Mai* (*Beltane* to the Irish) marked the beginning of the Light Half of the Year, when the summer began and the world was green and growing. Good weather and the good health of animals and humans alike were anticipated and the flocks and herds were put out to pasture. Communal ceremonies included driving cattle between two ritual fires to bless, protect, and purify them from disease-causing vermin left over from their long winter confinement.

At the clan central places, weather and marriage divination was performed, furious trading occurred, grazing land contracts were made, and rents were paid. Between the long winter and the preparation and planting of the crops, this was the first real opportunity for a tribe to leave their isolated farmsteads and travel for communal gathering. Trial marriages made from the previous summer were given the long isolation of the winter to test whether they would work out; if a pairing proved discordant, the couple would come before the judges at Calan Mai to have their union dissolved. Calan Mai was a celebration of the fertility of land, animals, and humans, and was one the greatest feast days—not surprising for an agricultural people for whom the land's abundance dictated their chance of survival.

Gwyl Awst

SOLAR OBSERVANCE: August 1
LUNAR OBSERVANCE: First full moon when the sun is in Leo

The festival of *Gwyl Awst* (*Lughnasadh* to the Irish) was celebrated as the beginning of the harvest. It was a time of thanksgiving for the bounty of the Earth and for the performance of sacrifices to ensure continued bounty for the rest of the year. Crops were welcomed and large communal meals of great ritual importance were held. Weather divination was practiced and seasonal harvest workers were hired.

Gwyl Awst was a festival known for its large, communal sporting events, especially horse racing, which served to reinforce the bonds between tribe members. Young men and women took this opportunity to prove themselves to the opposite sex, taking advantage of this rare occasion when a considerable amount of prospective mates was available. Gwyl Awst was when marriages were arranged, either for love or for economic/political purposes; the couple pledged to be married for a year and a day, and could part after that time should they find that they were not compatible. Along with marriage, the Celts entered into alliances of friendship and contracts at this time. This vibrant feast, said to commemorate the funeral games of the mother of Lugh, the Irish god of Light (perhaps also an analog to Lleu of the Welsh) was followed by several months of hard work until the last fruits were harvested, and Calan Gaeaf came around once more.

———————

The simple perfection of this cyclic system of risk sharing and communion is both admirable and successful. Although not everyone from a settlement was always able to attend any given festival, it was important for each homestead to be represented for both sacred and secular reasons. While individual farmers performed religious rites on their own land to ensure the fertility of their fields and to win the favor of the local deities and nature spirits, attendance at the greater communal rituals guaranteed the protection and blessings of tribal gods as well. However well these strategies may have worked, these agriculturalists used the amassed populace present at these gatherings as an opportunity to ensure economic stability through trade, the buying and selling of locally unavailable goods and products, and fresh bloodlines to strengthen herds and flocks.

The duality of communal participation and the cyclic work of each individual homestead underscores the ways in which we are called to participate in the cosmic dance. There is the call to work within, tending the fields of the soul, and there is the call to move without—bringing the bounty of harvest with us to share and exchange with others. The whole is nourished and strengthened by our personal contributions, and we in turn benefit from the bounty of the product forged at the hearths of others.

Although the Avalonian Tradition is a path that leads within, it is equally important to manifest our reclaimed wisdoms without. The beauty of the Tradition is that each woman's contribution is an important function of the whole. Together, we manifest as a self-sufficient community aiming to open and empower each individual soul. We cycle within and we cycle without.

The Neo-Pagan Wheel of the Year

Many Neo-Pagan traditions celebrate what are commonly called the Eight Grove Festivals. These are made up of the four solar-oriented Solstices and Equinoxes as well as the four lunar "Cross Quarter" holy days of Samhain, Imbolc, Beltane, and Lughnasadh. The Avalonian Tradition actively celebrates only the lunar holy days for several reasons. Their connection with the moon gives them greater correspondence with the inner feminine energies associated with Women's Mysteries, aiding us in our work and on the journey within. Indeed, we celebrate the holy days on the days of their lunar observance, rather than that of the solar Gregorian calendar, thereby reinforcing our connection with the female energetic and our Briton foremothers in honor of their lunar calendar.

The solar holy days are not Celtic but Germanic in origin. Celtic Britons began to be displaced by the Anglo-Saxon invasions of Britain in the fifth century CE; English Pagan traditions therefore strongly reflect these later Germanic influences. Celtic British culture survived to the west of Offa's Dyke, separating the Welsh kingdoms from the rest of England. The Welsh (or *Cymry*) then, are the descendants of the Britons, and inheritors of the Celtic language and tradition. As the work of Avalon takes inspiration from earlier Celtic materials, we draw primarily from the Welsh mythic cycle, seeing in it the remnants of the Celtic Briton belief system, and seek to reclaim the older archetype of the four Fire Festivals.

Interestingly, there is a degree of energetic redundancy in these two systems of celebration. A brief examination illustrates how the holidays of the Lunar Cycle reflect those of the Solar Cycle that directly precede them.

Samhain and Mabon/Autumn Equinox

Both are harvest festivals at waning threshold times. Mabon holds the point of equal night and day, moving into longer nights, while Samhain holds the point which bridges the old and new years. Depending on the tradition, either holiday is considered the beginning of the Dark Half of the Year.

Imbolc and Yule/Winter Solstice

Both are midwinter festivals at the point of greatest decrease. Yule marks the longest night of the year, while Imbolc marks the deepest depths of winter and its stillness—occurring exactly at the midpoint between the beginning of winter and the beginning of summer as conceived by Celtic cultures.

Beltane and Ostara/Spring Equinox

Both are fertility festivals at waxing threshold times. Ostara holds the point of equal day and night, moving into longer days, while Beltane holds the point which bridges the Light and Dark Halves of the Year, directly opposite Samhain.

Lughnasadh and Litha/Summer Solstice

Both are midsummer festivals at the point of greatest increase. Litha marks the longest day of the year, while Lughnasadh marks the very height of summer and its bounty—occurring exactly at the midpoint between the beginning of summer and the beginning of winter as conceived by Celtic cultures.

Wisdoms for Today

Over time, surviving through periods of socio-economic and religious change, the traditions and symbolic remnants of the four Great Festivals passed into folk usage, and have been carried down through the generations into modern times, allowing us a glimpse of what was. Old as these traditions may be, the relevance of these ancient wisdoms has not faded.

Details of an ancient culture's agricultural cycle may seem out of sync with modern Western realities of technology and urban living. What makes paying attention to this seemingly outmoded method of marking time so important? As with much of our work, reclaiming the wisdoms of those who have come before us is crucial to our process and is a step towards wholeness. The implication is not that agrarian peoples were inherently more spiritually advanced because their connection to the land was more profound than is our own; rather, those who worked the land and depended upon it for their survival understood great truths. These truths are hidden from us in the glare of artificial light and the extreme abundance on supermarket shelves.

The ebb and flow of the tides of the Earth, sun, moon, and stars are but repetitions of the Great Cycle, the very nature of the energetic workings of the universe. Understanding this cycle and learning to harness its energy through working within its parameters is one of the greatest gifts we can give ourselves... one of the greatest tools in our quest for inner growth and understanding. We are a part *of* the universe, not apart *from* it, and becoming conscious of the mechanics of the universe gives us great insight into our inner universe as well. As above, so below. As within, so without.

When we acknowledge and integrate the lessons of the Great Cycle into our work and into our lives, we can more fully participate in the promise of change and renewal that this great Cosmic Dance eternally brings. Not only can we come to better understand our own process of unfolding, we can actually, with consciousness, harness the energies that sweep over us and through us and use them to reinforce and empower our path to wholeness. Aligning our work with the Great Cycle allows us to plug into a great cosmic battery, which, by virtue of the Hermetic principle of correspondence, will energize our changes. What better ally on our quest for wholeness than the whole of the universe?

NOTE: The goal of the Avalonian Cycle of Healing is to help us recognize the unhealthy patterns of our lives and to lay down new energetic pathways in support of our personal growth and the actualization of our inner Sovereignty. The Cycle of Healing is a tool of self-exploration and personal empowerment, and is most effective when used in the context of a supportive community or in tandem with traditional therapy. Change can often be painful, and while this work can bring up unpleasant memories or trigger emotional reactions as we process and explore, these feelings should *never* become overwhelming or incapacitating. Should this occur, *immediately* stop your work and seek help from a qualified mental health professional.

5

THE STATION OF
DESCENT

Three things no being can be seen without: covering, movement, and shadow

CELTIC TRIAD

THE BEGINNING OF THE CYCLE of Healing, the Station of the Descent, marks the place in the Cycle where one turn ends and the next turn begins. Here we assess aspects of the self which are outmoded, restrictive, and are a drain of our inner resources; old, open wounds have nothing to do with the reality of the now. Here, we undertake the journey into the unconscious, the dark half of ourselves hidden from view. In this shadowy realm lies the root cause of our wounding and the ultimate treasure: the reclamation of energies tied up in our pain. It is here that we ask ourselves the grail question: Whom does this serve? If the answer is that these parts of our selves do not support manifestations of our higher self potential, it is time to look further.

Descent in the Cycle of the Year

The rites for honoring the ancestors and celebrating the lives of those who died during the last year have been performed. The harvest is complete and grain has been stored. Those animals not slaughtered and smoked are corralled and sheltered for the coming winter. The fields are bare and seemingly lifeless, surrendering to the replenishing slumber of the Dark Half of the Year. The coming stillness and silence of winter have been prepared for; with forethought and mindfulness, all reserves have been stored. Anything unnecessary has been cast aside.

Calan Gaeaf (Samhain) signaled the beginning of a time of forced inner contemplation; there would be little or no travel between the isolated Celtic homesteads during the long winter months. Rather than the outwardly focused concerns that are the primary occupations of an agrarian society, the dark time brought with it a new perspective—one that turned the eye inward, concentrating on the needs of hearth and home. How beautiful and right that the agricultural cycles mirror so very closely the tides of the soul's journey and the endless progression of all things.

Calan Gaeaf is the gatekeeper into the Dark Half of the Year. An old cycle ends and a new one begins. The paradox of Calan Gaeaf is that it is neither of the new order nor of the old. Rather, it is the doorway through which one must pass in order to begin the Cycle anew. In the same way that the Celts considered a new day to begin at dusk, Calan Gaeaf was both the ending of the old order and the beginning of the New Year. In this way, Calan Gaeaf is the sunset of the year, the transition period into a darkness that in turn begets newness.

Portal days like Calan Gaeaf are liminal periods: experiences that exist beyond the scope of everyday life and outside the limits of time and space. Many cultures set aside days that did not appear on any calendar but were used as sacred periods to mark the transition from one year to the next. These "non-days" were filled with ritual and celebration, and some sources believe the Celts did the same. An individual within society can often be seen as a microcosmic representation of the larger whole, and we see cultures all over the world using the concept of intermediary sacred periods to mark important life transitions. Rites of passage act as bridges between the old self and the new; they ritualize the shifts in societal stature that accompany these changes. At Calan Gaeaf and Calan Mai (Beltane) we, like the Earth, pass through the liminal gateway to enter into a new phase of existence.

There is no better time to announce our intention to undertake the inner quest to the universe than at the transitional time of Calan Gaeaf—the portal through which we enter into the Dark Half of the Year—the time when the veil between the worlds is most thin. In the time leading up to Calan Gaeaf, our work is to review our inner landscape to identify ways in which any blight upon our harvest has manifested, and to seek its root cause.

The Avalonian Cycle of Healing, then, begins at the Station of Descent—in a place between the worlds that straddles the light and dark, the conscious and unconscious, above and below, the self and the shadow. Here we enter the Cauldron of Ceridwen, seeking wisdom and rebirth in the darkness of the womb/tomb. We set into motion the work of the Dark Half of the Cycle … turning our attention within to see the root of our wounding, the cause of our pain, and all that prevents us from being whole.

At Descent, we prepare ourselves for the journey within, casting away that which will prevent us from having unobstructed sight. We gather our strength and pull our energies within, so that we may reclaim the energies tied up in shadow. We announce our intentions for wholeness and peel the first layer of energy away, getting deeper and deeper to the core. We must look behind at what was—honoring the ghosts of our past—and then move forward to begin the work of what can be. This is both a beginning and an ending … the death of the old self and the re-creation of the new.

It is important to remember that the shadow cannot be eradicated; it is a vital part of who and what we are. Energy can neither be created nor destroyed; it can only change forms. The work of the Dark Half of the Cycle is to uncover and understand the hidden ways in which the shadow has co-opted our personal energy—energy that would otherwise be available for growth and positive manifestation of our potential. By removing this energy from the lower self, the shadow is disempowered and the freed energy resources can be redirected into becoming the women we were meant to be.

This Station is where we set into motion the work of the Dark Half of the Cycle and commit ourselves to seek the truth of the inner self. Descent is aligned with the energies of solar Scorpio, the conscious regeneration of a lower energy into a higher energy, and lunar Taurus with its earthy chthonic energies directed within.

Descent in the Cycle of the Moon—Third Quarter

The moon is in her third quarter from the seventh through the tenth day after the full moon. During this phase, the left half of the moon appears to be illuminated by direct sunlight. The third quarter moon rises in the east at midnight, is at its apex in the sky at dawn, and sets at noon past the western horizon. Energetically, this is a time for descending into the darkness and seeking inner balance.

Self-reflective Questions for the Station of Descent

Take some time to meditate upon these questions while in a clear and receptive space. Use your replies to help form a focus for the work of the Station of Descent. Be sure to record your thoughts in a journal—this will help you chart your process of growth and change as you do the work of the Avalonian Cycle of Healing.

- *What perspective, situations, persons, and things in your life cause you pain? What things stimulate guilt? Sadness? Anger? Remorse? Embarrassment? Fear?*

- *In what areas of your life are there inequities of energy exchange—where your personal energy is being expended without being replaced? How does this make you feel? Would you like for this to change? Why has this been permitted to occur?*

- *In looking over the grand scheme of your life, what destructive patterns of behavior can you recognize? What effect do these patterns have on the quality of your life? In what ways would your life change if these patterns no longer existed?*

- *Think about yourself as a child and the life you imagined you'd have. What would you be doing? Where would you be living? Who would be in your life? Compare these aspirations and their natural growth and modification to your life at this very moment: Where are you in attaining these goals? Are you satisfied with your progress? What could you be doing differently? What obstacles have gotten in your way? How have you dealt with them? What prevents you from being the person you wish to be?*

· *What prevents you from manifesting your dreams and realizing your potential? When did you come to accept your limitations as unalterable? How much of this perspective is your own? How much of it did you learn from the people and experiences in your life? What keeps you anchored to this belief? In what ways would your life be different if you could change your mind about your worth and your abilities?*

The Avalonian Landscape—The Red Spring

ALTERNATIVE NAMES: Chalice Well, Blood Well, Blood Spring
CYCLE OF HEALING: Station of Descent
CAULDRON TRANSFORMATION: Salmon/Otter
ELEMENTAL ALIGNMENT: Water
ENERGY CENTER: Womb

We enter the manifested Cycle in Avalon's Sacred Landscape through the holy waters of the Red Spring. The physical landscape of old Avalon changed significantly over time. What was once simply a spring bubbling forth from the ground has undergone many transformations to become the healing garden and holy well so lovingly cared for by the Chalice Well Trust in present-day Glastonbury. What is today the shaft of Chalice Well was, in actuality, a well house built in the late twelfth century to protect the spring (then the main water supply for Glastonbury Abbey) at its source. This artifice disrupted the free flow of the stream that carried away the erosive silt, causing it instead to build up over the centuries. Ultimately, the silt buried the Well House in its entirety. The Well, then, is formed by the medieval Well House structure with the capstones removed.

Yet, even in the seemingly mundane, there remains mystery.

It can be no accident that here, in the power spot that is Glastonbury, we see the upper realms imprint themselves upon the lower realms—that physical form comes to reflect spiritual energy. Consciously constructed or no, the well shaft is adjacent to a pentagonal chamber, whose most elongated angle points west—the direction which, like Avalon herself, is associated with the Otherworld. The number five features prominently in the Avalonian Tradition; it is number of the quest, the number of goddesses honored by the Sisterhood of Avalon, and the number of seeds comprising the five-pointed star hidden in the apple so sacred to the Holy Isle.

Assailed by the forces of persecution, restriction, and co-option, the essence of what makes Glastonbury holy has survived over time, albeit through embracing new form. Once honored and free flowing, the Red Spring reacted to containment attempts by submerging herself and her mysteries deep into the sheltering Earth. There, protected, sustained, and robed in a new garment, she continues to flow and her energy remains intact, awaiting those who seek her. No longer only the Cauldron of Ceridwen, she is also the keeper of the Holy Grail—the sought and submerged power of the Sacred Feminine.

Over time, this ostensibly female object changed from cauldron to cup, from the Womb of the Goddess to the Holy Grail of Christianity. Accordingly, the Red Spring of Avalon transformed over time to the Chalice Well of Glastonbury. Hidden in the well by Joseph of Arimathea, legend tells us the Holy Grail stained the waters red, recalling Christ's sacrifice on the cross. Again, the water's healing properties are reflected in the Grail mythos—when found and lifted to the lips of the Wounded King, one sip returned vitality to the wasteland.

The many stories and traditions that have come to be associated with the Red Spring over the centuries have spun the many layers of archetypal garments now worn by the site. Interestingly, each overlay is connected to and builds upon the rest. Whether spiritual metaphor or psychological symbol, the Chalice Well embodies the urge to reconnect with the universal matrix of creation—the Source to which all things return.

The Red Spring has been venerated since time immemorial as holy to the Goddess. The water's high iron content stains red every fountain, basin, and sluice in the gardens, thereby evoking Her sacred blood mysteries. This obvious menstrual connection serves to further the message: we must shed the old to make way for the new—from death comes new life. The waters of Chalice Well have never been known to fail; they have sustained Glastonbury through various droughts over the centuries. These icy waters have been revered for their healing properties and have been a pilgrimage destination for hundreds of years.

The Chalice Well of modern times is sacred to spiritual seekers the world over, and has come to be symbolized by the *vesica piscis*, wrought into the well cover's ironwork. This image figures significantly in the sacred geometry of Glastonbury Abbey, as noted by Fredrick Bligh Bond in the early twentieth century, and it was he who commissioned the cover for the Chalice Well Trust. The interlocking circles of the vesica piscis, representing the duality of nature on a myriad of levels, create a yonic (suggestive of female genitalia) gateway, an apt symbol for this deeply feminine holy place of Descent and Transformation.

Immram to the Red Spring of Avalon

The Red Spring is related to the Station of Descent in the Avalonian Cycle of Healing. Stepping through the portal of this Station, we commit ourselves to the inner voyage of transformation this healing dance can bring to us. Use this holy site to help you clarify those things that hold you back from manifesting your authentic self. Clear away those things which block your sight so that you may honestly see where your fears and patterns prevent you from recognizing your wholeness.

Entering the shadow work of the Station of Descent takes great courage, for it represents a death of sorts as we enter the Otherworld in search of inner treasure. Know that you are supported in your journey, and that the universe will never reveal to you that which you do not have the means of handling. The work is uncomfortable, but should never be incapacitating; it is important to know the difference between the two and to seek the help of a professional counselor or therapist if you become overwhelmed with what surfaces. Having a good support system is always important when doing inner process work; part of personal empowerment is knowing when you need some help and then learning how to ask for it.

Perform the Immram to the Island of Avalon as described on p. 55. After disembarking the Barge to Avalon, proceed with the rest of this working.

The Journey

It is dusk. Stepping out of the Barge that transported you across the glassy lake to the Holy Isle, you meet your guide waiting for you on the shores of Avalon. Greet your guide and share your reason for undertaking this journey and your desire to visit the Red Spring; ask to be guided there.

The sharp scent of distant hearth-fires and the sickly sweet smell of fermented apples fill the air as you are led through the orchards. Nearby, you can hear the rooting of wild boars as they devour the last of the over-ripe fallen fruit. Time passes so differently here. Through the twisted branches of the nearly bare apple trees, you can already see the autumn stars twinkling in the velvet of the darkening sky.

The hilly terrain slopes up and down again, finally causing the slumbering body of the Tor to rise gently over the landscape. Take note of what you see along your path as you follow your guide, neither to the spiraled hilltop nor to the pregnant earthen mound silhouetted against the moonlit sky, but to the valley between these two hallowed promontories.

Softly at first, then growing louder as you approach, your ears pick up the gentle burble of flowing water. It is the Red Spring, fountaining out from a cleft in the spongy Earth, spilling the life-blood of the island, and making the air heavy with the tang of iron. Surrounded by red-stained stones creating a small dolman-like enclosure, it is guarded by ancient, brooding yew trees whose bark seems to shift into patterns of ancient symbols the longer you stare into them.

Red ribbons hang in the branches of these venerated trees, the tokens of those who have come before you asking guidance from these holy waters and giving thanks to the Goddess. Your guide hands you one such ribbon. Take your time and infuse the ribbon with the intention of this journey. When you are ready, and after asking the tree's permission to do so, tie it onto an empty branch. Feel your request being received into the night.

Gazing again at the simple beauty of the waters springing forth at your feet, you feel an inner thirst unlike any you have ever experienced, and are drawn to drink of this holy elixir. Although you feel that you are standing in a place pilgrims and priestesses have visited for countless ages, you see no cup or vessel with which to collect the water. Your hands begin to tingle, and you understand you are to put your hands directly in the spring; no human-made vessel, no matter how finely wrought, is worthy enough to touch these healing waters.

With great reverence, kneel and cup your hands, filling them with the icy water. Bringing the liquid thrice to your lips, take the time to drink in all aspects of the water—how it tastes, how it makes you feel, how it connects you with the Holy Island of Avalon. You have received a most blessed sacrament. Take the time to fully understand its meaning and consequence in your life.

After a while, you notice a stream of water flows forth from its source, gathering into a pool that darkly reflects the clear starry sky. Take some time to stand over the rivulet, centering yourself and slowing your breathing. Feel the deep magnetic pull of the water beneath you, and sense that it is drawing off any energies generated by your lower self, cleansing you of any blockages and removing any fear. Feel your womb stirring within you. Awakened by the power of the Red Spring, your own sacred flow begins, be you maiden or crone. (*NOTE: If you are pregnant, simply feel the energies cleanse you and bless the babe in your womb—do NOT envision your moon blood coming upon you.*) Spend some time standing over this cleansing stream and take note of how your energy has changed and what has been cleared from you; these are important clues for your inner process.

When you feel you have spent enough time straddling the flow, continue to follow its path to the glassy mirror formed by the pooling of the water. The clarity of the reflection of the waning moon on its calm surface is striking. Speak aloud the purpose of your quest to the Red Spring, and see your words carried on a soft wind, rippling magickally over the pool's taut countenance. Sit beside it and gaze into its depths, taking note of any images that may play across the water. The mirror pool draws you deeper and deeper into its cauldron-shaped abyss, and you find yourself slipping, headfirst, into its magnetic belly. Surprisingly, you have no trouble breathing as you become immersed into icy waters much deeper than you could ever have imagined from the surface.

You descend lower into the red-tinged otherworldliness of the sacred pool. The water spirals around you like a glass tower, drawing you towards the bottom where you see a glowing silver light. You can almost discern the faint outline of a fantastically constructed palace when a strong current begins to eddy around you, causing the vision to dissipate in the churning waters. Doubt clouds the water, keeping you from maintaining focus on that which beckons to you from below. What is the nature of this resistance—what within you prevents you from reaching this goal?

You struggle against the vortex, which increases in intensity the more you flail about. *Clear your mind and calm your breathing,* comes a thought and you comply. The waters still, the stirred-up debris settles, and your way is made clear to the bottom, where an entirely new world opens before you.

You find yourself standing before a majestic building, seemingly wrought from the water itself. The high walls and spiraled turrets appear as glass spun from the luminous currents swirling around them. As you approach the entrance of this incredible edifice, its shining doorway opens to you, and you enter into the underwater palace's grand hall.

A long and inviting table fills the hall, illuminated by candles and exquisitely set with a sumptuous feast of exotic foods. Although there are settings enough for a hundred guests, the banquet hall is empty and the translucent citadel is eerily quiet. Your eye catches the slightest hint of movement on the other side of the chamber, and you walk towards it, past the bountiful table.

There is a doorway here, draped from lintel to threshold with a dark opaque veil. Through the fine weave of the silken material, you can look into the room beyond just enough to make out the ghostly outline of figures, appearing to move to the rhythms of a soundless dance. Before your eyes, the smoky vision begins to shift, and the figures begin to take on more familiar forms. Their dance changes too, and within the space of a heartbeat you recognize that these are no longer featureless shadows, but people and events that have had deep emotional impact on your life and have contributed to establishing the negative patterns and perspectives that color your sight. Long-forgotten memories rise to the surface and play out beyond the fabric of the veil. As you watch these energetic echoes of what has passed, you realize these are people and situations which, through the workings of the shadow, still play an active role in what you do, how you feel, and what you think.

Deep within you comes the dawning realization that these dark specters need to be honored and laid to rest. As painful as some of these visions may be, they need no longer be woven into the fabric of the present. The shades of things past have no place in the reality of the now. Allow the images to run their course, taking note of all that you see and remember. When the cloaked apparitions cease shifting, take three centering breaths and ask to see that which lies beyc d the hanging pall. When you are ready, move the shroud aside with the intention to see things for what they are, untainted by the dance of shadows.

You pass through whisper-soft curtains and enter the room beyond the doorway. The shadows dissipate in your wake, insubstantial as the hazy smoke tendrils generated by the single candle illuminating the room. It is hard to see in the flickering light of the dim flame, but you realize the chamber is empty, save for a silvery object, gleaming from its very heart. You reach for it instinctively, knowing it is a gift meant for you. Your outstretched fingers make contact...

...And you find yourself standing in the orchard once again, under the crisp night sky. Looking down at your hands, you see that you are holding the object from the bottom of the mirror pool. Examining it, you realize it holds important information about your work, and you make note of as much detail as you can. You are back where you started, but a change has occurred, and you know something has been set into motion. Take some time to reflect on your experiences.

When you are ready, your guide leads you back through the orchard and to the shores of the lake, where the Barge of Avalon awaits you. Turn once more to face the island and thank the Lady and all the guardians of this sacred space for supporting your work and allowing you to visit. Bid your guide farewell, and climb aboard the Barge to complete your journey to the other side, bringing with you the memory of all that has come before.

Revisiting the Self

As you continue making your connection to the Red Spring and participating in the process of descending into the unconscious aspects of the self, go back and re-read the self-reflective questions above. How have your answers changed? What catalyzed any changes? What underlying energies are you now aware of which were previously unconscious? What patterns have become visible? How can you put your insights and connections to work in order to bring change into your life?

Tool for the Station: Developing Inner Sight

The women of Avalon were renowned for their powerful use of the Sight. This was not a supernatural ability; rather, the priestesses of Avalon learned how to read the greater patterns around them, and from that, could predict how things would likely unfold. We can make use of this ancient art in our personal process; the more we understand the mechanisms of our inner landscapes and the more we are able see the way in which our own patterns manifest, the more we will be able to effect deep and lasting change in our lives.

It is this change which allows us to rise above the lessons being presented to us over and over again, giving us new eyes with which to see ourselves and the world around us. The more we change and grow, the greater becomes our ability to perceive the pattern. Therefore, we can say the Sight is not the goal of spiritual attainment, but rather, its byproduct.

Scrying is a potent tool for uncovering and deciphering the individual parts that make up the greater pattern. Like any other tool or esoteric art, learning to scry successfully takes a great deal of dedication, patience, and practice. You needn't be "psychic" in order to scry; we already have this ability within us. Scrying is a simple way to bypass the conscious mind, allowing us to connect with the wisdom inherent in our higher selves. The biggest challenge of this discipline is honing the ability to obtain clear focus. This can be achieved in a number of ways.

There are many objects that can be used as a focus for scrying. Crystal spheres or points, the embers of sacred woods, standard silvered or specially blackened mirrors, candle flames, intricate mandalas, or a bowl or body of still water are but a few examples of tools traditionally used in this art. One medium may have a greater draw over others, or it may be necessary to explore and experiment with several before finding the focus that works best. As with all things, personal experience is the most important element in the decision making process.

The women of Avalon made special use of the sacred waters gracing the Island. To honor the wisdom of our foremothers, we too make use of water as an instrument for scrying. Although we will focus on water here, the presented techniques can be adapted to other scrying methods that may work better for the individual.

It is important to select a scrying vessel suited to the process; many Avalonian Sisters use an iron cauldron or a silver bowl as a way of making a strong connection with our archetypal spiritual heritage. Other sorts of vessels may be used as they suit the individual, but it is best that there be no distracting patterns or textures which may interfere with the clarity of the reflective surface. Although there are special "magick mirrors" available for purchase, it is always better to make our own tools; doing so infuses them with our intention and facilitates our ability to connect with the tool for our workings. Whatever vessel is chosen, our efforts will be empowered if its use is exclusively for scrying. When not in use, wrapping the vessel in a piece of silk will keep it charged and protected.

Pure spring water is an excellent medium for scrying. Alternatively, consider making a magickal herbal infusion for this purpose. A particularly powerful elixir for Sight can be made in the following manner:

1. Boil spring water and let sit for five minutes.

2. Add a handful of vervain (*Verbena officinalis*) herb, a piece of silver, and a moonstone.

3. Let steep until cooled.

4. Strain liquid into a bottle or jar, retaining the silver and moonstone.

5. Place bottle in direct moonlight overnight. It is best to create two different elixirs at the full and dark moons; they can be used for different purposes and to seek different kinds of information. For maximum potency, keep the elixir in the moonlight for three consecutive nights.

6. To preserve the liquid, you may choose to add a small amount of brandy or vodka after it has been potentiated by moon energy. Store it in a cool place or in your refrigerator, if you do not wish to use alcohol. You may remove the silver and moonstone before storage if you wish.

7. When scrying, add three or nine drops of the Elixir for Sight into a water-filled vessel. Placing a few drops underneath the tongue before working helps to open the pathways to the Sight.

Note: Although vervain is safe, especially in the small dosages that come from elixir use, consult a health care professional if you have any questions about ingesting this herb. Do *not* use the Elixir of Sight if you are pregnant. Instead, make a gemstone elixir with moonstone by placing it in a glass bowl filled with spring water and follow steps five through seven, omitting the alcohol in step six.

Setting up the work beforehand is one of the most important elements of scrying. Knowing how to ask for information is critical to the success of the working. Take some time to meditate on what it is you would like to know before actually sitting down to scry; it is better to focus on one issue at a time. Preparation ensures you are spending as much time as needed concentrating on one topic rather than quickly running down a laundry list of concerns. Once you have chosen a topic you would like to receive more information on, or a situation you feel needs more clarity, you can begin work and set your intention accordingly.

When ready, gather your tools at a time and in a place where you will not be disturbed. It is best to work in low, indirect light; try scrying under the full moon or by the light of a single candle. Some women find that playing soft ambient instrumental music helps filter out distracting noises; if you do, it is best to use neutral music or rhythmic drumming so as not to have musical energy interfere with the information you are seeking. You may decide to hold the vessel in your hands, sit in front of it on the floor, or rest it on a table or altar in front of you. You may choose to use different positions for your vessel as you proceed in your scrying session, but before you begin, it is important to be in a comfortable position allowing a clear view of the inside of your vessel.

Always start your working by clearing and centering—this can be done through breath, sound, visualization, or burning sacred herbs like vervain or Balm of Gilead (*Populus candicans*). Fifteen minutes of Power Breathing is very effective for this purpose. Once you have cleared your physical and energetic spaces of distraction, sit with your intention and all that is connected with the issue at hand until it fills your very being. For example, if you have decided to work on understanding why you find it difficult to say "no" to others, even when you are already over-committed, bring to mind instances when this has happened and connect emotionally with how it made you feel.

When you are strongly rooted in this energy, call your guide and ask the Goddess to help you receive the information you need to understand this situation so that you may make positive growth changes. Place your hands around your scrying vessel—already filled with water and drops of the Sight Elixir if you have chosen to use it—and feel your intention for clarity on this *specific* issue flow out of your hands to charge the water and the vessel. When you feel you have put as much of this energy into the vessel as possible, take three deep breaths to settle your energy, and begin scrying.

A good way to start is by softening your vision as you stare at the still surface of the water. Keep your breathing deep and rhythmic as you work, and keep your mind clear of any doubts or expectations. Some women find it helpful to concentrate on their peripheral vision while focusing on the center of the scrying field; this creates a place in between for information to present itself. This information can come in many forms, and you may experience one or several of them at different times in your work. You may find that images, symbols, or even words form on the surface of the water, or you may see moving scenes unfold before your eyes. Whatever comes, don't judge what you see—

just accept and take note. There will be time later on to process what you have received.

You can continue to ask related questions based on insights you may have received in the moment, but resist shifting the focus away from the issue at hand. Follow the thread of revelation until no more images appear. Check with your guide, and when you are sure you are done, thank the Goddess for Her assistance. With intention, close down the energy of the scrying vessel by passing your hand three times over the surface of the water as if to close a window. Breathing any remaining energy down into the Earth, visualize the streams of energy pouring out of the bowl or cauldron and being absorbed into the ground.

Have your journal on hand so that you can record all of your insights and all that you have seen. This information can be the focus of your work for the lunar cycle, and you can use other tools, like the doorway working presented on p. 142, to help unlock the meanings of what you have seen. When you are done with your scrying session, it is a good idea to dispose of the water in a sacred way. Give thanks for the guidance you have received, and pour out the water on the earth or as a libation to a tree or plant.

Remember that scrying works by allowing your unconscious mind to speak to you without interference from your conscious mind. It may take a while to be able to bypass your conscious mind, but if you are diligent and disciplined, you can make a good and solid connection with the inner source of wisdom that lies beyond the unconscious. It is important to note that everyone receives information in a different way; it is not unusual to get auditory responses during a scrying session, or to get a sense of "knowing" that cannot be attributed to any physical sense. Do not judge the method of transmission; *what* is communicated is more important than *how* it is communicated.

The more you practice, the better your discernment skills will become. Frightening or negative images are more often than not a reflection of your own fears than an indication of your life's reality. Our higher selves mediate the voice of the Goddess for us; if you are not receiving constructive information—even in the face of bad choices you have made—you are probably not hearing with clarity. For this reason, it is important to clear out all negative energies from your personal energy field and to be centered in your work and your self before beginning to scry. In this way, you have fewer obstacles keeping you from accessing inner wisdom.

Once we begin to piece together the threads of underlying and unconscious energies that motivate our lives, we can begin to see the greater pattern. There is a saying:"That which is unconscious, controls us." Looking in the mirrors of our souls—beginning to descend into the hidden realms of the shadow—is a powerful way to take control over the tapestry of our lives, so that we may become all that we are meant to be.

The path of Sight always leads within.

6

THE STATION OF CONFRONTATION

Three things which continually grow less: darkness, falsehood, and death.

CELTIC TRIAD

CONFRONTATION IS THE DEEPEST POINT of the Cycle of Healing, the place where the roots of our disconnection and lack of wholeness are brought to light. These soul wounds may have their origins in childhood, past abuse, socialization, environmental stresses, or past lives. These hurts are reinforced by our perceived failures and shortcomings, leading us to believe in flawed perceptions of the self; they manifest in our lives as shadow tendencies. These cause us to repeat and perpetuate patterns; what we truly need is the ability to see our lives with eyes clear of past pain. Seeing the roots of our wounding allows us to throw back the veil of illusion and reclaim energies tied up in retaining these false beliefs about our abilities and ourselves. This reclamation is the gift that can only be found in the darkness. What was once a fallow field now holds the seeds of potential. What will this newfound energy be used for?

The Station of Confrontation in the Cycle of the Sun

In the heart of winter, the Celtic Britons subsisted on what they had in their stores and never traveled far from their homesteads because of the weather. Their attention was instead taken by what was needed in the home; they focused on repairs, weaving, and planning for the coming growing season. We too look within to see where the roots of our pain begin, and to plan for our healing. We cannot apply a cure when the source of the hurt is unknown. Gwyl Mair (Imbolc) is a time of expectant stillness, knowing that we have done all that we can this Cycle to see what lies unconscious within us. We can begin the upwards climb toward the Light Half of the Cycle, in motion once more, but only through commitment to the revelation of what we have worked to discover.

The Station of Confrontation is of extreme importance in women's Soul Work. Having undertaken the journey into the self at the Station of Descent, Confrontation marks the stillness before re-emergence. It takes great courage to immerse oneself in the darkness of the shadow, seeking out all that lies hidden, and working to reveal the mechanisms of the lower self. These revelations can heal the wounds that have motivated our actions and colored our perspectives. Armed with the knowledge that comes from exposing the root of our pain, we can begin the ascent, bringing our once-hidden issues with us back up into the light of consciousness.

This Station embodies the deepest depths of the Dark Half—the nadir of the Cycle and the very bottom of the Cauldron. The work of Confrontation is to come face to face with the core of the shadow aspect being sought. We must delve into the darkness so that we may see and name that which holds us back—there is great power in that naming. Facing the root wounding allows the freeing of psychic energy otherwise tied up in perpetuating lower self impulses. We can cease engaging in compensatory behaviors, allowing our actions and perspectives to better reflect our true selves.

The depth of the descent sets the height of the ascent; we can only reach as far up as we are willing to dig down. It is important to work to push past our limitations when confronting the shadow, for the more we are able to see of our wounds, the greater our capacity to heal. The energy released through the act of Confrontation is the resource from which the new self is created. To be sure, it takes great courage to look within, but the universe will not present to you what you are not yet ready to see. Everything is keyed to honor the seeker's limitations. Plumbing the inner depths will bring us as close to the root of our issue as can be processed with the tools at hand; we will never be given a burden greater than our ability to carry. That said, processing inner discoveries with a therapist, a trusted friend, or a circle of Sisters can contribute greatly to the individual process, especially when the need for support and encouragement are strong—growth and change are hard work.

This Station is where we sit in our stillness of honest self-contemplation and undertake the great magick of reweaving the pattern of our inner tapestry and setting our course to wholeness. Confrontation is aligned with the energies of solar Aquarius: drastic and sudden change, inquiry, and insight; and lunar Leo: reflecting the inner flame of transformation in order to understand the center of the self.

The Station of Confrontation in the Cycle of the Moon— Dark Moon

The dark moon phase lasts from the day of dark moon until three days after. During this phase, the moon's face is hidden by the shadow of the Earth, and so its familiar disk cannot be seen, except on the occasion of a solar eclipse. The dark moon rises and sets with the sun. Energetically, this is a time for turning within, confronting the shadow, and banishing negativity.

Self-reflective Questions for the Station of Confrontation

Take some time to meditate upon these questions while in a clear and receptive space. Use your replies to help form a focus for the work of the Station of Confrontation. Be sure to record your thoughts in a journal—this will help you chart your process of growth and change as you do the work of the Avalonian Cycle of Healing.

- *What keeps you anchored in negativity, hurt, pain, and suffering?*
- *What is your first response to a confrontational situation? Do you address the issue head on, or revert to a defense mechanism? When*

and why did you begin to use these methods of protection? How have these affected your quality of life?

- *What do you consider ugly about yourself—physically, emotionally, mentally, and spiritually? When did you learn to despise these aspects of yourself? How would your life be different if you could change how you felt about these things? What keeps you from making these changes?*

- *What would be the most frightening thing you could come to discover or realize about yourself? How would this affect you? Is there any truth in this fear? What makes you feel this way?*

- *What is the worst-case manifestation of your greatest fear? How would this affect your life? Is this a fear you learned from someone else? If so, is it truly relevant to your everyday life?*

- *If your life would be completely transformed by changing one thing about yourself, what would that thing be? In what ways would your life be different? How can you manifest this change in your life?*

The Avalonian Landscape: The Tor

ALTERNATIVE NAMES: Tor Hill, Glastonbury Tor
CYCLE OF HEALING: Station of Confrontation
CAULDRON TRANSFORMATION: Hare/Greyhound
ELEMENTAL ALIGNMENT: Earth
ENERGY CENTER: Root

The most commanding feature of Avalonian landscape is undoubtedly the enigmatic Tor, the center of Confrontation and the deepest point of the Cycle in the landscape. Rising to a height of over five hundred feet, the recumbent body of the Tor can be seen from a distance of twenty-five miles away; there is nothing like it in all of Somerset. For all its height and rarity, the most distinctive quality of the Tor is its terracing. It is possible the terraces are natural in origin, created by instability of the Tor's geologic makeup; these were later augmented or used as they were for agricultural pursuits in medieval times.

Alternatively, the Tor's undulating pathway may be what remains of a three-dimensional labyrinth created as a massive earthwork in the Neolithic period, around the same time as the Avebury complex. If so, the Tor Labyrinth is truly unique in scope and dimension. Taking the form of the seven circuit pattern called the Cretan or Classical labyrinth, a configuration seen the world over, it is the only such example created in three dimensions. Even archaeologists cannot discount the theory that the terraces on the Tor were once a massive labyrinthine earthwork; indeed, the Tor Labyrinth can still be walked today.

Perhaps both theories are true; the medieval usage of the Tor could well be agricultural, usurping its earlier usage as a sacred Pagan site. It is well known that other earthworks and stones from circles and henge monuments were reclaimed for building projects long after their original usage was forgotten. This is just one example of the many paradoxical dualities making up the Tor's essence.

Climbing its steep slopes, one is confronted with buffeting winds, wild and unsettling. Yet, even as one spirals up towards the crest of the Tor, there is an unmistakable magnetism, pulling one's energy down into its very bowels. It is disconcerting to be pulled upward and downward at the same time, and yet through this seemingly irreconcilable polarity, the Tor's power reveals itself.

Dual energy lines encircle the hill, following the path of the terraces, and merging near its apex. Feminine and masculine energies meet, symbolized by the Mary and Michael Lines—a geomantic resonance of the red and white dragons of British myth. Here then, on the slopes of the Tor, we experience the alchemical mingling of energy in this Sacred Landscape that sets the tone for the transformative power of place.

Red and white are the colors of the Celtic Otherworld. The merging of these two energies—and the Tor holding the place in the Cycle between the Red and White Springs of Avalon—creates a fitting portal into the chthonic powers associated with the Tor as a Gateway into the Underworld, the Celtic Realm known as Annwn. Ancient lore tells us that Gwyn ap Nudd—Light, Son of Night—rode out from his Otherworldly kingdom through the Tor, calling the spirits of those who had died to join the Wild Hunt with his white-bodied, red-eared hounds at his side. Interestingly, there is a long-standing legend of a cavern complex existing beneath the Tor, and that an entrance to these subterranean features can be found somewhere on its slopes.

Such an underground system of tunnels would further reinforce the "as above, so below" duality evoked by the energy of the Tor. On its surface winds the ancient processional way, recalling the stirring of Ceridwen's Cauldron. In walking this three-hour moving meditation, the women of ancient Avalon spun the landscape energies coursing through the ley lines up to the top of this earthwork spindle, all the while delving down deeper into the self. Once at the top and deeply entranced, the priestesses could connect more fully with the Lady and divine the needs of the Sacred Realm of Albion, the Spirit of the Island of Britain (Ynys Prydein), entrusted into their keeping.

The Three-Dimensional Tor Labyrinth—
After a drawing by Kathy Jones

The present-day tower standing on the Tor's crest dramatically punctuates the power of center. This last remnant of the second Christian monastic complex built upon the hill in the fourteenth century serves a powerful energetic purpose. Indeed, this may be the reason it endured when other buildings erected on the Tor have long given way to fire, earthquake, and Dissolution. St. Michael's Tower, without roof or doors, serves as a stone conduit at the Tor's energetic apex. The tower is a physical-world manifestation of the World Tree of Shamanic cosmologies that intensifies and focuses energies which course through it. The tower is the bridge between the realms, and by crossing this, the seeker can journey through time and space, and confront the very center of her existence.

Immram to the Tor of Avalon

The Tor of Avalon resonates most strongly with the energies of the Station of Confrontation in the Avalonian Cycle of Healing. This Station marks the nadir of the Dark Half of the Cycle, and represents our complete immersion into the realm of the Unconscious.

Stepping through the portal of this Station, we commit ourselves to acknowledging the root causes of our pain and naming the source of the involuntary manifestations of shadow in our lives. Use this holy site to unearth the root cause of the soul wounds hidden at the the core of your being. Clear away self-deceptions that block your sight, so you may look into this spiritual underworld with honesty and without fear. The ultimate treasure of the soul is found through the reclamation of energies tied up in our pain. The greatest growth occurs in the darkness.

Perform the Immram to the Island of Avalon as described on p. 55. After disembarking the Barge to Avalon, proceed with the rest of this working.

The Journey

It is midnight. Stepping off the Barge that transported you across the glassy lake to the Holy Isle, you meet your guide waiting for you on the shores of Avalon. Greet your guide. Share your reason for undertaking this journey. State your desire to visit the Tor and ask to be guided there.

Crystalline shards of frost crunch beneath your feet as you are led over the frozen ground through the heart of the orchards. The twisted apple tree limbs lift their skeletal arms skyward, as if to touch the cold and distant light of the stars shining in the moonless winter sky.

The hilly terrain slopes up and then down again, finally causing the slumbering body of the Tor to rise gently over the landscape. Take note of what you see along your path as you follow your guide to the foot of the imposing spiraled hill. At the mouth of the serpentine path are two stone markers, each carved with intricate and ancient designs. You feel drawn to touch the patterns, and find they have been made smooth by the finger tracings of countless pilgrims. You notice a walking staff propped up against the stone to your left. Sensing it is for you, you take it and examine the powerful glyphs etched into the yew wood. It feels solid in your hand, and you test your weight against it—it will be a perfect companion for what lies ahead.

Your guide steps aside, leaving you to stand alone between the guardian stones; it is clear that you must walk the rest of the way in solitude. Take a moment to revisit your purpose for making this journey. What insights do you seek at the heart of the labyrinth … the heart of the Tor … the heart of the self? Connect with the essence of the matter, concentrating on your breath to bring you clear focus. Release all fears, doubts and expectations. With a deep breath, plant your feet firmly on the path, and pass through the portal stones. Your journey begins.

One foot … then the other … you begin the ascent. Up and up and up you climb … each step brings you higher up the hill … and deeper within yourself. Every footfall becomes a rhythmic heartbeat, drumming your intention into the core of Holy Tor—reverberating in the sacred core of your soul. Every step awakens the energies of the landscape, and the twin coils of the Red and White Dragons of Albion arise in your wake. Encircling the sacred hill, the dragon lines empower the purpose of your journey, as you move with them through the sinuous terracing of the Tor.

Immerse yourself in these ancient and holy tracks of force—once stirred by countless priestesses in procession—once borne by humble pilgrims in solitude. Flowing around you and weaving their way to the hilltop, the energy currents begin to take on lives of their own. They appear powerful, moving you up the hill of their own accord, and you fall deeper into trance. Round and round, up and down, hill top and soul bottom … paths curving back upon themselves … the crest approaches, only to be taken once more from your line of sight by the next spin of the labyrinthine pathway.

Though leaden, your feet seem to move without conscious effort. You keep steady on the pathway aided by your yew staff, impelled forward with each breath. Dizzy with energy and confused by the endless series of twists and turns, you have lost track of time in the walking. The wind whips around you, sometimes chasing you up the path, other times causing you to struggle against its invisible resistance, holding you back from reaching the top of the Tor. The moonless sky is deep with stars, and shimmers, beckoning you forward—past the cold, through the dark, against the protests of your weary body.

Time passes … the stars move above you … And still you walk.

In and out.

Up and down.

Through and around again.

Spinning and weaving the energy up and back into itself.

At last, you find yourself making the final turn, bringing the crest of the Tor directly into your line of sight. Take a deep breath and proceed forward—each moment carries you closer and closer to the top. As you walk, the top of a standing stone comes into view, growing larger as you approach. Still others appear in your periphery, and at last you have reached the pinnacle. You draw a deep breath at the sight of what awaits you. With your eyes, take in all you can of the sacred precinct atop the Tor of Avalon.

You feel drawn to one of the enormous stones before you. With reverence, you walk forward and stretch your hand out to touch its lichen-mottled surface. The energy you have brought with you through the snaking pathway up the hill now courses through you and into the stone, and through it, into the others standing nearby. The entire breast of the hill is suddenly illuminated with the brilliance of the energy, almost blinding you with its intensity. You remove your hand from the stone to shield your face from the light, and just as suddenly, you are plunged into darkness.

Your eyes struggle to regain focus, and slowly notice a soft green-tinged glow. A few moments pass and you can see well enough to note that the vault of the sky has been replaced by the ghostly fingers of dripping stalactites above you, damply straining to meet the rising stalagmites below them. Somehow or other, you now find yourself in a cavern filled with a faint phosphorescence and the distant sounds of flowing water. You begin to move forward in the darkness, drawn towards an area of increased light. Moving slowly over the damp ground, and feeling your way through the forest of cave formations, you sense that you are less in a single cave than you are in a system of subterranean tunnels. With that consciousness, you suddenly feel—rather than see—the space in front of you open up into a large chamber.

You enter, tentatively, and feel the space brighten the further you move into the cavern. From out of the shadows, you catch an occasional glimmer of light or an odd glint of a sparkle. Though still dim, the light becomes strong enough for you to make out the fossil and crystal formations encrusting the walls and stone pillars of the cavern. The ground slopes downward from all sides, creating the effect of an underworld basin. As your feet take you forward and downward gently, you catch a glimpse of movement in the middle of the chamber.

Walking towards the center, you call out into the darkness, asking who is there. Silence and the quickening of your heartbeat are your only replies. You feel driven to announce your name and the reason for your journey. This time, your words echo around the chamber, each crystal facet reflecting the energy of your words back upon themselves until they are absorbed in the shadows. The chamber becomes silent once more. You take three steps forward and find yourself in the lowest point of the cavern.

Directly in front of you and spanning the distance from the ground to the ceiling of this subterrane is an enormous stone pillar, formed by meeting stalactites and stalagmites. The column is covered with arm-sized points of quartz crystals—some clear and pure, others clouded with mineral inclusions. Walking around the pillar to get a good look at this extraordinary formation, you realize that the movement you saw earlier was your dim reflection on the facets of the large crystals. Half-way around, you are confronted with what appears to be smooth sheet of raw quartz. Peering into it, you see your own reflection, warped and distorted by variations in the stone.

You are drawn to look deeply into your own eyes peering back at you from this underworldly mirror. Your eyes darken and swirl with subtle energies until all you can see on the stone's surface are the patterns playing out on the now-darkened surface. Unbidden, the key focus of your intention repeats itself over and over again in your head. The energy patterns begin to form coherent images and you find yourself unable to tear yourself away from the vision unfolding before you. The reason for your quest pounds loudly in your ears and above the din of your heartbeat. Looking deeply into the surface of the crystal, the layers of self peel away as the images before you hasten to bring forth the answers you seek.

Take what time you need to follow the branches of your work down to its very root, revealing its origin ...

When the images have stopped, take three deep breaths, fixing the visions in your mind and centering yourself in their energy. The calm surface begins to shift once again and the crystal begins to cloud and dim. The pillar of stone becomes an abyss of darkness that finds its resonance within you. Called forth from the deepest part of your psyche, the reflection of your shadow-self materializes in the obsidian-hued stone. Take a good long look at she who stands before you, familiarizing yourself with as many details as possible. When you feel you have fully explored the image in the glassy surface, ask her for her name. You hear it whisper in your ear as the mirror figure extends her hands to you. Repeat the name into the darkness of the chamber, feeling it reverberate around you. Extend your own hands to meet those of your shadow self, accepting the gift she presents to you. As you touch the surface of the stone, the world dissolves in a flash of light....

And you find yourself under a canopy of stars, on the steep slopes of the Tor once more. No longer at the crest of the hill, you realize that you are halfway down the spiraled path, facing the faint beginnings of a brightening horizon. The Red and White Dragon lines intersect at this point alone on the Tor, making it a node of power that bridges the worlds. You have returned from the underworld with the gift of the shadow in your hands. Examine it carefully and bring it back with you for it holds much that will aid you in your quest.

When you are ready, begin the slow descent that will bring you back to the two standing stones where your guide awaits you. The winds seem calmer now as you wind the pattern outwards, bringing the energies downward and grounding them within you. At last you reach the mouth of the labyrinth. Take some time to reflect on your experiences. Turn your face back to take in the sight of the sacred Tor, looking much like a goddess in repose across the landscape. Bow your head in thanks for the time spent in this holy place and for the insight and support you have received. Take three deep breaths and pass once more through the portal stones, meeting your guide on the other side.

Your guide leads you back across the island, through the orchard and to the shores of the lake, where the Barge of Avalon awaits you. Turn once more to face the island and thank the Lady and all the guardians of this sacred space for supporting your work and allowing you to visit. Bid your guide farewell, and climb aboard the Barge to complete your journey to the other side of the lake, bringing with you the memory of all that has come before.

Revisiting the Self

As you continue making your connection to the Tor and the shadow aspect of yourself, go back and re-read the self-reflective questions above. How have your answers changed? What catalyzed these changes? What underlying energies are you now aware of which were previously unconscious? What patterns have become visible? How can you put your insights and connections to work in order to bring change in your life?

Tool for the Station: Threading the Labyrinth

In Caer Pedryvan, four its revolutions;
In the first word from the cauldron when spoken,
From the breath of nine maidens it was gently warmed.
Is it not the cauldron of the chief of Annwn?

—FROM *PREIDDEU ANNWN—THE SPOILS OF ANNWN*

The poem *Preiddeu Annwn (The Spoils of Annwn)* is attributed to the great Welsh poet Taliesin, and has been dated to between the ninth and twelfth centuries CE. It is an evocative and symbolic piece detailing the voyage of Arthur into the Otherworld. The strong association of Avalon with Annwn is reinforced by several elements of this poem. It is not difficult to see the Tor, with its labyrinthine terracing, as the revolving fortress Taliesin described. The four-fold revolution of the fortress seems to suggest the four outer Cauldron Transformations, while its association with the Nine Maidens and their Cauldron make a strong connection to the Ninefold Sisterhood of Avalon. Further, this Cauldron of Inspiration—warmed by the breath of priestesses—seems to be the self-same vessel in which Ceridwen brewed the three drops of Awen.

The women of Avalon utilized the labyrinth as a great pattern of power, tracing its undulating form up the sacred slopes of the Tor. Drawing the dual energies of the Red and White Dragons up with them as they walked, the Priestesses of Avalon connected with the sacred landscape of mystic Albion in service to the Goddess and Her people. This holy walk enabled them to open the portal into the Otherworld, delving deeply into the realm of Annwn in order to receive the wisdom found only in the Cauldron's utter depths.

The labyrinth remains as important to us today as it was to our Avalonian foremothers. This effective tool for centering and balancing is also a potent ritual, facilitating our journey into the Otherworldly realm of our own unconscious. Literally retracing the footsteps of our foremothers, this sacred working ties us to the energy of the Avalonian Labyrinth and joins us to the ancient threading of the Sisters walking the ritual way up the Tor.

The labyrinth is a powerful tool for transformation, winding its single, irrevocable way to the center—and back out again. Primarily a walking meditation, it is also possible to harness the power of what in Welsh is called the *caerdroia* (named after the ancient city of Troy) by tracing a small replica called a finger labyrinth. Using a finger of your non-dominant hand to follow the serpentine path is an effective way of directly working with the mysteries of the labyrinth. The Avalonian Labyrinth is unique in its three-dimensionality, but it is the power of the symbol that it will work in any form—carved in a sacred hill or drawn with intent using pencil on paper.

The pattern cut into the slopes of the Tor is a Classical, seven-circuit labyrinth, often called the Cretan Labyrinth, pictured in this chapter. There is another pattern made up of eleven circuits called the Chartres Labyrinth, named after the cathedral in France where it is inlaid into the church's nave. At the heart of this grand cathedral dedicated to Mary, the Cartres Labyrinth was used in the Middle Ages as a symbolic representation of the piligimage to the Holy Land when the Crusades made it too dangers to travel there in person. Interestingly, the church itself is said to have been built on the site of a holy grove or nemeton sacred to the Gallic Druids. Both labyrinth patterns achieve the same ends, though the process of coming to center differs in each on many levels. Our focus is on the Cretan Labyrinth because of its direct connection to the Avalonian Tradition, but exploration and personal experience of both patterns is encouraged.

Always a sacred symbol, the labyrinth represents the process of going within. It is the quest for Center and the descent into the Underworld. More than a meaningful picture, it is a road map for growth. Labyrinths actively cycle energy in a very specific fashion, magnifying and condensing whatever energy is applied to it. Building a labyrinth on power spots will activate and intensify the natural energy of the space, pulling it in and sending it back out, changed and refined. Physically entering a labyrinth will have the same energetic effect on the seeker.

Comparison between Cretan Labyrinth (left) and Chartres Labyrinth (right)

Walking its course, insight and shift of perspective will rise to the top as one proceeds to the heart of the spiral—the heart of the self or the issue at hand.

This is the essence of all labyrinth work; its unicursal design winds the walker down to the center, into the stillness of the self. Walking the labyrinth aids us in divesting ourselves of our outer masks, allows us to pass through layer upon layer of illusion, and helps us to navigate through our sea of inner obstacles. Finally, at our center, all we are left with is the seed of truth—the potential to become all that we are and to face all that lies waiting in our inner darkness. Once we have touched this energy, we bring a thread of its revelation back up to the surface of our consciousness; retracing the same path outward, we unwind the energy and bring our wisdoms back out with us. We willingly enter the Otherworld and return changed.

Finding a Labyrinth

Learning how to draw the labyrinth pattern is a magnificent way to truly understand its energetics. Sig Lorngren of Mid-Atlantic Geomancy (www.geomancy.org/#labyrinths/index.php) presents a "seed pattern" which will allow you to draw it yourself.

Once you know how to draw the labyrinth, a good exercise is to create a left-handed pattern and a right-handed pattern side by side, allowing them to be traced with a finger from both hands concurrently, bringing balance to both sides of the brain. Learning how to draw a labyrinth is a magnificent way to truly understand its energetics. Below is a step-by-step guide on how to construct a seven-circuit labyrinth through the use of a seed pattern, based on the work of artist and labyrinth scholar Jeff Saward. You can take your paper labyrinth and laminate it, carve it yourself into wood or clay, or think about investing in one of many finger labyrinths available for purchase.

How to Draw a Seven Circuit Labyrinth

There has been a recent renaissance of interest in labyrinths; with some research you may find a public labyrinth to walk in your area. The Episcopal Church has done a great deal in reviving the Chartres pattern; many local churches have labyrinth walks open to the public. Many Avalonian Sisters have built labyrinths on their land using stone, plants, or other materials, and once you have learned to make the Classical pattern, it is an easy thing to draw it out in the earth, with candles or on sand for a temporary working. There are excellent resources available in the form of books and kits that will facilitate your creation of permanent outdoor or portable indoor canvas labyrinths.

The Working

A simple way to begin is to ground and center. When you are in a clear space, think about where you are in your personal process, especially as it concerns the work of Confrontation. Bring to the labyrinth an issue you are working on, a question you may have, an ongoing situation troubling your peace, or anything needing clarity. For which of your issues is it vitally important to see the root cause? What lies at the heart of the situation of which understanding is needed most? What do you need to see?

When you have decided on the focus of your work, keep the situation or question in your mind as you fall into your Power Breath. Standing at the threshold of the labyrinth, take a moment to recognize that you are about to enter into sacred space, and make some gesture to mark this passage; you can chant, ring a bell, make an offering of incense, say a prayer or affirmation—anything that is significant for you.

When ready, enter into the labyrinth with your mind centered on the intention for your walk. As you go, take note of what comes up for you—emotions, thoughts, symbols, and memories. Honor them and allow them to pass. Do not be fixed in your thoughts as you walk; you may enter the labyrinth with one thing in mind and find yourself exiting with an insight entirely different than what you expected.

This is the key to labyrinth work; we must release our expectations so we can be clear to receive what the universe sends our way. Not everyone receives a life-changing epiphany in a single labyrinth working; indeed, your experiences and the degree of clarity gained can change from working to working. Do not, therefore, judge your experience or compare it to an idealized scenario created in your head. The universe will send you exactly what you need, when you need it, and in a form that benefits you the most.

When you reach the center of the pattern, recognize where your journey into the sacred has taken you, and honor the space in a way you feel is appropriate. Take some time in the middle, awaiting insight or inspiration, before thanking the universe and taking your new wisdom with you. The heart of the labyrinth is not the only place to receive insight; many find small pieces of wisdom along the way, leading up to the greater whole in the center.

As you unwind the pattern, focus on the insights with which you were gifted, and contemplate how to integrate these gifts into your life. Like a pebble dropped into a still pool, the revelation at the center of the labyrinth will ripple out to touch all aspects of the self. Receive the vision of what this change will mean to you as you emerge from the heart of the pattern, and be open to the next level of insight these revelations can bring.

Upon exiting, thank the space for receiving you. Reflect upon the information you have obtained and the wisdoms you have been granted from your walk.

Oftentimes in labyrinth work, it is very effective to trace the pattern a set amount of times in a number sacred and meaningful to the user; walking sets of three, five, and nine bring powerful insights within the context of the Avalonian path. Many women comment that it takes a round or two to get settled into the walk or the tracing before they can focus on the work at hand, so keep this in mind as you begin to work with this transformational tool. The more familiar you become with the twists and turns of the labyrinth (themselves great lessons), the more you will begin to notice patterns in the type and tenor of information coming up for you at different points in the journey.

There are many ways to approach labyrinth work; some sources attribute a chakra, a musical note, a color and a healing focus to each circuit. It is empowering to take time to explore this incredible tool for yourself, coming to your own conclusion of what energy dwells where, before applying the external correspondences. When later comparing your insights with the work of others, you may discover a wonderful validation of your own innate wisdom, or find that the labyrinth interacts with your energy in a unique way.

A great many people use labyrinths as an element of healing work, and they can be walked or traced in a celebratory manner as well. They are used for rites of passage such as commitment ceremonies, consecrations, and baby blessings; to mark transitional holidays like New Year's Eve; on Avalonian Holy Days, especially Gwyl Mair and Calan Gaeaf; and even to evoke universal joy by moving through the pattern with song and dance.

The labyrinth is a powerful focus for the journey within; it is a symbol, tool, and metaphor. Although there are many applications for its use, labyrinth work is especially powerful when used as a focus to bring us to the center of our selves, to see the heart of a situation, and to bring the wisdom found within to a place of integration through emergence.

7

THE STATION OF EMERGENCE

Three things which constantly increase: light, life, and truth.

CELTIC TRIAD

W E RETURN FROM THE OTHERWORLDLY realms of the Unconscious with knowledge freed from its depths. Here is the sword taken from the stone—the freeing of truth from the grip of illusion. With this liberated energy at our disposal, we seek the vision of our higher self made manifest, and plant the seeds of wholeness in the receptive and fertile soil of our souls. Having drunk deeply from the well within, we are able to harness the endless potential of the revitalized landscape with consciousness. This inner renewal sprouts forth, fragrant with possibilities and garlanded with the beauty of choice. No longer limited by what was, we have the power to catalyze what can be.

The Station of Emergence in the Cycle of the Sun

The Light Half of the Year dawns with the cleansing flames of the Calan Mai (Beltane) fires. The world is awash with the vibrant intensity of all things green and growing as a fertile wave of vital energy crashes across the landscape. For Celtic Britons, Calan Mai marked the beginning of summer and catalyzed a shift in focus on both agricultural and societal fronts. Just as the natural world was bursting forth with new beginnings and the promise of grand potential in the frenzy of renewal, so too were Britons emerging from constrictive winter weather and homestead activities. Summer was the time to reaffirm bonds of community and economy with neighbors.

Gathering for celebrations at clan central places, Britons gave thanks for the return of the Earth's bounty and forged social and economic relationships to ensure continued survival for seasons to come. They made legal contracts, traded their goods and livestock, performed agricultural divination, and settled outstanding financial accounts. In all these things, we see the Celts took stock of what was important based on what the previous winter had brought. They used this information to decide and act on what they would need for a successful upcoming season of growth and abundance. Although today most of us are not directly concerned with raising cattle and producing crops, we can take these underlying wisdoms and apply them to our own lives so that we may support the self we wish to encourage and the inner gifts we wish to cultivate.

The great challenge of the Station of Emergence is bringing the revelation of the deepest depths—the transforming wisdom of the Cauldron—into the consciousness of the Light Half of the Cycle. It is not enough to be able to see, however. We must also act by making outward changes that reflect our newfound inward knowing. At Emergence, we plant the seeds of our intention into a ground made fertile by the energy freed up from the shadow. Through the marriage of what is within to what is without as we straddle the worlds of dark and light, we work to make the unconscious conscious, and seek an external manifestation of the true self revealed in the darkness.

The focus of this Station is to set the work of the Light Half of the Cycle into motion, committing ourselves to charting the course of consciousness and external manifestation. Emergence is aligned with the fertile energies of solar Taurus—the externalized beauty of abundance born of inner renewal reflected out into the world by lunar Scorpio.

The Station of Emergence in the Cycle of the Moon— First Quarter

The moon is in her first quarter from the seventh through the tenth day after the dark moon. During this phase, the right half of the moon appears to be illuminated by direct sunlight. The first quarter moon is visible throughout her course in the night sky. She rises in the east at noon, is at her apex in the sky at dusk, and sets in the west around midnight. Energetically, this is a time for emerging into the light, planting seeds for manifestation, and seeking outer balance.

Self-reflective Questions for the Station of Emergence

Take some time to meditate upon these questions while in a clear and receptive space. Use your replies to help form a focus for the work of the Station of Emergence. Be sure to record your thoughts in a journal—this will help you chart your process of growth and change as you do the work of the Avalonian Cycle of Healing.

- *What perspectives, situations, persons, and things in your life bring you joy? What things stimulate exhilaration? Happiness? Fulfillment? Pleasure? A sense of accomplishment? Balance? How often do you permit yourself to engage in these things?*

- *Make a list of your gifts, talents, abilities, and interests. How much time do you devote to the pursuit or development of the items on this list? How much of person that you are inside is reflected into the outside world? What is the reason for any dissonance between what is within and what is without? What can you do to change this?*

- *If there were nothing preventing you from achieving your ideal life, what would this life look like? What would you do for a living? How would you spend your leisure time? Where would you live? What would your guiding principles be? What can you do to manifest this ideal life? Create a plan of action—a spiritual road map—that will* bring you to this destination. What do you aim to accomplish in one year? In three? In nine? What can you change today that will set you down this path?

· Think about the times that you were able to achieve your goals. What did you do in those instances that was different from the times you fell short of manifesting your desires? Can you discern a pattern of decisions and actions that have held you back from doing and being all that you could be? What can you choose to do differently?

· Think about the insights you gained from the work you did at the Station of Descent and review your answers to the self-reflective questions posed. Revisit the work of the Station of Confrontation and the revelation of the shadow at the core of your being. How can you constructively apply these hard-earned wisdoms to the work of Emergence? In what ways can you work to reroute the energy freed from the shadow realm of the Unconscious and use it to empower the woman you were meant to become?

The Avalonian Landscape: The White Spring

ALTERNATIVE NAMES: Tor Springs, Well House Spring

CYCLE OF HEALING: Station of Emergence

CAULDRON TRANSFORMATION: Wren/Hawk

ELEMENTAL ALIGNMENT: Air

ENERGY CENTER: Throat

Moving out from the Underworldly realms into the shining brilliance of the light, the White Spring fountains out of the Earth like the freed-up energies of the unconscious rising to the surface to nourish whatever seeds we choose to grow. Moving into the active portion of the Cycle, the White Spring holds the energies of the Station of Emergence and serves as a portal moving outward, just as the Red Spring stands at the threshold of that which lies within.

There is great significance in the duality of these two springs. They resonate with the energy of the Celtic Otherworld, as white and red are emblematic of Annwn; we see these colors together over and over again in British mythology in connection to the Otherworldly realm. Essentially standing side by side in the Tor Valley, these springs are of completely different telluric origin, and their waters exhibit different properties of flow and mineral content. The Red Spring boasts a constant stream, having never failed in historical memory, even in times of drought. It has high iron content, a constant temperature, and its waters are thought to originate many miles from Glastonbury, perhaps as far away as the Mendip Hills to the north.

The White Spring's flow, on the other hand, is much more sporadic, and its high calcium content is attributed to the limestone Lias layers underlaying Glastonbury Tor. These waters rise from deep within the earth—perhaps originating from an artesian system—percolating through the limestone caverns beneath the Tor before emerging as a confluence of springs at the surface. The high calcium content is consistent with the formation of flowstone, the petrified mineral deposits laid down by a flow of water often found in caverns and caves. Indeed, there are visual accounts from the late nineteenth century describing the lush and verdant area surrounding the White Spring as being covered in white calcified material, creating natural pools and flow forms.

Once spilling from the mouth of a cavernous opening in an enclosed rock face hanging with flowstone, the waters of the White Spring—also known as the Tor Springs—were as venerated as the neighboring Red Spring. The flow of the two springs was thought to have commingled in symbolic marriage at some point in their journey towards the marshlands of Avalon. It is easy to see how the fantastic sight of this grotto, dripping with the ghostly echoes of calcified stone streaming forth from a cavern leading beneath the Tor, could suggest the entrance into the Underworld realm of Gwyn ap Nudd. What a vision it must have been!

Unfortunately, the construction of a stone reservoir in 1872 has completely obliterated the natural beauty of the White Spring, and has, over time, been converted from its original purpose for use as a café and jewelry shop in recent years. Even with the more commercial uses of the building, some acknowledgement of the spring's spiritual power has been made in the form of indoor shrines in areas where the water has been allowed to flow freely, and to run on the floor in channels reminiscent of some of the flow forms in the Chalice Well and Gardens.

Although the space has been altered by construction and commercial development, the spiritual nature of the White Spring is being reclaimed and honored today more than ever before. The Companions of the White Spring purchased the property in 2005 and began a staged process of converting the reservoir building into a temple. With shrines dedicated to the Lady of Avalon, Gwyn Ap Nudd, Brigit, and St. Michael, the building plans feature a series of pools both for immersion and for reflection. Outside of the building, White Spring waters flow freely from a spout directly across the lane from a similar one for the Red Spring. An outdoor shrine has been built where the waters collect, and is decorated with stones, flowers, and other offerings left by pilgrims.

White, nourishing, and transforming all it touches, the Tor Springs represent the milk of the Mother. It is the vital and fertile flow freed from the bones of the Earth, returning to the surface with the promise of new life and abundance. The fundamental nature of the White Spring speaks of laying down new pathways and re-channeling the essence of that which is found within. Complementing the menstrual energy of the Red Spring, the White Spring creates and builds up, while the other cleanses and breaks down. We enter the darkness through the cauldron womb of the Red Spring, and emerge from the Underworld through the shining portal of the White Spring.

These two sacred springs hold the essence of the dual nature of Avalon's transformational energy, mirrored in the Red and White Dragon

Lines that encircle Glastonbury Tor and arch out across the landscape. We must embrace the energies of creation and destruction, for it is only through the interplay of what is in the light and what lies in shadow—of that which is conscious and that which remains unconscious; of outward expansion and inward contemplation—that soul growth and personal evolution can occur.

Immram to the White Spring of Avalon

The White Spring is related to the Station of Emergence in the Avalonian Cycle of Healing. Stepping through the portal of this Station, we commit ourselves to the outer manifestation of the potential we have come to recognize within. Use this holy site to empower your journey of self-actualization as you begin to reroute energies once ensnared in shadow. Plant the seeds of your growth in the renewed and fertile soil of your soul.

The challenge of this process of self-revisioning is to break free of destructive patterns by rerouting your energy to flow in a new and personally empowering direction. At the Station of Emergence, the butterfly of our soul departs from the darkness of gestation's cocoon and is birthed into the limitless promise of the Light Half of the Cycle. All that we can dream, we can become. All that we strive for, we can obtain. All that wounds us, gifts us as well—which way the pendulum swings is a matter of choice. The Station of Emergence calls us to dip deep into the well of our potential and transform the prospective self within into an actualized reflection of Sovereignty without.

Perform the Immram to the Island of Avalon as described on p. 55. After disembarking the Barge to Avalon, proceed with the rest of this working.

The Journey

It is dawn. Stepping out of the Barge that transported you across the glassy lake to the Holy Isle, you meet your guide waiting for you on Avalon's shores. Greet your guide. Share your reason for undertaking this journey and your desire to visit the White Spring; ask to be guided there.

The landscape is painted with shimmering dewdrops, catching the first warming rays of the awakening sun. As you are led through the orchards, the crisp morning air is filled with the discourse of birds and the heady scent of apple blossoms. Time passes differently here. The shifting colors of daybreak provide a pastel backdrop for the white and pink flowers bursting forth to blanket the spindle-limbed forms of Avalon's apple trees.

The hilly terrain slopes up and then down again, finally causing the slumbering body of the Tor to rise gently over the landscape. Take note of what you see along your path as you follow your guide, not to the spiraled hilltop nor to the pregnant earthen mound silhouetted against the sun-brightening sky, but to the valley between these two hallowed promontories. Turning slightly to the right, the path you follow is lush and green, fragrant with the delicate scent of the opening blooms that ornament the plants and trees.

The energy of the narrowing trail begins to shift and you find yourself walking through a small copse of oak trees, garlanded with strands of tiny clusters of yellow flowers. The pathway leads to a sheltered alcove, encrusted with strange stone formations that seem to flow out from the hillside. Everywhere, small pools of fossilized ripples cover the ground; even the overhanging plant life is garbed in a cleansing sheen of white.

Peering into the alcove, you hear and then see a stream of water emerging throat-high from a small opening in the back wall. Looking up into the rocky crevice, you see that it widens into a passageway before diving deep into the hillside—evoking mystical images of crystal caverns below the Tor. The flowstone follows the path of the water, laying down new layers of mineral to renew the old channels; the entire alcove is encrusted in stone formations, creating a magickal garden of calcified movement.

Like Mother's milk spilled across the Earth, the flow of water winds its way through an enchanted landscape of sluices and tiny waterfalls into a naturally formed basin pooling beside the exposed roots of a gigantic oak tree. The ancient tree reflects upon the shining water, its roots nourished by the flow—its form straight and tall, its limbs hanging with yellow threads of flowers. Growing as high as its roots run deep, the oak tree bridges the worlds above and below, just as its roots now straddle the waters of the White Spring. Fed by the glistening waters from below, the mighty tree is able to stretch its limbs high above.

You notice a simple wooden bowl lying between the roots of the oak tree; it is a pilgrim's cup, worn smooth with use and seasoned with age. You bend to fill the cup with the calcium-rich liquid, and with awareness and intent, you take a drink. Like the whitewashed vision of the holy grotto, the cleansing energy of the water fills your soul. Take some time to experience this sacrament, being sure to take note of how it makes you feel and the way your personal energy shifts.

Sit down next to the tree and breathe in the essence of this place. It is serene beyond words, yet crackles with the vital energy that accompanies springtime newness. Take some time to watch the flow of the water, listen to the early morning birdsong, and experience the growing warmth of the new day's sun. Gaze at your image in the water, reflecting on all that you have learned about yourself during the work of the Dark Time.

Watch the water as it runs down the pathway, making its own winding way out of the mouth of the Earth, passing over the stones that seek to contain it, and laying down its own track through the lush plant life, transforming all it touches with its white and shining purity. Your soul resonates with the song of the White Spring: it is one of rushing waters, breaking free of old patterns, and finding ways to reroute that which rises to the surface from within the depths of the darkness—ever in pursuit of its goal. The soil of your soul has been renewed; receptive and fertile, what will you plant in your quest for Sovereignty?

Deep in thought and gazing upon your own reflection, you feel the rise of a warm breeze that stirs the limbs of the tree towering above you. Three golden threads of oak blossoms fall into the water, dispersing the image of your face as it sends subtle ripples across the pool's glassy surface. As the motion subsides, you watch as your reflection reforms itself into a symbol. As soon as the image completely resolves itself in the water, you realize it is a key to unlock the door to the inner change you are seeking to make. Be sure to take precise note of the symbol's details.

The tree beside you begins to vibrate subtly, and you rise to stand in front of it. As you do so, the oak begins to glow and the texture of the bark begins to shift before your eyes. The ridges rearrange themselves into a gleaming replica of the symbol you saw in the water. Curious, you reach out to touch the image, but your fingers pass right through it into the trunk of the tree. Fascinated, you feel drawn to walk into the symbol, and as you do so, the tree becomes intangible and you pass through easily.

Your vision tilts, the landscape shifts, and you find yourself looking out at the world from the perspective of the oak; everything around you has been transformed into a shining reflection of the world you left behind. You can see the luminous aura of every living thing, and the spring water pooling at your feet carries a stream of life-force energy emanating from the core of the planet itself. You can feel that your arms have become oak branches, your hair budding leaves and strands of flowers, your torso its trunk, and your legs and feet its roots. Take some time to experience what this feels like, and fully give over to the sensation of being one with the oak tree.

You become aware of something shining invitingly above the top of the tree. Although the details are not completely clear, you can see just enough of it to recognize that it is an image of your actualized self. You strain to touch the image, but for all of your efforts, it is just beyond the reach of your highest boughs. Knowing that this vision would not have revealed itself if there was no way for you to claim it, you consider how you might be able to reach higher.

The pool of milky water begins to tingle beside your feet and you feel your vast root system, anchored deeply in the ground, drawing nourishment from the rich earth. You feel new growth at the very tips of your roots and the recent underground extensions that have sought and found the underground flow of the White Spring. There, below the surface, you sense an abundant source of recently liberated energies awaiting a focus for use. With consciousness, you begin to draw the rejuvenating energies of the spring up from the earth and into the tree's vascular system. As it enters the roots and rises up through the trunk, the sacred waters transfer the potential from below into the ability to manifest a harvest above.

At last, the water spreads out into the tree limbs, expanding outward and entering into smaller branches and twigs. As its vibrant energy enters the smallest ends of every stem, the transformational waters catalyze an amazing burst of growth. Fresh green tips begin to telescope out from the sealed points where last year's growth ended. Burgeoning buds of leaves begin to unfurl and the last of the yellow oak blossoms open to the springtime air, high above the ground. The growth accelerates as the transfigured crown of the tree comes alive, reaching skyward—seeking to attain the potential height made possible by the new growth of the roots below.

Higher and higher and higher you reach, a bit disoriented by all the change. A sudden doubt halts the transfer of energy from below, and the growth stops, with your goal a mere hair's width away. You try to clear your focus and regain your momentum, but it is almost as if an invisible barrier is pressing downward on you, preventing any further upward growth. Your limbs feel heavy and the burden of holding them upward begins to feel more than you can bear. It's too hard... too hard.

The wooded area has grown hushed with anticipation, the silence unbroken except for the distant sound of a wave of wind through the trees. Rushing towards you and bearing the scent of apple blossoms up from the orchard, the current of air sets your branches into gentle motion as it sings the song of the breeze. Feeling renewed, your vigor returns. The wind seems to have shaken loose any lingering doubts and has freed you from weariness and stagnation. Your limbs start to grow again—reaching up and up until at last, it touches the image of your priestess self, no longer out of reach.

The moment you make contact with the image, the energy it contains bursts through your mind in a torrent of scenes and visions. Take note of all you see, for this is important information that will help you actualize the image of the Sovereignty you have just received. At the very point of connection between the oak tree and the vision above, the growth of the branch accelerates, and a tiny acorn is formed. This capped seed grows, ripens and then falls into the pool of water at your feet.

You bend down to pick the acorn up and find you have stepped out of the tree. Reaching into the puddle, you take the acorn in your hand and sense the powerful energies with which it has been imbued. You turn to thank the oak tree, still pulsing with a vital and renewed essence. The symbol you placed on the bark is still there, and with intent, you use a cycle of nine breaths to remove it from the trunk. Refill the wooden cup with water and pour a libation of gratitude over the roots. The branches light up once again, swaying back and forth in the returning breeze.

You look down at your hands and find them changed as well—bright, strong, and brimming with power. The whole of all that you can become is contained in the essence of the acorn, and you know you have the ability to bring yourself to full harvest. Having touched the potential realized in the light of the waxing sun, hold the thought in mind, and take one last drink from the White Spring. Allow its waters to empower the path you have chosen and the higher-self goal you have set, born of old perspectives, transformed by insights deep within, made conscious. Bring the acorn back with you to be planted in the prepared soil of your soul.

Take some time to reflect on your experiences. When you are ready, your guide leads you back through the orchard and to the shores of the lake, where the Barge awaits you. Turn once more to face the island, and thank the Lady and all the guardians of this sacred space for supporting your work and allowing you to visit. Bid your guide farewell and climb aboard the Barge to complete your journey to the lake's other side, bringing with you the memory of all that has come before.

Revisiting the Self

As you continue making your connection to the White Spring and participating in the process of recognizing the potential of the emerging self, go back and re-read the self-reflective questions above. How have your answers changed? What catalyzed these changes? How can you actively break free from outmoded patterns and lay down new pathways in your life? What choices now lie before you? How can you put your insights and connections to work in order to bring change into your life?

Tool for the Station: The Doorway

Doorway work is an incredibly empowering technique that will aid in uncovering the meaning of symbols—be they universal archetypes or holding personal significance. Upon mastering this tool, we will no longer be limited to the "accepted" meanings and general information found in symbol books. Looking to external sources for information can often leave one unfulfilled, especially when unraveling images received during Immrama, meditation, and dreams. When we receive information in our work, it filters through our energy field before becoming conscious, often in the form of a symbol. As such, the universe uses our personal energy to speak to us in a language we will understand. It is important, therefore, for us to learn to read our own code, rather than try to conform to someone else's—or worse, to restrict ourselves to the limitations of other people's knowledge.

Let us consider that there are two different types of symbols: universal archetypes and personal symbols. Universal archetypes will key into the same basic information for everyone; they represent wisdom encoded in the collective unconscious. Personal symbols will key into information meant specifically for an individual and directly addresses their work and personal process. There are times when universal symbols can also be personal symbols; working with them can yield two levels of information. It is therefore important to consider the context in which you received the symbol—was it as an answer to a specific question, or are you trying to undercover the hidden meaning of an object or magickal symbol? For example, the cauldron is a universal symbol, and doing doorway work to unlock the meaning of the cauldron can yield archetypal information. However, if you received the image of a cauldron in the course of your personal work or during an Immram, you may find that your doorway will yield information relating to you specifically and the situation about which you are seeking clarity.

The key to successful doorway work is not to edit, judge, or dismiss what you see when you walk through the gate. A huge part of the process of personal growth and inner empowerment is coming to a place where you trust the information you receive in your work. At the beginning, this trust may require you to suspend your disbelief long enough to develop new ways of seeing and to learn how to understand the language of the universe. This is not to say you should blindly accept everything as literal truth; at the beginning especially, much of what we see is allegorical and dealing with the personal.

Developed discernment accompanies our expanded sight with the clarity gained in working through the Stations of the Cycle of Healing; we can come closer to personal authenticity through issue resolution. Through this working, we will be able to perceive more of the greater pattern, for we will be able to separate our own stitches from the whole of the fabric; that is, we will know when we are looking at the world through the filter of our own issues or seeing things for what they truly are. Developing discernment and learning to trust in the self and our connection to the Divine is a difficult hurdle, but once conquered, an entirely new level of the work opens up before us.

When you are ready to begin, sit in your sacred space and start your Power Breathing until you find yourself centered, focused, and clear. Connect with the intention of your doorway and recall the circumstance in which you received this symbol. Was it in response to a question you asked? Was it a gift you received in one of the Landscape Immrama? Is it an element from a dream for which you are seeking clarity? This context is an important element of your doorway work and should frame every working.

Next, in your mind's eye, visualize a doorway or portal. It can take the form of any kind of door that you wish—from a standard wooden door to a megalithic dolmen, to a marble-hewn portico. Choose a doorway that feels best to you; if you encounter any difficulty, consider asking your guide for assistance in finding the right form for you. At the beginning, it is helpful to work with the same door whenever you use this technique. In this way you begin to associate that particular door with unlocking the information you need and it becomes empowered with the intention of each use. After you have become adept with this tool, you can do some experimentation with other kinds of doors with which to set up your work. Some women use a different door when they want archetypal information than when they are doing personal process work. Others find that their door seems to change over time. Be open to the possibilities, but remain focused with your intention.

When you have chosen the form of your doorway, sit with it and breathe it into existence. Create a mental image of the door and fill it with your energy and intention until it feels solid and complete. You should be able to clearly see it in the mind's eye. When it is as solid as it's going to be—the more you practice this technique, the more solid the doorway will become—put the symbol you want to work with on the door and breathe it into existence there in much the same way you constructed the door itself. It is important to record the details of symbols you receive as accurately as possible—color, direction, composition, dimensionality, and context—so that you can reproduce them faithfully when it is time to do a doorway. These subtleties can make all the difference when uncovering meaning of symbols.

When you feel the symbol is strongly affixed onto the door, open it and step through. You can "step" in one of two ways. You can accomplish this in your mind's eye, from either a first or third person perspective, or you can stand and trace your doorway and its symbol in front of you. Breathe it into existence with your will and intention, then open and walk through the energetic construct with your physical body. Either way, entering the doorway will open your conscious mind to information encoded in the symbol. There are many different ways this information may become available to you: you may meet someone, view static images, experience moving scenes, hear voices, see colors, perceive energies, trigger memories—there are endless possibilities. Don't be afraid to explore what lies beyond the door; look around and ask questions. You may find that each time you create a doorway, information presents itself in a different way—you are met by someone one time, but only hear voices the next. This is not uncommon. Accept the information in whatever form it is presented to you. Over time a pattern may emerge, so take note of differences as they occur.

Doorways can be a challenging technique to master; try not to become discouraged, because this is a tool well worth honing. As with any new skill, practice is the key to success. Oftentimes the more emotionally charged an issue is, the harder it is—and more important it is—to get the door open. Your guide is an excellent resource for this work and you can ask for her assistance in getting the door open and to obtain the information you need once you are on the other side.

When you feel you've received all the information you can in one session, return the way you came and step through the doorway once more, being certain to close it securely behind you. If you have drawn the doorway energetically in front of you, breathe it down into the earth to shut down its energy. As soon as possible, journal your experiences and draw all images and symbols found behind the door. Even if what you received does not make immediate sense, keeping a record of your encounters may provide greater insight later on your path of growth.

It is possible to work through doorways and see a symbol hundreds of times before you have fully unlocked all the information it bears, especially if it is a universal symbol. Don't be content with one go at it. At the very least, do an entire week of doorways for each symbol you are working on, making sure to work with any additional symbols that may come to you. If you go before the Goddess at the moon, as described on p. 264, ask Her for a symbol that will guide you in your work for the coming cycle, and do that doorway every night. At the next moon, you can come before Her again with insights gained, and ask for the next step in your work.

Doorways provide structure for your meditation that aid in receiving the inner wisdoms the universe seeks to impart to you. This work is powerful, and can be used in many ways. You can create doorways your name and your signature, something representing a choice that lies before you, a haunting image, a number, herb, Goddess symbol, something received in a dream or while scrying—the possibilities are endless.

Learning to hear the voice of the universe and find answers to your own questions by turning the eye within is key to personal empowerment and inner evolution. It reinforces the notion that you have the power to change your life as well as the wisdom to bring yourself to wholeness. Remember the old axiom: "If you can ask the question ... you already have the answer."

8

THE STATION OF
RESOLUTION

Three candles that illume every darkness: truth, nature, and knowledge.

CELTIC TRIAD

OUR PRIESTESS SELF IS REVEALED in the full illumination found at the apex of the Avalonian Cycle of Healing. The orchards of our souls hang heavy with the fruits of our becoming. The Station of Resolution is the point at which we gauge our success in bringing the energy of the shadow into the light of consciousness, thereby transmuting the power our wounds have held over us into the vehicle that brings forth our wholeness. Resolution is the crowning glory of the Cycle, where we give birth to an aspect of the actualized self and celebrate the passage of our inner Sovereignty into the outside world. Looking into the mirror of Resolution, we see the reflection of a woman made in the image of the Goddess—in truth, the woman we were born to be.

The Station of Resolution in the Cycle of the Sun

Gwyl Awst (Lughnasadh) was a time of great celebration for the ancient Celts. Finally able to take time away from their crops just before the harvest, families traveled to their clan central places for weeks of ritual, games, and festivities. They engaged in trading, entered into marriage contracts for a year and a day, and displayed and sold their crafts and wares. This festival marked the beginning of the harvest season, and the land around them was bursting with abundance.

Gwyl Awst is the height of the Light Half of the Year, the time when all is in full fruit and all is revealed in the dazzling power of the bright summer sun. It is a time to take inventory of our lives in order to see what we have brought into fruition and where we have achieved wholeness. There is a lull in activity, for our inner gardens have been tended and have reached their greatest potential. It is not yet harvest time and nothing more can be done to assure the quality of our yield. The Station of Resolution is the peak of all Stations preceding. This Station brings into manifestation revealed aspects of our authentic self once held hostage in the depths of our shadows. We now see a full harvest where once there was only the void of potential; we have come into full fruit. It is important for us to celebrate our accomplishments and to take the time to honor ourselves for how far we have come in our quest for self-understanding.

Yet here, in the culmination, are found the seeds for the next round of Cycle. We must look to see where the harvest was thin and take note of what did not grow at all. These are the considerations to take with us back down into the Station of Descent. Our shadow is the measure of our light ... our harvest, the measure of the sustenance that will carry us into the depths once more. We must remember the warmth of the sun—the glory of drawing closer to realizing the actualized self—and bring this light with us back down into the Dark Half in order to begin the Cycle anew.

This is a Station where we celebrate the joy of our achievements while also honoring the sacrifice that balances the abundance we have reaped. Resolution is aligned with the energies of solar Leo, vibrantly exhibiting the true essence of our core being, and lunar Aquarius, breaking free from old patterns and manifesting immense change.

The Station of Resolution in the Cycle of the Moon

The moon waxes completely full fourteen days after the dark moon. During this phase, the moon is completely illuminated by direct sunlight. A full moon rises as the sun goes down, or within half an hour of sunset. It is at its apex in the sky near midnight, and sets in the west within half an hour of sunrise. Although the moon appears to be full for three days, only the actual day of the full moon will see her rise at sunset and set at sunrise; the day before, she will rise an hour before the sun sets, while the day after the full, she will rise an hour after sunset. Energetically, the full moon is a time of revelation of the higher self, abundant manifestation, and unobstructed sight.

Self-reflective Questions for the Station of Resolution

Take some time to meditate upon these questions while in a clear and receptive space. Use your replies to help form a focus for the work of the Station of Resolution. Be sure to record your thoughts in a journal; this will help you chart your growth and change as you do the work of the Avalonian Cycle of Healing.

- *What keeps you connected to your personal vision of actualization? What can you do to reinforce this connection? How can you use this knowledge to aid in manifesting other not-yet-actualized aspects of the self?*

- *What is your first response to a situation in which your gifts are acknowledged or appreciated? Are you able to gracefully accept your accomplishments, or do you fall into a pattern of self-depreciation and false humility?*

- *When and why did you learn to devalue your abilities? Practice looking at yourself through the eyes of those who appreciate all that you are and can do. What do you think accounts for any differences in the way others perceive you and the way you perceive yourself? How can you change your opinion of yourself in order to see who and what you truly are more clearly?*

- *What do you consider beautiful about yourself—physically, emotionally, mentally, and spiritually? When did you learn to appreciate these aspects of yourself? How would your life be different if you* could fully birth the potential within you? In what ways have you already begun to become your authentic self?

· Who are your greatest heroes and role models? With which goddess aspect or myth do you resonate most? Why? Knowing what you hold sacred and what you admire in others reflects what is within your soul. How can you birth the person you aspire to become?

· What is the ultimate manifestation of your greatest dream? How would its full expression affect your life? What stands in the way of complete fulfillment? Do you have external support for this change? If not, how can you overcome this obstacle and gain complete Sovereignty over your life? What resources dwell within?

The Avalonian Landscape: Chalice Hill

ALTERNATIVE NAMES: Modron's Mound

CYCLE OF HEALING: Station of Resolution

CAULDRON TRANSFORMATION: Grain/Hen

ELEMENTAL ALIGNMENT: Fire

ENERGY CENTER: Heart

Rising gently from the ground at a height of 240 feet, the softly sloping dome of Chalice Hill holds the landscape energy for the Station of Resolution. Slumbering serenely beside the Tor (with which it forms Avalon's small Tor Valley), this rounded mound vibrates with the essence of the Great Mother, suggesting Her pregnant belly and the high point of the Cycle of Healing.

Positioned opposite the yoni-shaped portal to the Otherworld that is the Tor, this earthen womb burgeons with the energy of creation and underscores the pattern of alchemical polarity inherent in this Sacred Landscape. The Tor's deep magnetic energies allows us to birth our highest conscious calling. Just as the dark stirrings of Ceridwen's Cauldron-womb can be seen in the Tor's labyrinthine terraces, leading us down into the realm of shadow, so too can we visualize the overturned Vessel of Transformation in the guise of Chalice Hill. No longer concealing its mysteries within, the Cauldron of Rebirth has spilled the energies of its bounty outward across the land.

Chalice Hill is named for the legend that Joseph of Aramathea hid the Holy Grail beneath its slopes; belief holds that he returned to Glastonbury after the death of Christ to establish the first Christian Church in the British Isles. Symbolically, the sacred cup is analogous to the Cauldron of Plenty, and both are objects of quest in Arthurian mythos. Medieval tales speak of Arthur's knights seeking the Holy Grail in order to bring renewal to the land and to heal the Wounded King. As we have seen, the early Welsh poem *The Spoils of Annwn* depicts Arthur and his men traveling by boat into the Otherworld to obtain the Cauldron of Plenty. Both of these vessels of abundance represent the Sacred Womb of the Great Mother; seeking the Grail or Cauldron is a figurative embodiment of the journey into the unconscious and the inner quest for the Divine Feminine.

Just as the womb is the portal through which we enter into the physical plane, the Celts revered mounds as liminal places through which one could pass between worlds. Welsh mythology illustrates this in the First Branch of *The Mabinogi* where we see Rhiannon in the guise of the Otherworldly Maiden, riding out from the mound of Arberth. Folklore abounds throughout Celtic tradition extolling the mystical properties of the fairy mounds that dot the British landscape.

The veneration of mounds is a vestige of ancient Celtic ancestor worship. The importance of kin and clan finds no better manifestation than the sometimes-elaborate burial places of important persons and families. Although the method of burial differed through space and time in the British Isles—ranging from long barrows to cairns, and dolmens to tumuli—intention and symbolic resonance are a common thread. With the coming of new belief systems and the passage of time, reverence of these ancestors faded, and these great personages were preserved in folk memory as the Fair Folk or faeries. In Welsh tradition, these beings were called *Bendith y Mamau*—Blessings of the Mother.

Priestess and half-sister of King Arthur, Morgan le Fay is perhaps the most well-known inhabitant of Avalon. The appellation "Fay" or "fairy" denotes her Otherworldly status, hinting at her Pagan importance. There are clues that help us retrace her devolution, for her name is cognate with the Welsh goddess Modron, the Mother. Known in the Welsh Triads as the daughter of Avallach, the King of the Otherworld said to dwell below Glastonbury Tor, Modron is the Divine Ancestress of Avalon, perhaps the original figure come to be remembered in legend as Morgan of the Fairies. *The Spoils of Annwn* speaks of Nine Otherworldly Maidens who warmed the Cauldron of Plenty with their breath. These Maidens are the Nine Morgens of the Avalonian Tradition, powerful priestesses and teachers who serve as the Motherhood of Avalon. Morgen, in this case, is a title rather than a name, just as Modron may be an appellation of the Goddess rather than a specific deity. Perhaps originally an amorphic manifestation of the Divine Feminine, we know the mysterious figure of Modron tangentially through myth.

In *The Mabinogi* and its associated tales, Modron is the mother of Mabon, the Wondrous Youth after whom the collected stories of Welsh mythology may be named. In the story of *Culhwch and Olwen*, several of King Arthur's band search for this son of Modron, who, at three days old, was taken from his mother and held in captivity. They inquire of the five Oldest Animals, seeking his whereabouts and each, older than the last, had not heard of him. The procession of these marvelous creatures is an allegorical echo of the Cauldron Transformations, each of them speaking of the process of the Great Cycle, at the end of which the child of the Goddess within can be freed from his prison. These ancient races of animals are the totemic ancestors of the Cymry (Welsh), each a teacher of the mysteries and a guardian on the inner paths.

The Oldest Animals

The Blackbird of Cilgwri

MYTH: Blackbird had lived so long she was able to shrink an un-worked blacksmith's anvil to the size of a nut solely by pecking at it every night.

SYMBOLISM: Blackbird, the Otherworldly messenger that calls us to the quest, reminds us to listen to the voice of our inner Divinity.

ASPECT OF THE QUEST: Descending into the unconscious with the aim of getting to the core of the matter, eroding any obstacle preventing us from seeking our Center.

CORRESPONDENCES: The Station of Descent in the Avalonian Cycle of Healing; the Lower World.

The Stag of Redynvre

MYTH: Of the race older than Blackbird, Stag had lived so long as to witness the growth of an oak from a sapling to a mighty tree of one hundred branches, which then declined and died, leaving only a withered stump.

SYMBOLISM: Stag represents the fertile potential of the Land and the stillness of Sovereignty that lies within.

ASPECT OF THE QUEST: Uprooting the shadow aspects of the self that once fed upon our personal energy, and sent out tendrils of lower-self influence into our lives; death of the old self.

CORRESPONDENCES: The Station of Confrontation in the Avalonian Cycle of Healing; the Middle World; the Realm of Land.

The Owl of Cwm Cawlwyd

MYTH: Of the race of animals older than Stag, Owl saw three successive periods of uproot and reforestation of a wooded glen.

SYMBOLISM: Owl teaches us to see past the darkness of illusion to find truth and to hold fast to our convictions.

ASPECT OF THE QUEST: Creating new growth from that which is old and outmoded. Transformation of the self through the initiatory process of the triple rebirth.

CORRESPONDENCES: The Station of Emergence in the Avalonian Cycle of Healing; the Middle World; the Realm of Sea.

The Eagle of Gwern Abwy

MYTH: Of the race of animals older than Owl, Eagle witnessed the transformation over time of a stone which was once so tall he could stand upon it and peck at the stars every evening, to something just a span high.

SYMBOLISM: Eagle reminds us of the brightness of our potential and the new perspective that accompanies the quest for the actualized self.

ASPECT OF THE QUEST: Attaining the summit and achieving one's goals. While we cannot remain forever at the top, for the wheel will turn around and down once again, we bring our gifts with us, so that the peak of our next summit will be higher yet.

CORRESPONDENCES: The Station of Resolution in the Avalonian Cycle of Healing; the Middle World; The Realm of Sky.

The Salmon of Llyn Llyw

MYTH: The oldest of all animals, Salmon was once almost captured for food by Eagle, with whom he then entered into battle before making peace. On one of his journeys upriver made with every tide, Salmon discovered the location of Mabon's prison and was able to bring Arthur's men to free the boy.

SYMBOLISM: Salmon brings revelations of wisdom and connection to the essence of divinity that transcends all Worlds and Realms.

ASPECT OF THE QUEST: Freeing an aspect of Sovereignty from the prison of the shadow by successfully navigating the currents of the Unconscious and conquering the impulses of ego.

CORRESPONDENCES: The Station of Integration in the Avalonian Cycle of Healing; the Upper World.

As ancient as these animals may have been, only Salmon, the eldest and wisest of them all, knew the whereabouts of Mabon. Because of this, it may be that Modron and Her son existed before them all, reinforcing the notion that They are a primal Dyad—the Ancestral Creatrix and her Divine Son. In the creation stories of many cultures, the Primordial Mound is the first formation to rise out of the watery abyss. It seems fitting in many ways, therefore, that in seeking to reclaim the pre-Christian name of Chalice Hill, the name Modron's Mound was chosen—the Mound of the Mother.

Immram to Modron's Mound

Modron's Mound, or Chalice Hill, is related to the Station of Resolution in the Avalonian Cycle of Healing. Stepping through the portal of this Station, we enter into the direct light of complete inner illumination. That which we discovered hidden in the darkness of the unconscious has been brought full circle to complete conscious revelation. Seeing ourselves in the brightness of self-actualization, we are now empowered to bring ourselves to a full and abundant outer harvest.

Use this holy site to bring forth the full fruits cultivated in the orchard of your soul. Unleash the unbridled power of the soul's vital force into the world; it is a canvas awaiting your brush—a slab of marble awaiting your chisel. All you desire at the very heart of your being sings for release. The spark of Sovereignty reclaimed from the shackles of the shadow is fanned into flame, shining its warmth and light into the outside world—a herald of growth and transformation. The Station of Resolution inspires us to become all we aspire to be, teaching us to love all we are so that we may finally see the face of the Lady revealed in our own reflection.

Perform the Immram to the Island of Avalon as described on p. 55. After getting on the Barge to Avalon, proceed with the rest of this working.

The Journey

It is noontime. Stepping out of the Barge that transported you across the glassy lake to the Holy Isle, you meet your guide waiting for you on the shores of Avalon. Greet your guide and share your reason for undertaking this journey. State your desire to visit Modron's Mound and ask to be guided there.

The landscape is vibrant with a riot of color intensified by the sun's peak strength; the warming rays beat down upon you from directly overhead. The vivid blue sky is cloudless and clear. As you are led through the orchards, the day's heat is cooled somewhat by the shade of the apple trees, their limbs hanging heavy with ripening fruit.

The terrain slopes up and then down again, finally causing the slumbering body of the Tor to rise gently over the landscape. Take note of what you see along your path as you follow your guide, not this time to the Tor's spiraled terraces, but to the pregnant earthen rise known to those of this time as Modron's Mound.

You stand before the rounded hill, inviting in its resonant bounty and enrobed in a mantle of lush and vibrant green. The mound is hedged all around by wildly growing hawthorn trees and bushes. Their ripe, red berries are the delight of the congregation of birds moving in and out of the thicket, all the while deftly avoiding its thorn-armored branches. Accompanied by a chorus of cheerful song, the flurry of the birds' activity lends a festive quality to the air. Their industry inspires you; you feel drawn to ascend the hill.

After a short and invigorating climb up the gradual slope, you find yourself standing at the top of Modron's Mound. All of the Vale of Avalon opens before you: the Tor to the east, the fish-shaped Wearyall Hill to the south … the lush apple orchards … the sparking sun on the distant, encircling lake … the oak processional leading to the Tor … the ancient column of yew trees guiding the way to the cleft in the Earth from which the Red Spring flows …

You survey the landscape and take in the sights of the Sacred Isle. In the day's illumination, all things have changed. You see where you have come from—the orchards, the Tor, and the springs—the areas you have become familiar with in your work. You see that which is yet to come—the other hills on the island, the sanctuary, the timber halls, the roundhouses of the priestesses and teachers, and all other parts of the island you have yet to visit.

Turning your attention to the center of the curving hilltop, you find a woodpile built up into the form of a small bonfire. Walking closer, your expanded vision allows you to see that the pile is made up of nine sacred woods, and it comes to you that they have been gathered with great intention from all parts of the Holy Isle. Your guide gestures to two oak branches in the grass in front of the fire circle. You pick them up, knowing you are meant start the fire with these oaken staves.

Kneeling before the fire, you begin to rub the sticks together, hoping to release the spark that will set the bonfire aflame. The heat of the sun beats down upon your head and you begin to perspire, in no small part from the effort with which you work. With your breath, connect with the energies of the sun and pour it into the place where the two sticks meet. Like a magnifying glass, focus all the heat and light to the point of greatest friction, as if to harness the full strength of the sun's potential. The heat builds and the sticks begin to smoke. Suddenly a spark flies out and makes contact with the kindling below the crisscrossed fire, igniting it.

You gently coax the fledgling flame to grow, feeding it with your breath. Gradually the fire builds as scarlet tongues lap at the dry and ready wood. Soon the entire pile is engulfed, and you step back with a deep feeling of gratitude and accomplishment at what you have achieved with your own two hands. You can sense right away that this is no ordinary fire. Burning brightly, the flames devour the sacred wood, releasing the spiritual essences that dwell within. The smoke begins to shift, no longer only a physical byproduct of the burning wood, but now stirred by swirls of mystical power.

Each of the nine woods has its own distinctive energy signature, moving and vibrating at a different rate. Undulating above the fire, like energies are drawn to each other and coalesce into separate but harmonious streams of light. Nine women take form out of the pools of liberated energies—each one different in stature and appearance, but all of them strong, wise, and centered. Two of them approach, each taking one of your hands to include you in the circle of women forming around the blazing fire. Experience the oneness of this moment—the feeling of inclusion and acceptance. No woman standing in circle is of greater or lesser worth. All are Sisters in the Goddess; all are Modron's Daughters. The women who gather here now are your peers, your friends, your companion journeyers, your sister change-makers. Take some time to be in this space, and look into the eyes of the women around you. Who are these women? Why have you gathered here in this place and at this time? What message do they have for you?

Standing there, connected and connecting, you begin to feel another circle forming around you; each woman in the circle now has three women standing directly behind her, all holding hands in unison. These are your teachers, your role models, and your biological and spiritual mothers. Reflect upon all that you have learned from them and what they symbolize to you. How have they helped you become the woman you are today? As they have inspired you, what in turn has inspired them? What part of themselves have they passed along to you as your spiritual heritage?

The circles begin to turn now, one inside the other, moving sunwise around the center of the hill and expanding the energy outwards. Behind each woman comes to stand three more women, forming circle after circle of ever-increasing numbers. The ancestral lineage ripples further and further back through the pool of time. Women of every race, creed, age, size, ability, and social standing are there, representing the full spectrum of women's experience. Circles form around circles until at last there are nine circles in all … turning and turning, expanding the energy outward until the entire landscape thrums with the resonant heartbeat of the women gathered here.

Take some time to be with this experience … to feel yourself a part of a vast and supportive tapestry of women, each in her own right a woman of wisdom. Feel the drumming of the collective heartbeat fill your own chest, consciously aligning yourself with the sacred dance of women that moves to the pattern of wholeness and co-creation. At the heart of this dance is the truth of who and what you are, an ember fanned to flame, now burning brightly in your soul. Claim your place in the circle and radiate with the fullness of your joy.

Nine waves of women pulsate around you, drumming the guardians of Modron's Mound awake with each circling step. The energy reaches its peak, and all movement and sound comes to a pregnant pause as nine huge, misty forms rise to stand upright around the perimeter of the circle. These giantesses are the Mothers, the Triple Matronæ, and the Great Ancestresses of the Holy Island—the Nine Morgens of Avalon. These Nine attendants of the Cauldron of the Otherworld are the guardians of the Mysteries of Avalon, and it is through their teachings that the blessings of Awen can be obtained.

It is that very spark of Divine spirit that now begins to glow in the breasts of the Nine, forming a circle of Awen around the vast gathering of women. In unison, the Morgens bend to touch the heart space of a woman in the outermost ring, and immediately the hearts of all within that circle become illuminated. These women turn to the next circle, three hands on one heart, passing the flame to the next ring... and the next... each successive circle bursting forth with the fires of inspiration.

The fire moves quickly, and with a rush of wind in its wake, it is your turn to receive the sacred fire. You turn to face the three smiling women standing directly behind you; each places their right hand on your heart. With their left hand on their own hearts, you feel a surge of energy like a lightning bolt course through their arms as the three rays of light join to kindle a flame in the core of your existence.

As the inner warmth expands to every part of your being, take time to experience this complete inner illumination. All things are made clear in this moment. In the light cast by the fire within, the true essence of who you are and what you were born to be is fully revealed. The fire burns through any obstacles that prevent you from fully manifesting the woman that you are; the barriers are gone, the way is made clear. All that remains in the wake of this Divine and cleansing flame is the vision of the fully actualized priestess self. The goal has been reached... the Grail found... the Cauldron reclaimed from the Otherworld. The Wounded Queen within has been fully healed. Bask in the abundance of this moment. Feel your soul swell with the joy of actualization. Imprint this feeling into the very fiber of your being so that you may never forget what has been revealed.

You turn back towards the center of the circle, and the great assemblage begins to move once more, this time circling moonwise—moving the energies towards the center. It comes to you as you encircle the fire that you too must pass along the blessings of Awen. Take some time to reflect on all that you have to give to others. In what ways can you inspire? How will your life and the way you live it serve as an example to others? How can you cause the light of the Goddess to shine more brightly into the world?

With these thoughts in your mind, focus on the fire in the center as you circle around it. Envision each tongue of flame... each spark... each glowing ember... as the women to whom you will pass the sacred inheritance that you yourself have received. These are your students, your daughters, those unknown women who will be touched by your work or whose lives will be changed because of the impact you will have upon them. Breathe the energy of the Awen that burns in your breast into the bonfire, sending it to all women who will come after you seeking the way of women's wisdom, the way of the Goddess—the way of Avalon.

Just as you are able to stand in this company because of the work and sacrifice of the women who have come before you, so too will the path of those who come after be made easier because of the work you do now. You are an important link in the process of reclaiming the wisdom of the Mothers. The more you can connect with the energy of this sacred lineage, the more you can birth change and wholeness into the world.

See the faces of the women in the circles to come, dancing in the flame, just as those who joined circles before you dance on the roundness of the hill and beyond. All women who seek the way of Avalon with clarity are inheritors of this wisdom; they need but claim it through the workings of the Cycle.

Bless these women on their path, and send them a part of the divine flame within you, drawing back through the circles of the women, through the Morgens and past them to the Great Mother Creatrix, the Modron Revealed. Breathe that energy into the flame, feeling yourself joined by the intentions of all the women in the circle. The bonfire of the sacred woods arcs higher into the sky, burning with an intensity fueled by the collective spirit of sisterhood. The small fire has become a large and living flame encircling the entire hillside.

The sun shines high above, and Modron's Mound is alight with a turning, flaming wheel... a wheel that has grown so large it cannot be contained on the top of this one hill. The circles of women begin to move down the slopes of the mound, less a circle than an ever-expanding spiral. You descend the hill with the other women, and like them, you carry a blazing brand of Awen in your heart. The Morgens lift their hands in blessing as you pass, and like the touch of the sun on the morning mist, they disappear. Reaching the base of the hill, the circles open and the Ancestresses begin to fade. All that remains are the countless tongues of flame that expand outward over the landscape, blessing Avalon with abundance (for it is also named the Fortunate Isle). The orchards and vineyards are burst forth with ripened fruits; the crops ripple golden and sway heavily in the gentle breeze. The lake is alive with fish and waterfowl. The summer herbs are fragrant and plentiful. The beehives are filled with dark, sweet honey. Reflect upon the nature of your inner abundance. What is the harvest of your soul?

Take some time to reflect on your experiences.

When you are ready, your guide leads you back through the orchard and to the shores of the lake, where the Barge of Avalon awaits you. Turn once more to face the island, and thank the Lady and all the guardians of this sacred space for supporting your work and allowing you to visit. Bid your guide farewell and climb aboard the Barge to complete your journey to the other side of the lake, bringing with you the memory of all that has come before.

Revisiting the Self

As you continue making your connection to Modron's Mound and the revelation of your priestess self, go back and reread the self-reflective questions in this chapter. How have your answers changed? What catalyzed this change? What underlying energies are you now aware of which were previously unconscious? What patterns have become visible? How can you put your insights and connections to work in order to bring change into your life?

Tool for the Station:
The Glamour—The Mantle of Sovereignty

Spin, Spun, Spinning
Weave, woven, weaving
Let me reweave tapestries of light
Let me shine like moonbeams pierce the night
Through my darkness to that place inside
Where I can free all I once denied
Spin, spun, spinning
Weave, woven, weaving

—*TAPESTRIES OF LIGHT*, JHENAH TELYNDRU

The Avalonian Glamour is a positive exercise to facilitate the manifestation of priestess-self energies in our lives, and as such, is a powerful tool for the work of the Station of Resolution. When using the Glamour, we are not seeking to change how we look or are perceived; instead, we are drawing upon the potential within us with the intention that it be reflected without. Connecting with and projecting an image of our actualized self as an energetic overlay helps to draw corresponding energies to us. This energy will reinforce our intention and support our goals of growth and personal attainment. Using the Hermetic Principle of Correspondence (oftentimes expressed as the esoteric axiom "as above, so below; as below, so above"), the Glamour facilitates our ability to tap into our greatest potentials and allows us to act as if they have already been fully manifested in our lives.

The Cloak of the Priestess

The written record provides us with an account of the garb worn by Celtic priestesses. We find a description from the Roman commander Suetonius Paulinus who in 61 CE successfully lay siege to the Druid isle of *Ynys Mon*, known today as Anglesey. There, the Roman legions savagely slaughtered everyone they could find and burnt down sacred groves in retaliation for Druidic encouragement of resistance to Roman rule. Paulinus' account included a description of long-haired, dark-cloaked women carrying torches and shrieking at the Roman invaders, simultaneously trying to frighten them and summon Otherworldly aid. The historian Tacitus relays the scene thus:

> On the beach stood the adverse array, a serried mass of arms and men, with women flitting between the ranks. In the style of Furies, in robes of deathly black and with disheveled hair, they brandished their torches; while a circle of Druids, lifting their hands to heaven and showering imprecations, struck the troops with such an awe at the extraordinary spectacle that, as though their limbs were paralyzed, they exposed their bodies to wounds without an attempt at movement.
>
> —ANNALS, BOOK XIV, CHAPTER 30—TACITUS

The priestess cloak is of particular significance to the women of Avalon. It is the mantle of authority earned though self-transformation and progression on the path. The deeper one becomes immersed into the Mysteries of the Goddess, the darker the color of the cloak one wears. As the Druids wore white cloaks, which reflected the brilliance of light out into the universe, so the clositered priestesses wore black— the primal magnetic power that concentrates and absorbs all things unto itself. The color black corresponds with the energetic paradigm of Feminine Spirituality as a path of growth that spirals inward, always pulling the seeker towards the center.

Weaving the Mantle of Sovereignty

Creating a Glamour is an effective way to redirect the energies freed from the illusion of shadow during the Dark Half of the Cycle in support of the manifestation of higher self potential. When we first weave the mantle of Sovereignty, it is an empty vessel—a form to hold and focus our magickal purpose. With work and in time, the cloak becomes empowered with intention—an astral repository of refined and directed energy committed to our growth and transformation.

Like dressing for the job position we would like to have rather than the one we are currently in, enrobing ourselves in the completed mantle infuses us with an influence that both raises the vibratory level of our personal energy and draws a like energy to us. In this way, as we work to manifest our sovereign selves—whole, complete, and centered in the Goddess—we have the assistance of our mantle to support and generate the energy of all we wish to become.

STEP ONE: To create your mantle of Sovereignty, begin by reviewing your personal process since first beginning to ride the wheel of the Avalonian Cycle of Healing. Meditate upon the growth resulting from the seeds you have planted at the Station of Emergence. What shape is this energy beginning to take?

STEP TWO: Connect with your guide to help clarify your goals and recognize the form of the Sovereign Woman within you. As you explore, release your connection to the ways in which you have not already externally manifested your priestess self. When self-recriminating thoughts come up during this work, seek the ways in which you can work to bridge the gap between what is and what can be, rather than dwelling on the fact that disparity exists in the first place. Remember, the goal of this work is to move you into a place of actualizing your potential; focus your intentions there. If you find it challenging to visualize your Sovereign self, it can be helpful to ask your guide for a symbol that represents the woman you are working to become. This symbol can then be used in doorway work with the intention of seeking a vision of the priestess within so that you may begin to create your cloak.

STEP THREE: Once you can clearly see the woman you are meant to be, fully actualized and connected with the Goddess, open a dialogue with her. Ask for her story and about the path she has had to walk down in order to become who she is today. What will help you arrive at the place where she stands now? What insights into your process can she bring? How will your life be different once you have manifested the changes she represents? What can you do to facilitate these changes?

STEP FOUR: Perform an Immram to Avalon and when you arrive on the shore, ask your guide to take you to the Weaving House. There, at the center of this round house, next to the hearth, sit down at the wood-framed weighted loom awaiting your touch. You instantly know how to use the loom and it comes to life beneath your fingers. Take several breaths to calm and connect and bring forth the image of your sovereign self. Visualize a connection between your hands and this image in the form of a silver strand of energy; this will serve as the thread from which you will weave the material of your cloak. Take as much time as you need at the loom; it may take more than one session to complete the material. Should you need to return, ask that your work remain in Avalon's keeping until you can complete it. Do not take more than three days to weave your cloak; otherwise the energy will begin to dissipate and you will need to start over again. It is important that you remain focused in your weaving, taking care to exclude self-doubt or limiting thoughts from the matrix. A good way to imbue your cloth with intention and keep your mind clear as your weave is to repeat a chant or affirmation connected to your work. When you have completed your weaving, be sure to tie it off before removing it from the loom.

STEP FIVE: When you have completed the material, sit with it for a while and connect with what you have woven. When ready, visualize yourself placing this energetic cloak around your shoulders with great intention. As you do so, the material immediately takes the form of a hooded cloak. Fasten it and feel the energy of the mantle of Sovereignty envelop you. Take note of all you feel and experience. Visualize a mirror in front of you. How do you look in your cloak? What do you see? What color is it? What form is the clasp? What changes do you notice on all levels?

STEP SIX: Take some time to ground and center this energy, integrating it into your own. You have effectively brought energy of a higher vibratory state into your aura structure, and you may experience some light-headedness, giddiness, or euphoria upon donning your mantle. Make sure you are comfortable with the shift before moving out of a ritual space.

It may be useful to tie your cloak to something physical to help you connect with the essence of your Sovereignty once you are out in the world; a powerful way of doing this is to dedicate a pendant or ring for this purpose. Choose your piece wisely, as it will be a visual cue to connect you to your work. Have it on hand when you first put on your Mantle, visualizing it as a pin on your cloak. Once the connection is made, you can actively draw from your Mantle's strength as you work to actualize the potential it represents. You can also use the piece to empower your mantle's essence every month at the full moon; this recharging should be done whether you choose to use a physical tie-in or not.

Wear this mantle of Sovereignty from the Station of Resolution through to the next Station of Emergence. At the full moon after the portal work of Emergence, begin to explore and weave your new garment, connecting with your renewed and clarified vision of the Inner Sovereign. Every turn of the Cycle brings increased sight of who we are and what we have the potential to become. The work of Avalon is revealed only through the journey; the priestess within is ever unfolding.

9

THE STATION OF
INTEGRATION

Three things essential for the wise to know: their Gods, themselves, and the deceits of the world.

CELTIC TRIAD

HOLDING THE ENERGIES OF OUR Divinity and supporting the entire web of our soul's unfolding, the Station of Integration is the center around which the fabric of our lives is spun. Our internal *axis mundi*, pointing the way towards the unfailing Pole Star, this fifth Seed of Cycle holds the core truth of who we are—whole and fully connected to the Goddess. The work of the other four Stations is to manifest this complete and authentic self, and to cast aside the veil of illusion that prevents us from living fully from this center. Every consciously ridden turn of the Cycle of Healing allows us to spiral further up the path of our becoming, and further down into the Source of all creation. The more we are able to touch this Divinity, the more our sight will be blessed with a greater discernment of what is truth and what is shadow. The voracious hunger of ego is fed by the bountiful giving of the self; the joy reaped by clarity overwhelms the pain wrought by illusion.

The Station of Integration in the Cycle of the Sun

The wise woman who allies herself with the tides of the universe also comes to the understanding that our healing is cyclic as well. A deep-rooted issue does not go away with one turn of the Wheel. The wise woman has learned that the path of growth is spiraled. With each turn, we ascend upward. We may have to face the same painful lessons over and over again, but they change because our position on the spiral has changed. We look at it from a different perspective, and in so doing, reveal a deeper layer of the shadow and a higher level of the self.

The Station of Integration is found between all Stations and at the heart of the Cycle. Like the Fool card of the tarot, it both begins and ends each round of the Cycle, bridging the space between the works of each Station. Integration is the core around which the Cycle spirals; the work of the Cycle of Healing propels the energy ever upward. It is the path of individuation and transformation, the pulling together of all parts of the self into the wholeness of self-awareness. As the energy spirals up and the soul vibrates at a higher level, this Station's impact increases. It holds the sum of the reclaimed energy resulting from our process work and is the degree of realization of Divinity within and life's purpose without.

When all our soul's energy is reclaimed, oneness with the Divine is achieved; this is the work of lifetimes. As one successfully effects inner change and healing, the Cycle makes tighter and tighter spirals, gaining energetic momentum until the Stations and the turnings of the Cycle itself become less and less discriminate. Here the work of Integration is achieved. Paradoxically, as the energy freed from shadow increases and obtains a higher vibratory state, it also becomes more and more consolidated—in effect, reflecting the highest manifestation of pure yin energy—Goddess. It is *She* at our core, and through the Station of Integration we may achieve Divine stillness and unity.

The work of this Station is to do the work of the Cycle—acting to bring the self into awareness and full consciousness of the truth of its essence: We are Goddess.

The Station of Integration in the Cycle of the Moon— The Moon

There is no corresponding moon phase for the Station of Integration. Rather, it is represented by the moon herself, devoid of light or shadow and independent of the perception of external forces being overlain upon it. The phenomenon of lunar phases is simply the result of the angles made between the sun and the Earth and the visual changes these shifts in position create. The moon itself, its very core nature, is unchanged—the constant. Our work is to find and maintain this constant center in ourselves, unchanged in the face of expectation and external circumstance.

Self-reflective Questions for the Station of Integration

Take some time to meditate upon these questions while in a clear and receptive space. Use your replies to help form a focus for the work of the Station of Integration. Be sure to record your thoughts in a journal—this will help you chart your process of growth and change as you do the work of the Avalonian Cycle of Healing.

- *What contributes to your being in a place of calmness and balance? Are there specific activities, tools, or techniques you use to attain this state of being? How long does this feeling last? What can you do to prolong its effect? In what ways do you see the world differently when you come from a place of serenity and centeredness?*

- *What makes up the core of who and what you are? What is your ultimate definition of self? In what ways do you express the essence of self in your life and in your world? What prevents you from completely reclaiming what has already been revealed to you? How can you go about rectifying the difference? How do you envision the ultimate expression of self? What can you do to facilitate its conscious manifestation?*

- *What is your concept of the nature of the Divine? How would you describe your relationship with the Goddess? What helps you to connect with Her and receive Her guidance? To which archetypal aspect or energy of the Goddess are you most drawn? Why do you think this is? What lessons does She have to teach you? How comfortable*

ST. MICHAEL'S TOWER • Believed to date back to the fifteenth century, St. Michael's Tower is all that remains of the second church built on Glastonbury Tor's crest. The roofless stone tower stands between the worlds—neither a shelter nor completely open to the elements, and as such, is an excellent conduit of the liminal energies rising out of the Tor.

GLASTONBURY LANDSCAPE • In the Avalonian Tradition, the Tor Valley Complex is a physical manifestation of the Avalonian Cycle of Healing in the Glastonbury landscape. These sacred sites are abundant with transformational geomantic energies and are empowered by layers of myth and legend that span across millennia.

GLASTONBURY TOR • In winter, snow accentuates the unusual earthen features that many believe to be a three-dimensional, seven-circuit labyrinth carved by the ancients into the slopes of Glastonbury Tor.

MODRON'S MOUND • Commonly known as Chalice Hill, the softly rounded form of Modron's Mound rises alongside Glastonbury Tor. Folklore designates this gentle hill as the site of an ancient observatory as well as a potential hiding place for the Holy Grail.

ISLE OF AVALON • The prominent features of the Tor Valley Complex arise in the distance, while in the foreground, the river Brue's waters evoke a sense of how this sacred landscape may have appeared when the marshy waters of the Somerset Levels rendered ancient Avalon an actual island.

CHALICE WELL • The Chalice Well cover prominently features the *vesica piscis* symbol, a form common in sacred geometry. Representing the union of opposites, the yonic center of the symbol is significant to those who revere the Divine Feminine as a pathway to connection with the Source.

JACKIE HEWITT

RED SPRING WATERFALL The high iron content of the Red Spring stains red all of the water features in the beautiful Chalice Well Gardens, as seen in this waterfall — whose shape is suggestive of a Goddess figure — located in an area of the gardens called "King Arthur's Courtyard."

ROBIN L. WALLACE

WHITE SPRING • The White Spring's calcium-rich waters flow from a modern shrine inside the nineteenth-century reservoir erected to protect and contain the waters. The interior of the White Spring Wellhouse has changed greatly over the years, and its current caretakers have consecrated the building as a temple.

LABYRINTH • Creating a labyrinth is as sacred an act as walking one. Here, an Avalonian Sister ritually draws a Classical labyrinth in the sand, mirroring the seven-circuit pattern associated with Glastonbury Tor.

JACKIE HEWITT

HOLY THORN ON WEARYALL HILL • Adorned with colorful prayer ribbons and framing Glastonbury Tor in the distance, this is a descendent of the original hawthorn tree said to have sprung up from the staff of Joseph of Arimathea when he arrived in Glastonbury with his followers after the death of Christ.

JACKIE HEWITT

WEARYALL HILL • Legend teaches that the small island that is today Wearyall Hill was a place of purification, where pilgrims to Avalon were required to stay overnight before journeying to the Holy Isle. During the early Christian period, Wearyall Hill was home to a women's monastic settlement.

GLASTONBURY ABBEY
Built around the wattle and daub church at the heart of the first Christian settlement in Britain, Glastonbury Abbey grew to possess great prestige and wealth. Purported to be the burial place of King Arthur, the Abbey was destroyed during the Dissolution and remains a major pilgrimage site to this day.

JACKIE HEWITT

GLASTONBURY TOR
The enigmatic Glastonbury Tor seems to change its shape depending on the angle from which it is viewed, appearing sometimes to recline like a Goddess across the landscape, while other times assuming a pyramidical form. Here, the unusual light underscores the Tor's Otherworldly essence.

ALICIA GROSSO © 2005

GLASTONBURY TOR • This stunning aerial view of Glastonbury Tor highlights its feminine, yonic shape, and fully reveals the labyrinthine terracing that spirals around the hill. The two white pathways are modern additions, intended to reduce damage caused by people climbing the Tor.

are you with the idea that the self and the Goddess are one? What can you do to become fully conscious of your connection with Her?

- *What is the nature of service to the Divine? How do you serve the Goddess today—right now? How would you like to serve Her in the future? If you were a priestess of ancient Avalon, what would have been your service to the island? What does it mean to be a priestess in today's world? How can you initiate the journey down the path to reclaiming the priestess within?*

- *In Arthurian legend, the story of Sir Gawaine and the Loathly Lady teaches that our very lives are transfigured when we reclaim and obtain our personal Sovereignty. What changes will result from the acknowledgement of your authority over your life and your vision of self? How can you empower your Sovereign nature? How can you use your Sovereignty to midwife the birth and emergence of the priestess within?*

The Avalonian Landscape: The Island of Avalon

ALTERNATIVE NAMES: Ynys Afallon, Ynys Witrin
CYCLE OF HEALING: Station of Integration
CAULDRON TRANSFORMATION: Gwion/Taliesin
ELEMENTAL ALIGNMENT: Spirit
ENERGY CENTER: Third Eye

Ynys Afallon. Ynys Witrin. Ynys Glas. The Isle of Apples. The Island of the Blessed. The Island of Glass. The Western Isle. The Summerland. The Gateway to Annwn. Avalon.

Known by many names through many times, the site of the present-day town of Glastonbury holds a deep resonance with the energies of ancient Avalon. Some of the most evocative descriptions of the Otherworld found in the Welsh poem *The Spoils of Annwn* are suggestive of some of the unique features in the Glastonbury landscape. Caer Siddi, the Spiral Castle or Fortress of the Fair Folk, could refer to the spiraled terraces of the Tor and its entrance into the Otherworld. Caer Wydr, the Glass Fort, could be connected with the British name for Glastonbury—Ynis Witrin—the Island of Glass.

It is tempting to connect the name Glastonbury itself to the glassy imagery, but etymology suggests that the word *glaston* refers to the woad plant and the Welsh word *glas* means "blue." A sacred plant to the Celtic Britons, woad was used to dye textiles and can be used medicinally to treat infection, inflammation, and cancer. While a popular theory holds that woad was used to decorate the bodies of British warriors entering into battle, the plant's use in dyeing and healing certainly holds Avalonian significance and may provide a clue to Glastonbury's sanctity.

Yet, beyond the veil of lore and word paintings composed of poetic imagery, the physical elements of the Glastonbury landscape certainly lend themselves to support a tradition of enchantment. Rising from a mist-ringed marshland, the enigmatic figure of the Tor punctuated the landscape of southwest Britain and could be observed from as far as twenty-five miles away. Perhaps first drawn by this awe-inspiring sight, settlers in the area (known as the Somerset Levels) found the region blessed by water's embrace—they could find food in abundance, rich soil, and means of transportation and communication—and perhaps a sacred precinct of great power and mystery.

It is no surprise that what would become modern-day Glastonbury was once a place of deep reverence for the ancient Britons. Almost entirely surrounded by water, the peninsula was set apart from the mundane world, imparting a liminal quality upon the land. Wrapped in ethereal mists, guarded by a strangely formed hill that may have been further altered to create its labyrinthine terracing, and supplied with fresh water from bountiful springs, the area must have indeed appeared magical.

Not an island proper, Glastonbury was once surrounded by water on three sides. Before the area was tamed by sea walls, flood banks, drainage, and modern-day water channels, the Somerset Levels were prone to flooding. Seawater egressed from the west and heavy rainfall caused the swollen rivers to abandon the confines of their banks. In periods of flood, Glastonbury could be accessed by boat or through rivers and waterways leading to the peninsula.

The marshy and oft-flooded Somerset Levels evolved through many stages of settlement and development. From the timber trackways crisscrossing the landscape of the Neolithic period (4000–2000 BCE) to the rise of the Iron Age Glastonbury Lake Village (circa 300 BCE), people gathered to live along the water and in the shadow of the strange, spiraled hill. The villages were a wonder of adaptation, comprised of distinctive roundhouses with central hearths, constructed on large platforms over and next to the marshes.

Amidst all this water, the sole means of reaching Glastonbury on foot was by a strip of land enhanced by a feature known today as Pointer's Ball. This earthwork bank and ditch resembles the type used for defense or to mark sacred space, as used in the nearby megalithic complexes of Avebury and Stonehenge. While there is still debate as to the period in which the earthwork was constructed, it bears similarity to structures known to date to the Iron and Dark Ages. Either as a boundary marker enclosing a religious site or a defensive structure associated with a hillfort said to be located in Glastonbury, Pointer's Ball suggests the peninsula of Glastonbury held special significance to the peoples of the Somerset Levels through time.

Archaeological analysis provides for additional intriguing possibilities. There is evidence that the Lake Villages contained areas of specialized activity and included buildings that were exclusively occupied and used by women. No burial places were ever found for these lake dwellers, contributing to the notion that Avalon's first association with the Otherworld—the land to which the dead traveled—is tied to its use by the inhabitants of the Lake Villages as a sacred precinct where the dead were buried. This is not a unique occurrence in Celtic lands. The archaeological record of the Scilly Islands off the western tip of Cornwall, shows the number of found burial chambers far exceeds that of the island's population, supporting the idea that bodies were taken from the mainland to be buried on one of the holy islands of the dead.

Other evocative features lent their aura of mystery to the power of the island. During times of flood, the hills of Glastonbury became an association of small islands. The rounded belly of Modron's Mound (present-day Chalice Hill) is an unusual feature; it has been suggested that a prehistoric observatory once stood on her crest. The fish-shaped body of Wearyall Hill at the southeastern part of the Sacred Isle connects with the vesica piscis symbolism—as it relates to both the yonic form of the Divine Feminine as well as the symbol of the fish, iconographic of the early Christian Church. This connection is especially significant as the story of Joseph of Arimathea is directly connected with Wearyall Hill.

Joseph of Arimathea was a tin trader and Jesus' uncle. Legend teaches that Joseph brought Jesus with him on one of his trips to the British Isles, where it is said the youth studied with Druids. The famous English hymn "Jerusalem," written by William Blake, commemorates this journey, asking:

> And did those feet in ancient time
> Walk upon England's mountains green?
> And was the holy Lamb of God
> On England's pleasant pastures seen?
> And did the countenance divine
> Shine forth upon our clouded hills?
> And was Jerusalem builded here
> Among those dark satanic mills?

During their pilgrimage to the Island of Avalon, tradition holds that the pair built a small wattle-and-daub church—the first in the British Isles—marking it as the holiest earth in England. It can be no coincidence that this famed church, at Avalon's heart, was dedicated to Christ's mother. Christian sacred sites often claimed those venerated during preceding Pagan periods, and just as we see the remains of the church of St. Michael the Dragon Slayer in the tower on the Tor with its two Dragon Lines, so we observe the symmetry of a church to the Blessed Mother marking a place of deep veneration to the Goddess.

As Christianity spread, Glastonbury Abbey arose around this wattle building until the old church was destroyed by fire in 1184, and replaced by a chapel to St. Mary known today as the Lady Chapel. As further indication of the holy nature of this site, analysis of the plan of the Lady Chapel reveals patterns of sacred geometry that appear to also have been used at Stonehenge and other holy sites. A place of deep reverence to this day, Lady Chapel is said to be the burial place both of King Arthur and Joseph of Arimathea.

According to tradition, Joseph returned to Glastonbury after Jesus' crucifixion. Near the end of their journey, Joseph and his twelve followers stopped to rest on the crest of Wearyall Hill. There, Joseph drove his staff into the ground where it miraculously took root.

The famed hawthorn tree found at the top of Wearyall Hill today (and in several locations in Glastonbury including the Abbey grounds and Chalice Well Gardens) is a descendant of that tree, a species native to Palestine. Unlike other local varieties, the Holy Thorn of Glastonbury blooms every year at Christmastide, and by tradition, a branch is brought to the reigning British monarch as part of the holiday celebration.

Tradition states that Joseph founded the first Christian community in the British Isles and that he brought from the Holy Land either the Cup of the Last Supper or two crystal cruets holding the blood and sweat of Christ—surely a symbolic echo of the red and white alchemical energies of Avalon. Before his death, Joseph is said to have hidden the relics at the foot of the Tor, thereby coloring the Red Spring, a reflection of the blood of Christ. According to another legend, Joseph buried the grail in the mound of Chalice Hill, which today still bears the name of the sacred object.

The small hill of Beckery, located near Wearyall Hill on the banks of the River Brue, also became an island during times of inundation. Legend recalls that it was a place of vigil where all visitors would have to spend the night in prayer before they could enter the Holy Island of Avalon. It was there that King Arthur is said to have received a vision of the Holy Mother and the Grail. *Beckery* means "Beekeeper's Island," undoubtedly reflecting both the island's honey production and the symbolism of bees as a potent goddess totem. A small Irish community dwelt in the area and an alternate etymology posits that Beckery means "Little Ireland" from the Gaelic *Beag Erie*.

Legend holds that St. Brigid of Ireland came to Beckery in the fifth century CE, to visit a shrine dedicated to Mary Magdalene. It later became known as Bride's Mound in honor of this goddess-saint, and a well associated with the mound was named for her. Until modern times, local women came to dress the well and hang prayer ribbons over its waters. Bride's Well is where the famed Blue Bowl of Glastonbury was discovered in the early 1900s and is a place of deep reverence.

Wellesley Tudor Pole, the founder of the Chalice Well Trust, received a vision that led him to seek an object at Bride's Well which could only be uncovered by a pure maiden. After searching the waters of the well at Tudor Pole's direction, three young women happened upon a blue glass bowl, featuring the renowned Venetian millefiori motif. This vessel had been deposited in the well years before by a local doctor who had found the bowl in Italy, and was later led by some inner impulse to place it in Bride's Well. The discovery of the bowl caused quite a stir at the time; some believed it to be the Holy Grail, while others acknowledged that its resonance with that holy vessel was more symbolic than actual. Ultimately, the bowl was revealed to be of nineteenth-century origin and is today in the keeping of the Chalice Well Trust, always watched over by the Well's female guardian.

Joseph of Arimathea and his followers were granted a large piece of land known as the Twelve Hides of Glastonbury, a 1,440-acre area that included seven sacred islands. These islands are believed to have held ritual significance during an earlier Pagan age and were later sites of Christian hermitages and chapels—among them, the Island of Avalon and Beckery. In his book *New Light on the Ancient Mysteries of Glastonbury*, British author and mystic John Michell plots the positions of these seven islands on a map of the region, and reveals that together they directly correspond to the form of the Big Dipper constellation, an important part of the larger constellation known as Ursa Major (the "Great Bear"). King Arthur is related totemically to the bear (Artos), and Michell suggests the stories of Arthur's exploits were based on tribal memories of a chieftain called Arth Fawr—the Great Bear. Perhaps only an intriguing coincidence, this is yet another reiteration of the connection between Avalon and Arthur.

This formation of the seven sacred islands is one of several striking connections between celestial representations of Arthurian mythos and the landscape of ancient Avalon. The axis star of the Big Dipper is the one around which the constellation appears to rotate though the cycle of the seasons. This star, on the upper lip of the star-drawn vessel, points to Polaris, the Pole Star. Interestingly enough, the island that corresponds to the axis position terrestrially is Glastonbury. There is a sense, then, that Glastonbury exists at the center of a grand, rotating cycle of cosmic proportions, perhaps suggested by a description of the Otherworld from *The Spoils of Annwn*—the Revolving Fortress, *Caer Pedryvan*.

An apparent manifestation of this cycle can be found in the mysterious Glastonbury Zodiac. This Temple of the Stars, so named by Katherine Maltwood, who discovered these figures in the landscape surrounding Glastonbury in 1929, are gigantic effigies created by natural and man-made boundaries across the Somerset countryside. These images correspond to the constellations of the western zodiac in the correct astrological order, yet are represented in an Arthurian context. Maltwood considered this landscape zodiac to be the original Round Table, and found that the images held great resonance with characters and events in the stories of King Arthur.

The Glastonbury Zodiac is ten miles in diameter and some of the figures are five miles long. Drawn on the canvas of the landscape by streams, hills, and valleys, these images were further developed by human hands as evidenced by field boundaries that contribute to the outline of the figures. Interestingly, some of the geographical locations that fall within these giant figures bear names that reflect a degree of consciousness of the effigies, citing body parts or related words. The figure that encompasses the Tor is, appropriately enough, the Phoenix—representing the sign of Aquarius. It is symbolically apt that this powerful symbol of death and rebirth overlays the entrance to the Otherworld where the Cauldron of Rebirth can be found, marking Glastonbury Tor as a place of pilgrimage for the Aquarian Age. In contrast, Wearyall Hill falls within the figure representing Pisces, symbol of Christianity and the era that began with the return of Joseph of Arimathea to the Holy Isle.

The overall essence of Avalon lies in its function to unify dualities. Star patterns from above take shape in its landscape. For a time, two different faiths are able to peaceably coexist on its shores and evolve to share a common symbol set. Legend and history both have powerful footholds in the countryside. Past and present intermingle as the ancient traditions of the island are reclaimed, while mystics forge ahead, gaining new wisdoms from this sacred site. Land and water ebb and flow, turning hills into islands and drowned Roman villas into underwater palaces. Cauldrons become grails, springs become wells, goddesses become revered saints. Layer upon layer of metaphor and allegory form the foundation of this unique place, becoming mirrored in its geography and taking root in the spirit of all who spend time in its embrace. Above all, *Ynis Witrin*, the Island of Glass, holds up a mirror to all who will embark upon the quest—asking that we take that which is within and manifest it without.

Immram to the Sacred Center of Avalon

The whole of the Island of Apples is related to the Station of Integration in the Avalonian Cycle of Healing. Stepping through the portal of this Station, we allow ourselves to experience the truth of our innate beauty, perfection, and oneness with the Goddess. Use the Holy Isle to assist you in seeing the big picture and overall pattern of your personal process. Take the time to see yourself as the whole and sacred being that you are, blessing your shadow for the gifts it brings while owning your priestess self and all the ways you have already reclaimed her. Accept that where you are on your journey is exactly where you need to be, without judgment or expectation. Never forget that you are already whole…already One…already a cherished and vital part of the body of the Mother. You need only release and remember.

Perform the Immram to the Island of Avalon as described on p. 55. After arriving on the shore, proceed with the rest of this working.

The Journey

Stepping out of the Barge that transported you across the glassy lake to the Holy Isle, you meet your guide waiting for you on the shores of Avalon. Greet your guide and share your reason for undertaking this journey and your desire to visit the very core of Avalon; ask to be guided to the center of the island.

Everything about the isle seems different; it is completely still and calm, yet tinted with a hue of expectancy. As you move through the orchard, you are greeted by the curious sight of trees with limbs blossoming, bearing fruit, and bare—all at the same time. The apples that do grow seem to glow silver with their own luminescence, small and rounded moons reflecting an inner light onto the meandering pathway through the trees, tinkling softly in your wake as you pass.

Leaving the orchard, your guide turns down a path you have not yet taken, though it feels both strange and familiar to you. Take note of what you see as you follow your guide, passing low, darkened buildings and silent, tidied workshops … carefully tended gardens and mist-ringed circles … tree-lined processionals and venerated sacred precincts … There is so much yet to learn and explore here on Avalon, but now is not the time. You are brought instead to a shining meadow—a place set apart, yet at the very center of the web of energy that crisscrosses the whole of the island.

The time of day shifts around you—the stars shine then fade with the rhythm of a heartbeat. Shadows point first west, then east, as the sun rises one moment and sinks back behind the distant hills in the next. The moon waxes full and bright before fading to a pearl and silver sickle in the woad blue sky. The rose gardens bud and bloom and shed their leaves within the space of a breath, while the level of the lake rises and recedes according to its own inner tide.

Everything around you cycles and changes in perpetual movement, yet where you stand at the center of it all is serene and unaffected, save that your perceptions begin to grow more sharp and clear. Your peripheral vision expands and the horizon that bounds the landscape moves further and further away; you become increasingly able to take in more of the whole all at once. There is no place on Avalon you cannot see, feel, or experience. Here, there is nothing that is beyond your reach.

Your consciousness begins to envelop the whole of the island and its sheltering lake … the woolly flocks and fruit-laden orchards … the long timber halls and thatched round houses … the twin mystic pools and the mysterious green hills … the working songs of novices and the solemn chants of priestesses … the sounds, scents, and energies surround you, weaving themselves into a singular tapestry of experience here at the Heart of Avalon.

The unified calmness settles upon you like a blanket, and you lie upon the clover-carpeted ground. Feel your breathing become synchronized with the inner rhythms of Avalon, pulsing through each stone, tree, and hill. Your energy becomes one with the patterns of the landscape—the Dragon Lines, the nodes of power, the Divine essence permeating the sacred places. With every breath, you feel yourself being enveloped in the Spirit of Avalon, and in merging, you begin to experience the Holy Island unlike never before.

Bring your attention to the center of Earth energy in your body—that nexus of heavy, receptive forces pooling at the base of your spine and the opening of your vulva. Spend as much time as you need focusing on this Root Center, until your consciousness is able to perceive the entirety of the Earth energy within you. When this connection is complete, you feel a line of resonance arcing from your body to link with the labyrinthine-sculpted Tor. Take some time to fully experience what it is like to be the Tor—simultaneously in your body and the landscape. When the two become one, you become aware of the sound of a deep resonant tone or feel its accompanying energy, enveloping the totality of your experience.

With your breath and intention, move the energy of your consciousness up into the place in your body where the elemental energies of water are concentrated—your womb space or abdomen. Here the energy is fluid and magnetic, vibrating at the same frequency as the Red Spring. Immersed in the inner totality of this deeply feminine force, you feel your womb space reaching out across the landscape to combine with the red-tinged waters. Take some time to fully experience this connection—feeling the water energies expand and overtake the whole of your energies, rising side by side with the earthen essence of the Tor. Feeling deeply and fully connected with the Red Spring, you hear or feel a high-pitched note rise from the merging of the watery inner and outer landscapes to join with the tone of earth power.

Breathe the energy up higher along your body, bringing your focus to the fire nature of your Heart Center. Begin to kindle your Heart space energy until it expands, becoming an actively pulsing and raging fire. Feel the flames spread out from your chest and into the Avalonian landscape, finding resonance in the essence of Modron's Mound. Spend time fostering the bridge between the similar energies of that which is within and that which is without. When the two vibrate as one at last, a fiery third note rings out, and you feel it perfectly harmonizing with the tones of water and earth.

When it feels right, breathe the energy up your spine until you become fully aware of the Throat Center, the dwelling place of all that is aligned with the element of air within. Feel this center of active, expansive energy become fully activated with each intention-filled breath. Connect with all that is airy within, and when you are as conscious of this energy as possible, another beam of light bursts forth from your Throat Center into the Sacred Landscape, rushing to connect with the sparkling waters of the White Spring, where it emerges from the mouth of the Earth. Experience what it is like to be the Tor Springs, and sublimate its energy with your own. You will know you have made a strong and enmeshed connection when a fourth tone, of a higher pitch yet, beings to vibrate alongside those of the Heart Center, womb space and the Root.

When you are ready, bring your attention to the Third Eye Center in the middle of your forehead. Here dwells the essence of all that is of the Spirit and is your place of union with the Divine. Breathe this energy center wide and open as you experience all that connects to your sacred nature within. When you are as fully conscious of this energy as you can be, use it to connect with the island's Divine essence, rising forth to merge with the indwelling Spirit of the entire Avalonian landscape—the universal energies that underlie the archetype of the

Holy Island. A fifth tone sounds out, a result of the union of energies of Spirit within and without.

When you are fully conscious of the energies flowing through and around you, gather the vital force within you using your breath; begin with your Root. Breathe it up through every energy center—from earthy Root to watery Womb, through fiery Heart up to airy Throat, into the etheric Third Eye, building to fountain out through the crown of your head. There, the force meets and merges with the Modron— the essence of the Goddess that inhabits the Holy Isle. This union of the outer and inner Avalon is mirrored by your now-conscious connection to the indwelling source of Goddess—inseparable from the All.

In the wake of this acknowledgment, the five tones become intertwined, plaiting their ethereal concord like shining knotwork across the land. Their mingled vibrations release a powerful harmonic and everything shifts, everything changes. The veils between the realms are pulled aside, and the core nature of the whole of Avalon is revealed. There is no thought, no way to understand. You can only *be* in this energy, and feel its resonance within your own soul. The pall of pain and illusion, ego and expectation, fear and limitation, is lifted from your soul. In this enlightenment comes the revelation of your Divine truth; the fundamental essence of all you are, have been, and will be.

Take as much time as needed to fully experience this space—without thought, without judgment. Do not try to make sense of it all—simply *be* and receive all you can. When you feel it is time to return, fill yourself with feelings of openness and connectedness and ground yourself in the knowledge of your sacred nature. Breathe the energy of Avalon down through the top of your head, through all your energy centers, and through the bottom of your feet, closing the energetic circuit but retaining the essence of Sovereignty within you.

When you feel centered and grounded once more, your guide leads you back through the orchard and to the shores of the lake, where the Barge of Avalon awaits you. Turn again to face the island, and thank the Lady and all the guardians of this sacred space for supporting your work and allowing you to visit. Bid your guide farewell and climb aboard the Barge to complete your journey to the other side of the lake, bringing with you the memory of all that has come before.

Revisiting the Self

As you continue making your connection to the Island of Avalon and your fully actualized Sovereign self, go back and re-read the self-reflective questions above. How have your answers changed? What catalyzed this change? What underlying energies are you now aware of that were previously unconscious? What patterns have become visible? How can you put your insights and connections to work in order to bring change into your life?

Tool for the Station: The Three Realms Working

The essence of our being is a cosmological echo of the whole of Creation. As the Hermetic Axiom states: "As above, so below; as within, so without." We can use this wisdom to tap into our full potential as women and apply universal principles to our own process of unfolding. From what we understand about the Celtic worldview, they held a tripartite paradigm of cosmic organization we call the Three Realms.

> **The Realm of Land** is the physical plane, where the majority of our conscious experiences occur. This is the Realm of manifestation and the dwelling place of plants, animals, elementals, and entities connected to the land.
>
> **The Realm of Sea** is the dwelling place of the Ancestors, the Underworld to which souls return before again seeking manifestation; the maternal waters of birth and rebirth and sacred Cauldron of the Goddess.

The Realm of Sky is the abode of the Divine; the final destination of souls who have completed the cycle of bound and rebound, rejoining the All once more. Here too are all things celestial; the patterns of sun, moon, and stars exist here and derive from this progenitor of Cycle.

This triple division of the All is reflected in the microcosm of the self. Each of the Three Realms has a corresponding province in each of us, governing particular aspects of the self. Learning to navigate this inner landscape with consciousness is a key skill to master on the voyage to self-actualization.

The Land Within encompasses everything we manifest in the material world. It also determines how we create the outward circumstances of our lives. This inner realm holds the energy of our physical health, our ability to create abundance and stability in our lives, and our overall capacity to survive and thrive in the mundane world. The Land Within holds the energy of the present, the stage upon which we either play out our shadow patterns or choose to walk a new path.

The Sea Within is the medium through which we relate to the inner and outer world. It is the sphere of the emotions, connecting us to spiritual planes and granting us access into the collective unconscious. This inner realm is the receptacle of our innate wisdoms, the source of our intuition, and bears the reflection of our relationships to ourselves and others. The Sea Within holds the energy of our past—our memories, our fears, and our greatest hopes and dreams.

The Sky Within is the filter through which we view our world and understand our place within it. This inner realm holds our perspectives, the functions of the higher mind, and determines our ability see truth with clarity and discernment. The Sky Within generates our ideas for the future; how it will unfold depends upon the choices we make, our mental outlook, and our degree of conscious communication with the higher self.

These Three Realms compose the whole of who we are; their existence in our lives is immutable. What can change, however, are the ways in which each realm influences our lives. The ideal is for all three Realms to be in perfect balance with each other, gently overlapping in energetic interchange and synchronized clarity. Cleansing these energy fields of lower-self impulses and shadow patterns will bring them back into balance, and allow us to experience the gifts of spirit available to those in alignment with the whole. Consciously clearing and activating the highest vibration of the inner realms will ensure that we come to our work, and indeed our lives, from a place of center and discernment.

When used daily, the Three Realms working is an exercise that will cleanse, connect, and activate each realm of the inner self.

The Three Realms Working

Find your Power Breath, and sit with it for a space of nine cycles of inhalation and exhalation, finding your center. Bring your awareness in turn to each of the three inner realms, beginning with the Land Within. As you connect with each in the manner described in these pages, begin by taking note of how each inner realm feels. Is it heavy or light, active or still, clear or dense? Are there vestiges of other energies being carried around? What color is this realm? How is it the same or different from the last time you performed this working? Can you discern any energetic pattern for this realm—swirling motions of energies or subtle etheric textures? Does connecting with this inner realm evoke symbols, memories, or insights? Take the time to experience everything that comes up for you, making sure to write anything you feel is important in your journal later.

1—The Land Within

This Realm exists as an energetic overlay of your physical body and the space immediately surrounding it. It is anchored to your body through the Root Center, at the base of the spine. Bring your awareness to your Root Center, and from there, feel the energy radiate outwards, enveloping your body. Once you have taken inventory of the Land Within in the manner described above, connect with and breathe through all the issues connected with this realm: issues of abundance, physical ailments, mundane-world impediments to your growth and actualization, shadow impulses, self-indulgences or denials—anything which interferes with the clear flow of energy and brings this realm out of balance. Gather these energies with your breath, and breathe them down into the Earth, the planetary vibration of the Realm of Land.

Once you have removed these impediments to your inner realm, connect with the outer Realm of Land and breathe its influence into your energy field. Visualize the Land Within being filled with the clear, clean, balanced energy of its macrocosmic template. Bring your consciousness deep within the earth, connecting with the dark, rich soil that supports the Middle World. Breathe that energy up and into your personal energy field, replacing what you've released with a firm, stable foundation and a fertile field to yield inner abundance. Expand your consciousness outward to connect with all of the spirits of nature, feeling yourself a part of the greater pattern. Breathe the energy field associated with the Land Within as far out beyond the boundary of your physical body as you can, expanding your connection with the All, and your ability to live in the now.

2—The Sea Within

This realm exists as an energy field directly touching and surrounding the perimeter of the Land Within. It is anchored to your body through the Womb Center, just below your navel. Bring your awareness to your womb space and from there, feel the energy radiate and envelop your body and the inner land energy. Once you have taken inventory of the Sea Within in the manner described earlier, connect with and breathe through all the issues connected with this realm: issues of attachment, emotional imbalances, relationship concerns, disconnection to your innate wisdom, sorrow, pain—anything that interferes with the clear flow of energy, unbalacing this realm. As before, gather these energies up with your breath, and breathe them out into the waters, the planetary vibration of the Realm of Sea.

Once you have removed these impediments to your inner realm, connect with the outer Realm of Sea and breathe its influence into your personal energy field. Visualize the Sea Within being filled with the clear, clean, balanced energy of its macrocosmic template. Bring your consciousness to the maternal waters, connecting with the red, life-bearing power of the Cauldron of the Otherworld. Breathe that energy up and into your energy field, replacing that which you released with a fluid, receptive relationship with the cosmos and a clear connection to your inner wisdom. Expand your consciousness outward to connect with your ancestors, the Celtic Matronæ and the women who have walked the path of Avalon before us, feeling yourself a link in a sacred chain extending back into eternity. Breathe the energy field associated with the Sea Within as far beyond the boundary of the Land Within as you can, expanding your connection with the All and your ability to give and receive with clarity.

3—The Sky Within

This realm exists as an energy field directly touching and surrounding the perimeter of the Sea Within. It is anchored to your body through the Head. Bring your awareness to the area spanning from the crown of your head to the Throat Center and from there, feel the energy radiate and envelop your body and the energy of the inner sky. Once you have taken inventory of the Sky Within in the manner described earlier, connect with and breathe through all the issues connected with this realm: issues of perspective, lack of clarity, problems with discernment, blocked communication—anything interfering with the clear flow of energy and brings this realm out of balance. As before, gather these energies up with your breath, and breathe them out into the air, the elemental vibration of the Realm of Sky.

Once you have released these impediments to your inner realm, connect with the outer Realm of Sky and breathe its influence into your energy field. Visualize the Sky Within being filled with the clear, clean, balanced energy of its macrocosmic template. Bring your consciousness high above the clouds, connecting with the white, higher-self energies dwelling in the Upper World. Breathe that energy down and into your energy field, replacing that which you released with a clear, objective perspective and open channels of conscious communication with Divinity. Expand your consciousness outward to connect with your guides, your higher self, and the all-embracing essence of the Great Goddess, knowing without a doubt the truth of your Divine nature. Breathe the energy field associated with the Sky Within as far out beyond the boundary of the Sea Within as you can, expanding your connection with the All and your ability to set your sights—with consciousness—on the far horizon.

You are now enveloped with three interconnected strata of energy—fully clear, open, and connected with their interpersonal resonances. Visualize the three layers—black, red, and white—meeting at a point at your Heart Center. Feel these energies touch each other, and with your breath, move the energies around in a clockwise motion, forming a triple spiral radiating outward from the center made up of three streams of different colored energies. Expand this spiral until each stream is balanced and extended to the farthest expanse of your energy field. Hold this energy and set it with your breath for nine cycles of inhalation and exhalation, feeling it expand beyond the personal into the cosmological transpersonal realms. When you are ready, reverse the spin of the spiral in a counterclockwise motion, drawing the energies back into your center, bringing the higher vibrations back down into the realm of the personal, empowering the Land, Sea, and Sky Within. Feel this energy once more fill your personal energy field, and set the energy again with your ninefold breath.

Consistently performing the Three Realms working will facilitate and improve your ability to receive, process, and act upon information from the universe in a place of clarity and connection.

10

PILGRIMAGE
OF THE SPIRIT

So they rode till they came to a lake, the which was a fair water and broad, and in the midst of the lake Arthur was aware of an arm clothed in white samite, that held a fair sword in that hand. Lo! said Merlin, yonder is that sword that I spake of. With that they saw a damosel going upon the lake. What damosel is that? said Arthur. That is the Lady of the Lake, said Merlin; and within that lake is a rock, and therein is as fair a place as any on earth, and richly beseen.

LE MORTE D'ARTHUR, SIR THOMAS MALORY

As PASTORALISTS AND AGRICULTURALISTS, THERE was perhaps nothing more honored and revered by our Celtic forebears than the very land they lived on. Subject to the cycles of the moon and sun, and the ebb and flow of the ocean tides, ancient Britons aspired to align themselves with these forces for their survival. They sought the good favor of the spirits of nature—the indwelling life force of Land, Sea, and Sky—and requested their intercession for abundant harvests and healthy livestock. They created earthen burial chambers in honor of the sacred dead and used these sites as places to connect with their ancestors through the veil of the Otherworld. They acknowledged the power of the landscape by erecting megalithic monuments along ley lines and by worshiping the Divine in natural settings—especially those with the power to inspire.

Ancient Avalon's physical location was specifically chosen because of the uniquely powerful landscape features that comprise the Holy Island. These features—which include springs, hills, sacred groves, and an surrounding lake—both generated and supported Avalon's transformational energies. Although Avalon no longer exists on this plane, the powerful energies of Glastonbury provide portals through which we can connect with the Avalon of old. Journeying to Glastonbury in pilgrimage is an incredible spiritual experience but we need not physically travel to the site to connect with Avalon's essence. Firmly rooted in the archetypal realm, Avalon can be accessed through focused and disciplined inner questing.

We have used the Immram as a powerful tool for journeying to the spiritual landscape of ancient Avalon, yet there are as many ways of knowing as there are portals to the Otherworld. The Immram is an active process: we journey across the waters of the unconscious to access the realms of the spirit and connect with the Holy Island's archetypal essence. Another effective technique takes a more receptive approach, allowing us to bypass the material plane and enter into a shifted state of consciousness through the act of merging. Using this physical meditation discipline, one can connect directly with the energies of the Avalonian landscape, so revered by the ancient Britons.

Synthesizing Gnosis

One of the most exciting revisionings of recent years is a holistic tool called ecstatic trance postures, a synthesis of many different disciplines: psychology, anthropology, neurology and shamanism. Anthropologist Felicitas Goodman studied figural artifacts from many cultures around the planet and, through her work, realized these images were specific records of ritualistic poses intended to induce a particular state of consciousness.

Like the mudras of the East, these meditational postures seemed to evoke a particular experience in people who assumed them in a ritual manner. Uncanny similarities were noted in the trance visions of people practicing a particular posture; the end result of Dr. Goodman's research is the cataloging of over fifty different shamanic postures. It is truly a universal language that uses the body to form words and sentences.

Neurologically speaking, the brain and nervous system are affected by the body's position. Information is sent along the neural pathways, giving information to the brain. Trance postures posit a sort of kinesthetic memory, that when reactivated by holding the body in a particular position will trigger a shift in the practitioner's consciousness. Coupled with rhythmic breathing and drumming to occupy the left side of the brain, these postures facilitate the right hemisphere's ability to transcend bodily limitations and enter a different realm of awareness. It is believed these records of the ancients were meant to preserve techniques of spiritual awakening and provide the seeker with helpers and guides from the spirit world.

Celtic Images

Inspired by the work of Dr. Goodman and her students, I have done trance work with the few anthropomorphized images that remain available from the Celtic people. Either because they did not believe in creating images of the Divine in human form, or because, as the archaeological record suggests, they created such cult objects out of materials that would not have survived through time, there are only a few such images known to us today from pre-Roman times. The Gundestrup cauldron, an incredible silver ritual object that dates back to the first century BCE, boasts some of the best examples of such figural work.

This unique vessel was found in a peat bog in Denmark, of possible Gaulish or Thracian origin, and is believed to have been intentionally dismantled as a religious offering. It depicts people, animals, and plants in the La Téne art style. The seven outer plates of the cauldron feature busts of figures believed to be gods and goddesses, and each is rendered holding a specific (perhaps ritualized) pose, sometimes holding symbolic objects. Replicating these postures for trance journeying has resulted in powerful shamanic experiences, and the author is continuing research into their lessons and uses.

One of the most well-known images from the Gundestrup cauldron is found on one of the inner plates. Depicting what is believed to be the Celtic god Cernunnos, an antlered figure sits cross-legged and wearing highly stylized garments including striped breeches suggestive of those believed to have been favored by the Celts. In his right hand he holds aloft a torc, a symbol of sovereignty, and in his left he holds a horned snake, perhaps referring to his role as a fertility deity. Taken alone, this plate is a masterful religious icon in its own right, but when compared to an image that comes to us from the Indo-European peoples of the ancient Harappan culture of the Indus Valley, it takes on a deeper meaning.

Found in Mohenjo-Daro, an Indus Valley city that existed between 2600 and 1900 BCE, an object known as the Pashupati Seal bears many similarities to the Gundestrup Cernunnos image; the seal depicts a crossed-legged, horned male figure surrounded by animals. Pashupati ("Lord of the Animals") is seen by many to be a precursor to the Hindu god Shiva, and most scholars agree the stylized posture in the seal represents one of the earliest depictions of a yoga pose.

Although the Pashupati image predates the Gundestrup cauldron by more than a thousand years, it is significant when we consider the Indo-European mother culture that birthed the Celtic people. Could it be that the Celts practiced a physical meditative discipline similar to yoga, as demonstrated by the Gundestrup Cernunnos? It seems especially significant, as his entire body was intentionally depicted, whereas an overwhelming majority of the other images are rendered as busts. Perhaps the artisans were trying to communicate something important about the stance of the Cernunnos figure. Whatever their intention, these clues—while far from conclusive—paint a picture that makes use of a physical spiritual discipline in a Celtic context seem more plausible.

Avalonian Landscape Postures

When it comes to the Avalonian Tradition, there are no figural images to use for trance journeying that are directly related to the Holy Island. What we do have, however, are the very distinctive and prominent landscape features that drew ancient Britons to settle in and around Glastonbury. Taking these into consideration, a system of unique postures was developed that emulate and connect to power points in the Avalonian landscape. These postures provide vehicles for journeying to specific sites on the Priestess Isle, and each opens a specific doorway of inner understanding and transformational energies into our lives. The complete system of Avalonian Landscape postures permits the seeker to embark upon a series of spiritual pilgrimages that facilitate work with the spiritual essence of the Holy Isle. Such a journey allows us to discern meaning and to identify the Isle's role on our paths to the Goddess.

These postures have several goals. They provide a mechanism by which we can explore the sacred landscape of Avalon, learning thus the importance of each site, its relevance to the work of Avalon, and its usage by the priestesses of old. As well, the postures stimulate and awaken specific transformational energies in your own life, bringing forth insights and wisdoms related to your personal process and your soul growth. The postures are doorways of understanding to both the Avalonian Landscape and the Sacred Landscape within.

The five postures presented in this book correspond with the landscape areas related to each of the Stations of the Avalonian Cycle of Healing. There are several ways to approach the use of these postures. You can use the cycle of the moon, performing the appropriate posture at each lunar phase, or you can align your work with the cycle of the sun, using the posture that relates to the upcoming holy day for as long as you need to prepare for the deep work associated with each Station.

Avalonian Landscape Postures and Cycle Correspondences

Posture Name	Station	Cycle of the Moon	Cycle of the Sun
Y Tarddell Rudd	Descent	3rd Quarter Moon	Calan Gaeaf
Y Twrr	Confrontation	Dark Moon	Gwyl Mair
Y Tarddell Wen	Emergence	1st Quarter Moon	Calan Mai
Bryn Modron	Resolution	Full Moon	Gwyl Awst
Ynys Afallon	Integration	Any and All Time	Any and All Time

Once you have spent an entire yearly cycle working with these postures, documenting your insights, experiences, and personal processes, you can then work with individual postures at your discretion, connecting with those sites and energies you feel you need most to experience based upon discernment built during your month of workings. For example, if connecting to the Red Spring helped provide insight for your shadow work, you can return to this site through the landscape posture, bringing with you specific questions relating to the work at hand.

Before you begin to cycle through the postures—each one moving you deeper and deeper into the energies of Avalon—you may consider dedicating an entire month to the exploration of one sacred site at a time. In this way, you can fully explore this aspect of Avalon and experience the resonance of this sacred site in your life. It is recommended you perform each posture at least three times a week during the course of the month; more is ideal.

Applying the Postures

This deceptively simple technique is incredibly powerful, and one which works well both in group settings and for a solitary practitioner. Following these steps will move you down the path of experiencing a rewarding and transformational physical discipline with limitless potential for insight and personal growth.

For each posture:

1. Wear loose, comfortable clothing.

2. Use a fifteen-minute recording of rapid drumming or rattling, which you can purchase or make for yourself. In her research, Dr. Goodman found that a rhythm of 200–210 beats per minute seems to trigger the nervous system into entering the altered state of consciousness desired for these postures. A metronome or other such repetitive sound will have the same effect. This is an important ingredient, but if you simply cannot make a tape or find a pre-recorded CD, focus on your Power Breath, which

should be performed for at least fifteen minutes before beginning any landscape posture session. A callback drum beat or a gentle alarm set to go off after fifteen minutes will bring you back from your journey. An MP3 of a drumming session is available on the author's website (see appendix).

3. Work in your sacred space, surrounded by those things that trigger entrance into the realm of the spiritual. The simple act of spreading a sarong or cloth dedicated solely for use in these workings can help move you into a receptive space for journeying.

4. Clear and center and fall into your Power Breath for fifteen minutes before assuming the posture you are working on.

5. When ready, play your drumming recording and assume the position of the posture using the following photographs as a visual guide. Practice the posture before journeying so you are sure that you know it well and can make any necessary adjustments for comfort.

6. Should you feel you must adjust your posture for comfort's sake during the fifteen minutes, do so briefly while holding the intention of the posture clearly. Resume the posture when you are able. Some of these postures can be physically challenging, especially when held for a lengthy period of time. Always keep in mind that your best approximation of the posture will unlock its transformational power in your life. It is better to do the best you can than not to do the postures at all.

7. Keep your focus clear as you journey, allowing insight to flow. Spend the entire fifteen minutes of drumming or breathing in this posture, remaining as clear and open to the experience as you can. Pay attention to any and all visions, scenes, emotions, insights or information presented to you. How does the posture make you feel? What would you name this posture? What is this posture's lesson? How does it relate to you and your process?

Are there any issues this posture brings up for you? In what way does this sacred site find resonance in your soul?

8. It is important to ground and center after every posture session. This is discussed later in this chapter.

9. Be sure to journal your experiences.

Please note: As with any exercise routine or physical discipline, it is recommended you consult your health care practitioner before undertaking these postures. The creator of this work accepts no responsibility for injuries or issues that may arise from the use of these postures.

Y Tarddell Rudd—The Red Spring

THE LANDSCAPE

The sacred, iron-tinged waters of the Red Spring have been a source of reverence and inspiration for thousands of years. Although its outward appearance has shifted over the centuries, the waters of the Red Spring have maintained a constant flow, a consistent temperature, and a continuous connection to holy and healing energies. The Y Tarddell Rudd posture emulates the bubbling forth of these waters at its source—intentional, contained, and reflecting the deep chthonic symbolism of this liminal site—and is closely aligned with the Station of Decent.

POSTURE DESCRIPTION

- Kneel with your legs close together.
- Keep your back straight and your torso upright.
- Extend your arms at a 30-degree angle from the body.
- Flex your hands at the wrists, keeping your fingers together. The position of the arms and hands suggest the fountaining forth of the waters from the ground.

Y Tarddell Rudd Posture

- This posture may be difficult on the knees, so it may be helpful to kneel on a cushion. Alternatively, you may perform this posture sitting upright at the edge of a chair with your feet flat on the floor and your legs and knees held tightly together.

- Once you have settled into the position, hold it for fifteen minutes with a rhythmic breathing pattern. Playing a shamanic drumming track while holding the posture is ideal.

As you perform this posture, connect with the corresponding energies within you as well as the archetypal essence of this aspect of Avalon. What does the Red Spring bring to the surface from the depths of your soul? What can it teach you about the hidden nature of Avalon—both within and without?

Y Twrr Posture

Y Twrr—The Tor

The Landscape

A holy site and ritual center, the labyrinthine terraces of the Tor spin the great magicks of Avalon. Often compared to the body of a woman in repose over the landscape, the slumbering silhouette of the Tor lends itself naturally to imitation as a trance posture. Glastonbury Tor is believed to be a gateway into Annwn, the Celtic Otherworld, and Y Twrr posture opens many a doorway into the realms of the unconscious, facilitating the work of the Station of Confrontation.

Posture Description

+ Lie on your left side with one leg on top of the other and both bent at hip and knee. Keep your calves parallel to your torso, with both feet pointed in the opposite direction of the head.

+ Your upper left arm is on the floor and bent at the elbow. Rest your forearm against your abdomen and place your left hand face-down on the crest of your right hip.

+ Keep your upper body propped up on your left side with your right shoulder rolled back and your chest twisted to point towards the ceiling. Your head is facing forward with your left cheek on the floor. Extend your right arm behind your head and rest it on your right wrist and hand, which is palm up on the floor.

- Once you have settled into the position, hold it for fifteen minutes with a rhythmic breathing pattern. Playing a shamanic drumming track while holding the posture is ideal.

While performing this posture, connect with the corresponding energies within as well as the archetypal essence of this aspect of Avalon. Why is the Tor considered the entrance to the Otherworld? What is the importance of this sacred Avalonian hill?

Y Tarddell Wen—The White Spring

THE LANDSCAPE

The natural beauty of the White Spring has been disrupted by the presence of a reservoir built in 1872, and we are haunted by eyewitness descriptions of a flowstone-encrusted coombe (a small valley), issuing forth waters which have percolated through the limestone layers of the Tor. The Tor Springs, as it is also called, is actually made up of a confluence of waters that connect underground before gushing forth from the surface. The calcium-rich waters of White Spring are as unpredictable in their flow rate and temperature as the sources are varied, and can remake the environment with their limestone deposition. Y Tarddell Wen reflects the active, far-reaching essence of the White Spring and its connection to the renewing energies of the Station of Emergence.

POSTURE DESCRIPTION

- Kneel with legs hip distance apart.
- Extend your legs straight back from the knee at right angles to your torso.
- Keep your back straight, your torso upright, and face your head forward.
- Raise your arms at a 60-degree angle to your body, keeping them bent at the elbows.

Y Tarddell Wen Posture

+ Flex your arms at the wrists, keeping your fingers together. Position your arms and hands to suggest the fountaining forth of the spring waters into the air.

+ This posture may be difficult on the knees, so it may be helpful to kneel on a cushion. Alternatively, you may perform this posture sitting upright at the edge of a chair with your feet flat on the floor and your legs and knees opened in front of you, hip distance apart.

+ Once you have settled into the position, hold it for fifteen minutes with a rhythmic breathing pattern. Playing a shamanic drumming track while holding the posture is ideal.

What does the White Spring bring to the surface from the depths of your soul? What is the lesson of its calcium-rich waters?

Bryn Modron—Modron's Mound/Chalice Hill

THE LANDSCAPE

The pregnant silhouette of the rounded rise of Chalice Hill overlooks the Avalonian landscape. Said to be the resting place of the Holy Grail, our retraced work remembers this hill as sacred to Modron, the Mother. The faerie hills and earthen gateways to the Otherworld that feature prominently in the myths of the Celts evolved from the ancient British reverence of ancestral burial mounds. The door swings both ways and, burgeoning with possibility, Bryn Modron births forth the energies of manifestation aligned with the Station of Resolution.

POSTURE DESCRIPTION

- Kneel with your calves extended behind your torso, keeping them parallel and close together.
- Support the weight of your upper body with your arms straight forward and parallel to each other, bent slightly at elbows for comfort.
- Round your back to approximate the shape of the hill.
- Tuck your head slightly to round your shoulders.
- Once you have settled into the position, hold it for fifteen minutes with a rhythmic breathing pattern. Playing a shamanic drumming track while holding the posture is ideal.
- You may find you need to relax your back for a few moments, or lean back on your knees to relieve strain on your back. This posture may be difficult on the knees, so it may be helpful to kneel on a cushion. Resume the posture when you are able. Remember, your best approximation of the posture will unlock

Bryn Modron Posture

its transformational power in your life. It is better to do the best you can than not to do the posture at all.

While performing this posture, connect with the corresponding energies within as well as the archetypal essence of this aspect of Avalon. What is the importance of this sacred Avalonian hill?

Ynys Afallon—The Island of Avalon

The Landscape

The Island of Avalon is the embodiment of the wholeness of the Goddess in the landscape. A place of pilgrimage since time immemorial, the unique transformational energies of the Glastonbury landscape have always been considered sacred. Believed by some to be the Heart Chakra of the planet, the place where ancient Avalon once abided still draws seekers worldwide. These profound energies of oneness and connection evoke the transformational powers of the Holy Island that, when taken together, call forth the Station of Integration.

Ynys Afallon Posture

Posture Description

+ Sit with your right leg extended outward from your body at a slight angle. Fold your left leg towards the body, creating a space between the leg and your slightly left-leaning torso.

+ Round your arms in front of your body with open, palm-up hands resting on the floor between your left leg and your body.

+ Face forward with your shoulders slightly rounded.

+ Once you have settled into the position, hold it for fifteen minutes with a rhythmic breathing pattern. Playing a shamanic drumming track while holding the posture is ideal.

While performing this posture, connect with the corresponding energies within as well as the archetypal essence of the totality of Avalon. What is its ultimate expression in your life?

Grounding and Centering

After each posture session, sit in a neutral position with your hands flat against the ground. Continue with your Power Breath, bringing your attention to your personal energy. Feel yourself as present in your body as you can, returning fully from your journey. Breathe any residual energy—any emotional, mental, or physical responses to the posture—through your root and hands and deep into the Earth. Feel these drain away and return to the physical landscape; you maintain the memory of them, and should journal your experiences as an ongoing record of your process and inner revelation.

When you have discharged this excess energy, reach down deep into the planet, and breathe up rich, vibrant, vital Earth energy into your body and energy field. Feel yourself coming to a solid, centered, stable space as you breathe in this energy, and continue to do so until you feel fully relaxed, fully connected to your body, and fully present in the here and now. Take as long as you need to move into this space. No posture session is complete until you have grounded and centered in this manner.

Moving Deeper

As you work with each of these Avalonian landscape postures, consider the following questions to help you deepen your connection to these sacred places and their corresponding energies within you.

1. How does this posture make you feel emotionally? Physically? Spiritually?

2. How easy or difficult did you find this posture? Was it easy to assume? Were you able to maintain the form for the entire trance session? What would have better facilitated the experience for you?

3. Were your sessions accompanied by shamanic drumming? What effect did the drumming have on your work? Did you

use drumming at certain times and not others? How did the presence or absence of the drumming affect your experience?

4. What Western energy center (Root, Womb, Heart, Throat, Third Eye) or Eastern chakra (Base, Sacral, Solar Plexus, Heart, Throat, Third Eye, Crown) feels activated by this posture? In what part of your body does this posture seem to resonate most?

5. With what elemental energy (Earth, Water, Fire, Air, Spirit) or realm (Land, Sea, Sky) does this posture resonate most? What makes you feel this way?

6. What images, memories, emotions, or process-oriented thoughts did assuming this posture evoke for you? How did this change over time, if at all?

7. How did your experience of the posture change over the course of several working sessions, if at all? To what do you attribute any change?

8. What did your experiences of this posture teach you about Avalon? How did it affect your connection to the Holy Island? What do you think the purpose of this posture is in the context of the work of Avalon?

9. What did your experiences of this posture teach you about yourself? How did it affect your understanding of your inner process? What do you think is the overall lesson of this posture?

10. What would cause you to use this posture again? What do you feel it would help you accomplish in your work?

11. If you had to sum up the energy of this posture in one word, what would it be? How would you sum it up in one sentence? If this posture were a tool, what type would it be and what would it do?

12. Was this posture similar to any other metaphysical trance experiences you've had? If yes, why?

13. Have you worked with trance postures before? How has your work with the Avalonian landscape postures been the same? How has it been different? Why?

The Power of Pilgrimage

Undertaking a spiritual pilgrimage is a sacred act of devotion and personal sacrifice. These Avalonian landscape postures are a form of pilgrimage that strengthens our bodies as well as our connection to the Divine—both the inherent Divinity of the sacred Avalonian landscape as well as our own indwelling Divinity—the Goddess within.

In assuming these postures, we are able to experience facets of the Avalonian landscape even as we awaken their transformational energies in our own lives. As we explore the Holy Island, we come to a deeper understanding of our own sacred nature. As we connect with Center, we are drawn nearer in relationship with the Source.

11

THE MIRROR
OF THE SELF

*Three kinds of knowledge: the nature of each thing, the cause of
each thing, the influence of each thing.*

CELTIC TRIAD

A RARE AND CELEBRATED FIFTEENTH-CENTURY WALL painting in Wedmore Church near Glastonbury depicts a being that is half woman and half fish, holding aloft a round looking glass. That this unusual iconography was included in a Christian painting of St. Christopher may point to a continuation of affection for a local Celtic deity or water spirit; some believe her to be the Lady of the Lake herself. The symbol itself is very much in keeping with Avalon's spiritual essence. The human half represents consciousness, while the fish tail is symbolic of the submerged unconscious. The raised mirror is a call for us to look inside of ourselves with intention, to discover the truth of our inherent Divinity, while also pointing the way down the path of wholeness—the path that leads within.

An important component of the inner growth process is to bring all parts of the self into consciousness so that we may effect change in our lives. We are each beings of light and shadow, the two parts of ourselves which as the Hermetic Principle of Polarity describes, are the same in nature, differing only in degree. This means that our greatest flaws are often the antithesis of our greatest gifts, and for every issue holding us back, we already have the corresponding tool to propel us forward.

Though we may desire to, we cannot rid ourselves of our shadow side; it is irrevocably a part of us. Instead, our goal is to move energy from one end of the inner spectrum to the other, so the gift is nurtured while the flaw is starved. Casting light on the inner shadow can be painful work but it is a crucial step along the path to wholeness. Remember—that which is unconscious controls us. If we do not know the nature of our shadows, we cannot know the ways in which they manifest in our lives, and therefore cannot know how to transform their energy to something supportive of our growth.

The Cauldron Within

Just as the Cauldron of Ceridwen reveals itself in the Sacred Landscape of Avalon, its transformational powers are reflected in our process of self-understanding. We can apply the major themes of Ceridwen's story and the Stations of the Avalonian Cycle of Healing to guide our inner course of self-reflection and personal revelation. Unlocking these mysteries of the self is a key element in the journey towards actualizing the priestess within; it gives us the power to consciously choose our Sovereign nature over the unconscious reflexes of the shadow.

As inspired by an exercise by Franz Bardon in his book *Initiation into Hermetics*, let us look now into the Mirror of the self—seeking out the building blocks of our essences to understand the people we presently are and to obtain insight on how to become the women we wish most to be.

Creirwy and Afagddu: Personal Polarities
THE STATION OF DESCENT

As with all journeys, it is helpful to create a travelogue of your progress. Set aside a blank journal specifically for this mirror work; it will become your Book of Light and Shadows. To set up this journal, write "Mirror of Light" on the first page of the book, and on the last page, write "Mirror of Shadow."

After doing some clearing breathwork and grounding, turn your eye within and seek the inner mirror, assessing yourself with clarity and honesty. Concentrate first on the positive aspects of yourself—attributes and potentials that are facets of your priestess self, regardless of how actualized they are in the present. On your Mirror of Light pages, list your constructive qualities: your gifts and talents; special abilities and accomplishments; positive character traits, and challenges you have overcome—everything that supports your growth and connection with the Goddess.

When you are ready, turn your eye within once more, this time seeking those aspects of the self that dwell in darkness, and list these characteristics on your Mirror of Shadow pages: your fears and wounds; flaws and failings; pain and limitations; doubts and destructive patterns—all those things which are reactionary manifestations of shadow your life.

These lists are an ongoing record of the inner process and will change over time as we gain inner clarity and effect healing in our lives. For this reason, it is imperative that we be brutally honest with ourselves in this inner inventory. We must see ourselves as objectively and with as much clarity as possible so that our work will be as effective as it can be; do not edit yourself in your mirror work.

Interestingly, women seem to find it easier to list their shadow aspects than those that dwell in the light. Pay special attention to those things that perhaps have not been supported in our lives—gifts and talents that have gone underused or undervalued. We must learn to live from a place of light and not allow social conditioning or the mechanisms of the lower self or shadow to keep us from being all we can truly be—all that we were meant to be.

Creating these lists need not be accomplished in one sitting. Take as much time as you need to be as thoughtful and thorough as you can in this process. When you are satisfied with your mirror lists, look at them side by side to see where your shadow aspects find balance in your priestess-self qualities. How are these dualities related? How can you reroute your personal energy and replace a destructive pattern with a constructive trait? Where are the gifts that illuminate the shadow?

The Dance of Gwion and Ceridwen: Elemental Assignations

THE STATION OF CONFRONTATION

After working with your personal Mirrors of Light and Shadow for a while, return to the pages in your journal and begin to look at them with an elemental eye. For each trait, gift, and shortcoming, assign an elemental alignment which best describes its fundamental energy, using the elemental overview from chapter ten as your guide. For example, you could assign the element of Water to your artistic gift, and the element of Fire to your tendency to be quick to anger.

Go through each list and take your time with this elemental typing; spend a few days working on it until you feel satisfied with your choices. When you are finished, begin to look for any patterns that emerge: Is there one element you have in abundance or which seems lacking? Do you have a preponderance of one element on one mirror and not on the other? Do you seem to have a balance of energies? What would you say is your overall elemental energy? How does this feel to you? Do you notice any common threads with those entries to which you have assigned the same elemental quality?

Assessing your energy in this way provides many insights into your personality and can shed light on the ways you perceive your environment and choose to act in the world. Working with elemental energies is a powerful method to overcome the well-established patterns in your life. Once the elemental alignment of an issue has been determined, you can make use of what you know about the nature of energy to your advantage. You can augment or negate an elemental energy by introducing another elemental energy into your life using the "Rock, Paper, Scissors" rule of the elements. The following chart gives a general description of actions the elements have on each other:

Chart of Mutual Elemental Actions

	Air	Fire	Water	Earth
Air	Empowers	Feeds	Disengages	Stimulates
Fire	Activates	Empowers	Dissipates	Catalyzes
Water	Condenses	Douses	Empowers	Dissolves
Earth	Grounds	Smothers	Moderates	Empowers

Let us say, for example, that you are working on an issue that has a very powerful emotional content. Emotions are aligned with Water. If you wanted to delve deeper into the emotion to learn all you could from it, bringing additional Water into your life would increase your ability to connect with this emotion, expressed in the Hermetic principle "like attracts like." Performing an Immram to the Red Spring and doing the work of the Station of Descent are effective ways to gain insight and work through these issues; they are also aligned with the energy of water and therefore possess elemental correspondence.

However, if you were to find that water energy clouds your judgment, you could bring in the element of Air to disengage yourself from the emotion, leaving you with some detached clarity. If this emotion threatens to overwhelm you, you could bring in Fire energy to dry it up, or earth energy to bring yourself into balance. Again, performing the corresponding Immram and working with the tools of the Station of the Cycle of Healing aligned with these elements is very helpful in this process.

The art of the work is to decide which tactic will best address the issue at hand. The beauty of magick is that you can shape your tools to fit your needs; there is always more than one way to attain a goal. If you are trying to dissolve a negative pattern from your life, you can have your work concentrate on the element that best represents the issue, and then reroute that energy into something positive. Conversely, if you are working with a mirror aspect and are looking to encourage the growth of a potential within you, surrounding yourself with a like or compatible energy is appropriate.

For example, if you are quick to anger and have assigned Fire to this aspect of yourself, infusing your personal energy field and environment with Earth energy, the grounding elemental principle that is the opposite of Fire, will bring you back to balance. In the same way, if you need to magnify an ability to be empathetic to others' feelings in a particular situation, you can come to the situation having previously channeled Water energy. Further, if you are working on building self-esteem (which we have decided to equate with the element of Fire), you could bring in more Fire to bolster the ability to express your will and perhaps incorporate some Air energy to feed that flame.

Once you have established elemental alignments for all of your mirror aspects, see if you can group these facets of the self into related families. Are there issues that branch from the same tree? Are they symptoms of the same problem or facets of the same inner endowment? In what way does knowing the elemental alignment of these parts aid in recognizing patterns that run through the whole?

When you have bundled related issues together and discovered their causes, you can address the bigger issue rather than the smaller tributaries. For example, say you have discovered that many of your shadow traits are born from a sense of low self-esteem. How do you perceive low self-worth, in and of itself, from an elemental perspective? Does it feel earthy to you—being low and humble and on the level of dirt? Is it watery—being too compliant, submersing yourself into each situation, not making any waves, taking the form you feel is expected of you? There is no right or wrong answer in this; what's important is that the alignment resonates true with you. Once you have whittled down your mirror lists to the main themes and prominent energies running through your life, decide which element you feel best represents these key points and keep them in mind as you proceed in your mirror work.

Nine Moons in the Womb: Creating Personal Symbols
THE STATION OF EMERGENCE

As we have seen, assigning elemental alignments to each entry on the mirror lists of light and shadow provides us with insight into our predominant energetic, in addition to giving us a tool we can use to compensate for shortcomings, or fortify gifts and talents. Understanding our inner processes allows us to have a great deal of control over shadow instincts. We are also empowered to develop and use gifts and talents that support the actualization of the priestess self. With these insights in mind, let us take our mirror work one step further.

Look over your lists and create personal symbols representing each aspect of yourself found in your mirror of shadow and mirror of light. Do not rush through this process; take as much time as you need to create a symbol set that is meaningful and connected to your soul work. After choosing which aspect of the self you wish to focus on, quietly sit and do your best to immerse yourself in its energy. With which energy center does this issue resonate most? What alignment is the issue? How does being immersed in this energy make you feel? What memories, aspirations, and emotions does it bring up? These are all important clues that will aid in creating your symbol.

Say in the course of your inner exploration about a mirror aspect, you recall an incident from your childhood. Perhaps you were camping one summer, and an older sibling decided to push you out of the boat and into the lake, knowing full well of your fear of water snakes. You were terrified and almost drowned, but mocking laughter made you feel ashamed at your perceived weakness. This memory is important on many levels, as it could be one of the key experiences contributing to the formation of an inner wound. Perhaps then, you can create a symbol integrating images of the boat, a snake, and the water rushing over your head.

This is an example of a personal symbol, one that cannot be interpreted by anyone else, nor can it be confused with any other symbol.

If distilling a mosaic experience into one image is difficult for you, ask your guide or the Goddess to give you a symbol to represent the mirror aspect upon which you are focusing. No matter how you obtain it, be sure to thoroughly doorway the symbol, as described on p. 142, in order to obtain a deep understanding of this part of yourself.

While they need not be elaborate, it is important these symbols resonate only with the aspect of self they are meant to represent; that is, try to avoid using universal symbols (such as the cauldron) as a personal symbol. You can use a universal symbol as a part of your personal symbol—for example, you could depict a fear of change as a purple giraffe with a cauldron over its head—as long as it is sufficiently personalized so as not to cause confusion in your work. Taking each issue's elemental alignment into account when creating your symbol can strengthen the symbol's usefulness.

This long-term project will establish a working language between you and your priestess self; you will create a vocabulary all your own as you delve further within and begin to peel your onion of self-knowledge. Through ritual, Immrama, and sessions with your guide, you can gain greater insight into your work and clearer answers to your questions, especially if you begin to see symbols you have created as direct responses, or find them appearing in your dreams or even in the everyday world.

Continuing the earlier example, say you are driving to work and see a purple giraffe on a bumper sticker, followed by a billboard advertisement for a bean pot that looks a great deal like a cauldron. Chances are, seeing these things will trigger the memory of your personal symbol and make you realize the universe is trying to bring this issue to your attention for some reason—maybe it's related to the Immram you performed the night before or in answer to the focus of your Station work. Pay attention to the cues the universe is presenting you—this is an important step towards increased perception and sensitivity; your perspective on the world expands as you begin to notice subtle signs around you.

Gwion Reborn: Manifesting the Mirror Runes
THE STATION OF RESOLUTION

You have taken a huge step towards creating a personal language that will facilitate communication with the universe and your priestess self in creating a unique symbol system representing each aspect of your inner self from your mirror lists. The symbols you've created are important in passive communication—both in seeing symbol elements appear "spontaneously" in the world (synchronicity), as well as through active communication. Consciously seeking out insights using your inner symbol system can be useful for understanding your personal process and in uncovering energies that may be active in your life without your awareness. This seeking is accomplished by creating physical representations of your mirror symbols—manifesting the Mirror Runes.

There are many ways to create your rune set, and it is important for you to meditate on the medium that will best resonate with you and your work. Several construction methods are discussed here, but each is open to personal interpretation; there is no right or wrong way to create your Mirror Runes so long as they make an energetic fit and are imbued with a sacred sense.

To begin, review your personal symbols and ensure you are satisfied that each symbol accurately reflects the energy of the aspect of self they were created to represent. Take some time to fine-tune your symbols; creating a doorway to each of them is a good way to ensure they have the correct correspondence. Count how many symbols you have; if there are a great many, see if you can find common themes in them to distill them into a smaller number. There is no right amount, however; if you have a large symbol set, you might find it easier to begin this work with no more than thirty-three symbols in all. This system is dynamic, and you should expect to both add and subtract runes from your set in the years to come so they better reflect your work and growth.

Once you are sure of your symbols, spend time with each of them and make only one rune per session, taking care to imbue each with the energy of its symbol. This will greatly increase your rune set's power and usefulness. Consider the following media for construction:

WOOD: Wood is an excellent choice for creating your Mirror Runes. You can purchase or make wooden disks—or any other shape that works for you (apples, crescents, yonis)—in the amount needed to represent each symbol. Paint each disk either black or white, to represent whether the symbol comes from your Mirror of Shadow or Mirror of Light. You can then paint your symbols in the elemental colors you have assigned to each, to remind you of the energetic quality of the sigil. A powerful use of wood for your set is to cut the runes yourself from magickal trees representing the dark and light energies (for example, apple and oak) and painting or wood-burning your symbols onto each.

STONE: In the same way as using sacred woods, you may choose to carve your symbols on two different types of stones representing the dark and the light mirror energies. Some stone pairs to consider are hematite and moonstone, jet and amber, and onyx and quartz. These make lovely rune sets that hold the energy of each symbol well.

CLAY: You can purchase self-hardening clay, clay that needs to be baked, or you could make your own dough clay. It is best to use a natural clay rather than the artificial polymers used for many crafts. Hand-form a set of sigils in whatever shape moves you; you can carve your symbols directly into the clay or paint them on after they have dried. Consider adding herbs or stones of like elemental energies into the clay to augment the energy you are representing for each rune.

GLASS: Round-edged glass stones can be engraved with your symbols. They can be tinted to represent light, dark, and elemental energies.

METAL: Use two different metals, one active and one passive, to create your runes. Gold and silver, brass and pewter, and copper and iron are good choices, budget permitting.

CARDSTOCK: Cutting uniform shapes out of cardstock is an option for those who like working with decks. You can use markers, colored pencils, or paint to make the back of the card black or white, and the same to draw each symbol in their elemental color on the reverse side.

These are simply suggestions for creating your Mirror Runes; let your imagination take you to what will work best for you. You can create a powerful working tool keyed specifically to your needs and energies, keeping your intention focused and the elemental essence of each symbol in mind.

After creating your rune set, find or make a bag in which to store them. Silk works best to keep the energies of your personal runes intact.

The Radiant Brow: Divining the Self

THE STATION OF INTEGRATION

Once your rune set is complete, there are many ways to work with it to obtain guidance and clarity.

If you feel drawn to add another layer of interpretation to your rune workings, you could consider what the universe is trying to communicate to you when you pull a reversed (upside-down) rune. Some people read reversals as holding the opposite meaning of the upright symbol, while others consider them to be indications of blocked energies, or the foreshadowing of a challenge to whatever aspect of the self the rune represents. You can decide ahead of time how, if at all, you want to read a reversed rune. Of course, always trust your intuition in the moment.

ONE-RUNE PULL: It can be helpful to begin each day by pulling a rune to see what energies will be influencing you throughout the day. Pulling a Rune of Light can indicate an opportunity to develop or use this aspect of yourself sometime during the course of the day. Pulling a Rune of Shadow can warn you against allowing this aspect of your lower self to have any kind of control, and to ensure the issue is not unconsciously motivating you. A one-rune pull can also be used at the full moon to ask the Goddess for your work for the upcoming month. Concentrating on this aspect of yourself every day for the entire lunar cycle can bring about many insights and unexpected changes.

MIRROR BALANCING: Separate your Runes into Shadow and Light. With a situation or a desire for clarity about a circumstance in mind, randomly choose a Rune of Shadow and a Rune of Light. The Shadow Rune represents the underlying energetic of the situation operating unconsciously, and the light rune is the balancer—what you need to augment or use to insure that the situation is one of growth. The Light Rune will provide you with a way through the shadow.

THREE-RUNE SPREAD: This working is helpful to understand cause and effect in your life. Concentrate on an issue or situation at hand, and then pull three runes from your bag.

> *Rune One*—The energy you are bringing into the situation
>
> *Rune Two*—The energy of the situation itself—how it challenges you
>
> *Rune Three*—The energetic outcome of the situation—what you learn from it

THE AVALONIAN CYCLE OF HEALING: Using your Mirror Runes in this layout can be helpful to receive an overview of the present or upcoming cycle's energies, especially when done at the Station of Descent during the solar or lunar cycle. It can also be used to understand the way in which a specific situation is unfolding in the context of the Cycle of Healing. Decide on your focus, sit with your intention, and draw five runes from the bag. Lay them out in the following order, and meditate upon their meanings based upon their positions.

Rune One: Station of Descent—The shadow manifestation of the issue at hand or the hurdle you need to overcome for your growth this Cycle.

Rune Two: Station of Confrontation—The origin of the issue at hand or the root of the soul wound that is the core of your healing work this Cycle.

Rune Three: Station of Emergence—The priestess-self manifestation of the issue at hand or the bridge you need to create for your growth this Cycle.

Rune Four: Station of Resolution—The potential liberated by overcoming the issue or the fruit of your labor to manifest this aspect of your priestess self this Cycle.

Rune Five: Station of Integration—The gift that lies at the heart of this issue or the growth achieved and the lesson learned by completely realizing the potential at the core of the work of this Cycle.

DREAMWORK: The Mirror Runes are an excellent tool for use in dream interpretation. After waking, list major symbols, people, and situations found in the dream. Assign numbers to each and give each number a position in the spread; it is helpful to keep track of this by writing down what position corresponds with which number. Randomly pull a rune for each position with the intention that each element of your dream is an aspect of yourself; the rune will provide insight into its symbolism. For example, if you dream about a beach ball and pull your purple giraffe symbol representing your sense of self-worth, the message is that the ball is talking about how you feel about yourself— what the ball did in the dream (bouncing, floating in the ocean, rolling down a sand dune) provides further insight into what the universe is trying to tell you through your dreams.

TALISMANS: You can wear a personal rune or a combination of runes in a pouch around your neck for a period of time with the intention of bringing its energy into your life, or reinforcing exploration work you are doing on a particular aspect of yourself. You can consciously choose which rune you are going to wear, or ask the universe for the one you need most to be working with at that time, and pull one from your bag at random. You can include herbs and stones in your neck pouch to further amplify energies with which you are working.

TAROT SPREADS: You can use your runes as if they were tarot cards, reading them in your favorite layouts such as the Celtic Cross. This will give you a very personalized reading which will address your specific needs and gifts.

Let your intuition guide you with additional uses. Magick is adaptable; you can create a working layout custom-built to fulfill your needs. It is important, however, that you are the only person who touches or works with your runes. They are keyed directly to your process and geared specifically for your growth. Your Mirror Runes are a sacred tool—a physical manifestation of your energetic makeup. They are a part of you and should be treated with reverence.

12

THE GODDESSES
OF AVALON

*Three slender things that best support the world: the slender
stream of milk from the cows dug into the pail; the slender
blade of green corn upon the ground; the slender thread over
the hand of a skilled woman.*

CELTIC TRIAD

THE GODDESSES OF AVALON ARE the heart and soul of the sacred landscape, each weaving a transformational energy into the matrix of the archetypal realm. Once we have successfully made contact with the landscape areas and established a good working relationship which each of these places of power, we can use them to connect with the Ladies of Avalon. These five Divine Ancestresses will further our quest for positive change, personal Sovereignty, and the wisdom that comes from drinking deeply from the cauldron of our souls.

The Avalonian Tradition draws its inspiration from British, rather than English, culture. As we have seen, Wales was able to maintain and preserve the culture, language, and traditions of Celtic Britain far longer than the rest of England, so we look to Welsh language, literature, and folklore to understand the beliefs of the Britons. The Welsh mythic cycle contains the first references to King Arthur, and through him, to Ynys Afallon—the Island of Avalon. Therefore, to discover the Goddess as She has revealed Herself to the Britons, and as She was likely worshiped on Avalon, we must turn to Welsh mythology.

While we know the names of hundreds of Celtic divinities, many of them are mentioned only once and are associated with burials or local shrines and wells. There are a few deities, however, whose stories have survived the passage of time and have made it into the written record, accompanied by a rich tradition of legend and symbolism. It may be possible to conclude that there were two levels of worship in Celtic lands; local and clan divinities as well as tribal and regional gods. We cannot know this for sure, but there is iconographic and etymologic evidence enough to consider this possibility.

For example, the symbolism and attributes of the Welsh goddess Rhiannon bear a strong resemblance to those of the continental Celtic goddess Epona as well as to the Irish goddess Macha. The Irish Lugh and Welsh Lleu are both gods associated with light, while the Welsh Don and Irish Danu are both Great Mother goddesses from whom dynasties of gods have descended. It may well be that these and other such similarities point to a main pantheon of gods common to the mother tribe of all Celtic peoples in their collective past.

Modron and Mabon

There is only one goddess name that has any direct literary connection with Avalon. From *Trioedd Ynys Prydein* (the Welsh Triads), a compendium of lore and genealogy, we learn that Modron, daughter of Avallach, is the mother of Mabon—an associate of Arthur and the imprisoned youth of *Culhwch and Olwen*. Avallach is said to be an Otherworldly king who dwelt upon Glastonbury Tor, indicating the Divine stature of himself and his daughter. The Welsh Triads also tell us that:

> Owain son of Urien and Mor(fudd) his sister … were carried together in the womb of Modron daughter of Afallach.
> —TRIAD 70, PEN. 50—*TRIOEDD YNYS PRYDEIN*

Later Arthurian legend tells us Morgan le Fay was the wife of King Urien of Wales and the mother of Owain. This overlapping of Modron with Morgan further validates Modron's connection with Avalon, especially in an ancestral role.

Not only is Modron of Avalonian lineage, but she is also the mother of Mabon, the wondrous youth after whom the tales of *The Mabinogi* may be named. *The Mabinogi* is a collection of Welsh mythos thought to have been committed to writing sometime between the twelfth and fourteenth centuries CE and is believed to derive from an ancient, oral tradition. It is interesting to note that while Modron and Mabon do not appear in any of the Four Branches that compose *The Mabinogi* proper, they appear to represent a template after which each of the branches are patterned; indeed, their very names seem to validate this observation. *Modron* means "the mother" and *Mabon* means "the youth," and a major motif that runs through *The Mabinogi* is that of the youth separated from his mother. We have already seen this play out in the story of Mabon found in *Culhwch and Olwen*, a Welsh tale of Arthur often associated with the Four Branches of *The Mabinogi*.

In the first branch, *Pwyll, Prince of Dyfed*, we see Rhiannon's newborn child taken from Her bed by a hideous monster. Fearing for themselves because they fell asleep instead of watching over the baby, Her nurses frame Rhiannon for his murder. She is punished by Her husband Pwyll and forced to serve for seven years as a workhorse, carrying visitors to the court on Her back, and recounting Her tale of loss. In the end, Her child Pryderi is returned to Her and Rhiannon is restored to the throne. In the second branch, *Branwen, Daughter of Llyr*, Branwen suffers great injustice at the hands of Her husband, the King of Ireland. When Bran, Her brother and King of Britain, comes to Her rescue with his war band, Branwen's young son is thrown into a fire, initiating a ferocious battle that all but destroys Ireland and Britain's warriors.

In *Manawydan, Son of Llyr*, the third branch, we again see Rhiannon separated from Pryderi. In this story, he is imprisoned in an enchanted fort, and when Rhiannon tries to release him, She finds Herself captured as well. Manawydan, Rhiannon's second husband, eventually frees them both. In the fourth branch, *Math, Son of Mathonwy*, we see the virgin goddess Arianrhod bear twin boys. One crawls off into the sea, while the other is cared for and raised by his uncle Gwydion. Arianrhod places three prohibitions upon Her second son—refusing him a name, arms, or a wife of the Earth—setting up a tension between mother and son, who eventually gains the name *Lleu* through trickery.

The goddess Blodeuwedd serves as the catalyst that helps Lleu fulfill His Divine destiny, allowing Him to take His place as a god, beside His Divine Mother.

The Tale of Gwion Bach is sometimes included in collections of Welsh mythology along with the Four Branches. In it, the pursuit, devouring, and ultimate transformation of Gwion in the womb of Ceridwen, who then casts him into the sea as the reborn Taliesin, is yet another manifestation of the archetype of Modron and Mabon. In all these tales, the distance between the mother and son is very similar in energy to the Grail quest and the search for the Otherworldly Cauldron. The stories set up a pattern where there is a desire for a reunion between masculine and feminine principles, and an acknowledgment of the pain that exists where no union is to be found. This is echoed in the work of the Avalonian Cycle of Healing, where we seek to bring the darkness of shadow into the light of consciousness.

It is therefore appropriate for us to seek the Goddesses of Avalon in *The Mabinogi* for two reasons. First, this collection of stories represents the surviving body of Celtic British mythology and is worthy of study. Second, the spirit of Modron serves as a bridge between Avalon and the stories of *The Mabinogi*, as evidenced in its relationship to Her son and in the archetypal pattern that runs throughout the Four Branches. In many ways, the amorphous figure of Modron holds the primal feminine energy of the Great Mother Goddess, and can be seen as the collective essence of the Goddesses of Avalon—the five who are cooperatively One.

Decoding *The Mabinogi*

It is imperative to honor these goddesses by studying Their myths, seeking out Their symbolism, and coming to understand the lessons They bring to us. In reading *The Mabinogi*, it is especially important to identify those elements which reflect the patriarchal Christian world in which the stories were written; these have nothing to do with the true essence of the goddesses and the teachings inherent in Their myths.

We must remember that the social standing and privileges of British Celtic women were very different from those of women at the time the stories of *The Mabinogi* were committed to writing. Once we can read the stories of the Welsh goddesses without the filter of medieval mores and Christian philosophy, a very different portrait of Them emerges. The "betraying harlot" becomes the Giver of Sovereignty, free to choose Her mate as She wills, granting kingship to whom She deems best. The "abandoning mother" becomes the Great Teacher and the "devouring witch" is revealed as the Initiatrix into the Mysteries.

The fact that these stories were written down by people outside the original cultural context that revered these figures makes all the difference in the tone of their portrayal and the overall interpretation of story elements. As befits oral tradition, the Divinities of the British Celts did not benefit from having their myths written down by those who worshiped Them. We are not inheritors of an intact tradition, and must look between the lines to discover symbols that have made the transition from oral to written form. It is for this reason that we must immerse ourselves in studying Celtic culture so that we may piece the bigger picture together and reclaim what we can.

Avalonian Cosmology

Just as the cyclic patterns of the universe repeat in all aspects of creation, the Great Cycle is reflected in the cosmology of Avalon. Manipulating the matrix of the All into its various forms, collecting energies and transforming them into the thread of infinite manifestation, we see the Goddesses of Avalon working through the mechanism of what we have come to know as the Divine Spindle.

One of the most universal symbols of women's work, the spindle is an apt archetypal resonance for a female-centered cosmological para-

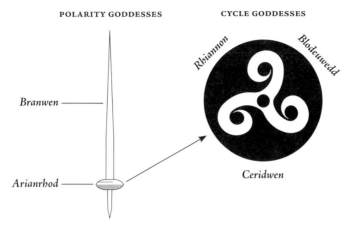

Rhiannon

Blodeuwedd

Branwen

Arianrhod

Ceridwen

The Divine Spindle

digm. It is a tool that transforms raw materials into a basic resource for creation: the cyclic pattern that gives form to energy, creating the thread out of which the warp and weft of all life is created. The central axis of the spindle serves as the focus around what spins is concentrated. Surrounding and grounding this action is the whorl, the circular object that transforms raw substance into a usable form. The Cycle, therefore, is the Universal Whorl—that which changes and is itself unchanged.

Following this pattern, the Avalonian cosmology can be represented in this way:

THE SPINDLE: the long central axis—is Branwen, the fixed and steady center.

THE WHORL: is Arianrhod—movement around stillness, embodying the Cycle and yet not of it.

THE CYCLE GODDESSES: Blodeuwedd, Rhiannon, and Ceridwen— divide the Cyclic Whorl into thirds, three being the number of physical manifestation and the Celts' sacred Triad of Existence. Each of these three goddesses presides over a corresponding aspect of the Cycle, each third transforming into the next in an ever-shifting continuum.

It is the motion of the Whorl, impelled by the spark of creation and through the lessons of its three aspects, which fuels the transformation of all that rides the Cycle. The female aspect of the Divine thus transforms the amorphic essence of the universe into a specific pattern—as the Kabalah teaches—the creation of form from force.

The Spindle of Transformation can only work the materials presented to it; it cannot determine, therefore, whether it spins rough wool or golden thread. Learning to consciously ride the Cycle gives us an opportunity to affect the degree of our transformation because it is we who provide the energetic materials to be spun. The harder we work and the deeper we look, the more profound the change we can accomplish; the depth of our efforts is what determines the quality and quantity of the fiber we have gathered to be spun. The more thread we have at our disposal, the greater the tapestry we can weave. The finer the filament we have created, the more elegant the stitch work we will be able to execute. Our choices determine our changes; the universe can only magnify that which we set into motion ourselves.

In general, therefore, following the paradigm of the Divine Spindle, we can sum up the functions of each Avalonian goddess in this manner:

The Cycle Goddesses: Blodeuwedd, Rhiannon, and Ceridwen

These goddesses are concerned directly with personal process. They advise and support us on our journey to wholeness through issue resolution and alignment with Cycle. Blodeuwedd is the Lady of Initiation. She calls us to cast off the garments of expectation and to peer into the darkness of the self to find and ultimately live our inner truth. She teaches us to fly where others would see us grounded. Rhiannon is the Lady of Manifestation. She calls us to stand strong regardless of the challenges to our truth. She teaches us to ask for what we need, and grants abundant and loving support to carry us through our dark times.

Ceridwen is the Lady of Transformation. She calls us to enter into our darkness to seek out the seeds of our wholeness. She teaches us that the only path to wisdom is through trial and experience. In Her Cauldron, the mysteries of death and rebirth are revealed, and we emerge to initiate the process once more. We ride the Wheel with our newfound insight and understanding, so that we may illuminate the next phase of our journey with what we have learned.

The Polarity Goddesses—Arianrhod and Branwen

These goddesses are concerned with creating the fabric of existence; Arianrhod is the weaver and Branwen is the web. Together, they represent the interplay of force and form, the active and passive essences that are the primary energetic differentiations of the All. Holding the energy of the active principle, Arianrhod is the Great Teacher. She is the embodiment of the Wheel, yet not Herself subject to it. She is the force of bound and rebound, the karmic Lesson Bringer that brings the universe into balance. All cycles and time are within Her realm of influence. Arianrhod is the source of Awen, the Divine spark of Inspiration, although it is through Ceridwen that Awen is bestowed.

Holding the energy of the passive principle, Branwen is the embodiment of Sovereignty and is the Guardian of Avalon. She is the whole, the center, the *axis mundi*. She is the goddess of the land made manifest, as well as its spiritual essence. On Avalon, Branwen was primarily consulted in matters dealing with Her realm—that is, concerning the full tapestry of Avalon, rather than the individual stitches. She is the goddess of the grand scheme of things, the broader perspective that allows the greater patterns to be revealed.

The Avalonian Pantheon

We who walk the path of Avalon primarily work with the Cycle Goddesses, riding the wheel of personal growth and evolution. This work is the *Service to the Self*, coming to understand ourselves so that we may come into our wholeness. By embracing this rarifying process of issue resolution, we progress into greater clarity and deeper understanding of our potential, our life purpose, and ourselves. The work of the Cycle never ends; we are constantly in progress, always unfolding.

It is then that the lessons of Arianrhod come to us, through the Cauldron of Ceridwen that holds the Cycle in its depths. Arianrhod will set our tasks before us when we are ready to embrace them; to hear Her clearly, we need to have bypassed the twin pitfalls of fear and ego. The work of Arianrhod is that of *Service to our Sisters*, for our work not only brings change and growth to us as individuals, but it is through acting in this world that we also catalyze growth and change in others. The deeper mysteries of the Avalonian Tradition are revealed through this service.

Service to Avalon is the work of the goddess Branwen, and necessitates a high degree of clear self-knowledge, a strong foundation in the Tradition gained through the teachings of Arianrhod, and a calling to selfless service. Working with Branwen means being concerned with the greater whole, almost never addressing the individual. Concerned with the totality of Her realm, Branwen brings large-scale awareness and the revealed wisdom of the full tapestry.

While all five goddesses have correspondences with the Landscape and the Cycle, the majority of the work of the Cycle of Healing is done with the three Cycle goddesses—Blodeuwedd, Rhiannon, and Ceridwen—leaving the two Polarity goddesses—Arianrhod and Branwen—to provide periodic "big picture" insight into the pattern and the whole, respectively. It is for this reason that the Cycle goddesses predominate during the turning of the wheels of moon and sun, while the deep reflective work of the Polarity goddesses sees Them honored during very specific lunar events—Arianrhod at times of full lunar eclipse, and Branwen during the Blue Moon, which occurs every three years and is reckoned using its original definition as being the second full moon during the sun's transit of an astrological sign.

Numerologically, five is the number of the quest and three is the number of physical manifestation; both numbers have powerful Avalonian associations and represent different approaches to the work. While exploring the landscape in search of the wisdom of the Cauldron and at the heart of the Apple, it is appropriate to connect with and gain experience from all five Ladies through Immrama. As we quest for the grail of our personal Sovereignty, the fivefold scheme provides us with the ability to map out the Avalonian archetype, seeking to understand the lay of the land and the geography of the soul.

Yet, when riding the Cycle for personal growth and evolution, we use the primary perspective of the Threefold. The whorl of the Divine Spindle represents the Cycle goddesses as it spins the transformation of the individual. Present, but outside of the sphere of the day-to-day personal growth tended by the three Cycle goddesses, the Polarity goddesses guide the motion of the Spindle and hold its still center, providing insight into the whole and the understanding of the great pattern.

Although there is a specific structure and path of progression to working with these Ladies, it is important to not equate work being done and goddesses being served with a hierarchy of achievement. It is not an indication of spiritual accomplishment or level of ability within the tradition to be working with, say, Arianrhod rather than Blodeuwedd. Attachment to such ideas is counterproductive to one's growth and is a function of ego rather than spirit. There will be women for whom service to Ceridwen and the work of the Cycle will be their spiritual calling. Others will feel the steady hand of Branwen on their shoulders. There is no meaning in this beyond the path of service to which each woman has been called.

Let us begin our journey to understanding the nature and lessons of these powerful allies on our path to Sovereignty. What follows is a brief overview of each of the five Avalonian goddesses as they relate to the Avalonian Cycle of Healing, providing resources for further study and important correspondences that will help foster a relationship with the Lady of the Land.

The Ladies of Avalon

Rhiannon

AVALONIAN LANDSCAPE: The Red Spring

AVALONIAN CYCLE OF HEALING: Station of Descent

SACRED TIMES

Cycle of the Sun: Full moon before Gwyl Awst to full moon before Calan Gaeaf*

Cycle of the Moon: Waxing gibbous to waning gibbous (tenth night after the dark moon through the seventh night after the full moon)

Cycle of the Stars: House of Cancer to house of Libra (cardinal to cardinal)—The Changer

MYTHOLOGICAL SOURCES: *The Mabinogi—Pwyll, Prince of Dyfed* and *Manawydan, Son of Llyr*

Rhiannon is a powerful ancestress who holds the key that allows passage between worlds. Hers is the Silver Branch that calls the seeker to the Otherworld. Through Her, we pass into the Beyond. The song of

---

*Note: Each Cycle goddess (Rhiannon, Ceridwen, and Blodeuwedd) presides over four full lunar cycles, remaining in ascendance until the night of the full moon that begins the next goddess' run of moons. For example, Blodeuwedd's time begins at the full moon after Gwyl Mair/Imbolc, when Ceridwen's time comes to a close, and ends on the night when Rhiannon's time begins, at the full moon before Gwyl Awst/Lughnasadh.

Her birds lulls our souls to sleep—opening us to receive unconscious wisdom as we enter that which lies within.

Riding out from the Otherworld on a pure white horse, Rhiannon's face is veiled, representing the inner mysteries. Though we may seek to obtain this knowledge, the object of our quest will forever elude us until we can ask for that which we desire. Verbalizing our intention to walk the path leading to our inner Sovereignty is the beginning of the work—and the universe stops to listen.

To lift Rhiannon's veil we must seek the Divine Queen within. Unhindered by illusion, we must connect with our inner essence to reveal the truth about the self. To reveal the beauty of what lies beneath, we must remove the masks forged by our fears, wounds, and by the expectations of others. Often, we must endure much to hold fast to our authenticity, and Rhiannon teaches that no burden borne of truth will ever be too great.

Pulling back the golden veil, we strip away consciousness, and with intention, enter the realm of the unconscious. Rhiannon guides us into the Otherworld, sitting astride the dark and light halves of the Cycle—the dark and light halves of the self. Descent into the unknown is the first step in the quest for wholeness. With trust, we lift the Apple of Wisdom to our lips—not knowing if it will be sweet or sour, pure or poisoned—and take the first bite.

INVOCATION TO RHIANNON

Holy Rhiannon, Lady of the Otherworld, fill me with your boundless love and endless compassion. Great Queen, teach me to ask for that which I need most and to endure the trials set before me on the path to obtaining that which I most desire. Nurturing Mother, help me to bear my burdens with strength and grace so that, empowered and empowering, I may serve others in turn.

Ceridwen

AVALONIAN LANDSCAPE: The Tor

AVALONIAN CYCLE OF HEALING: Station of Confrontation

SACRED TIMES

> *Cycle of the Sun*: Full moon of Calan Gaeaf to full moon of Gwyl Mair
>
> *Cycle of the Moon*: Last quarter to dark moon (seventh night after the full moon to the night of the dark moon)
>
> *Cycle of the Stars*: House of Scorpio to house of Aquarius (Fixed to Fixed)—The Unchanged

MYTHOLOGICAL SOURCES: *The Tale of Gwion Bach; Hanes Taliesin*

The goddess Ceridwen is the keeper of the Cauldron of Inspiration—the pearl-rimmed vessel from which all knowledge can be obtained. In the dark abyss of Her Cauldron, Ceridwen brews the Graal of wisdom—a powerful potion that requires much time and many components. When complete, the liquid will yield three potent drops containing all wisdom—the rest is a poison that cracks the vessel open. We must drink of this cauldron to obtain the three-fold gift found in the shadow's darkness.

Ceridwen teaches us that we can transform the darkness within us into the greatest of beauty though obtaining the illumination of Wisdom. This transformation is not without its price; we must change ourselves on every level and a part of us must die so that we may be truly reborn in wisdom. The Draught of Illumination is brewed only by the distillation of the self—that seeking of our inner truths mired in the poison of shadow. Connecting with these energies causes us to break our vessels open, catalyzing the death of our old selves and the freedom of our truths from outmoded perspectives and limitations of our beings.

Through this alchemical process we gain the Three Rays of Awen—the triple illumination that activates the dormant seeds of wisdom within us. Once obtained, these seeds must be incubated and brought to the surface, breaking through the once-fallow ground to sprout with new potential for a bountiful harvest. It is only when we allow our old selves to be consumed by Ceridwen that we can be born anew.

Invocation to Ceridwen

Holy Ceridwen, Lady of the Cauldron, fill me with Your streams of illumination so that I may find the depth of my vessel and test the true nature of my mettle. White Sow, teach me the art of transformation, that I may come to embrace the changes that bring me ever back into Your womb to be reborn again—ever in pursuit of all wisdom. Sacred Muse, inspire me to peer into the utter darkness of my limitations that I may find the fairest one of all—the Divine potential of my soul.

Blodeuwedd

AVALONIAN LANDSCAPE: The White Spring

AVALONIAN CYCLE OF HEALING: Station of Emergence

SACRED TIMES

Cycle of the Sun: Full moon after Gwyl Mair to full moon after Calan Mai

Cycle of the Moon: New moon to first quarter (night after the dark moon through the tenth night after the dark moon)

Cycle of the Stars: House of Pisces to house of Gemini (Mutable to Mutable)—The Changed

MYTHOLOGICAL SOURCES: *The Mabinogi—Math, Son of Mathonwy; Hanes Blodeuwedd*

Blodeuwedd is both Flower Bride and owl of wisdom—She who blossoms by day and hunts by night. Leaving the shade of the Otherworld behind, Blodeuwedd dances into the returning dawn to don Her blooming mantle of rebirth. Her energy rejuvenates the land, granting

Sovereignty to those She deems worthy. Rejecting the confines created by the expectations of others, it is the choice to live Her truth that causes Blodeuwedd to trade Her fragile petals for a feathered cloak of Her own design.

Sharp-taloned and keen-eyed, the transformed Blodeuwedd helps us see through the shadow's darkness so that we may grip tight to that which we wish to reclaim and all that we wish to become. No wilting flower, Her owl aspect is filled with wisdom only found through liberating the authentic self from the fetters of external influences and the parts we are expected to play.

Having faced the challenges of the shadow, and uncovered the gifts that lie within the deepest depths of the self, we too must return into the light in order to actualize the promise and potential unearthed in the darkness. Like Blodeuwedd, a coat of expectation is overlaid upon our person, and we are consigned to repeat our outmoded patterns of limitation and to perform the roles demanded of us in our daily life—unless we consciously choose otherwise.

In the wake of the renewal that comes with the Light Half of the Cycle, we are faced with a choice: to manifest the authentic woman found deep within, or to remain in the roles others would see us fulfill. With the choice to be true to the self comes wisdom gained, earning our spiritual wings for flight and lifting us above all that we have been. Our perspective shifts and our eyes become owl-wide, granting us the ability to see the truth through the shroud of the darkness that once hindered our sight.

Invocation to Blodeuwedd

Holy Blodeuwedd, Lady of Nine Flowers, fill me with Your
blessings of renewal and the joy of empowered flight. Flower-Faced
One, teach me the power of my choices so that I may embrace
my authentic self, even in the face of others' expectations. Keen-
Eyed Hunter in the Night, help me see past the illusion-shrouded

darkness, that my eyes may stay focused on the essence of my being, my sharp talons never losing their grip upon the Truth.

Arianrhod

AVALONIAN LANDSCAPE: Modron's Mound

AVALONIAN CYCLE OF HEALING: Station of Resolution

SACRED TIMES

Cycle of the Sun: All time

Cycle of the Moon: Full lunar eclipse

Cycle of the Stars: Band of the zodiac

MYTHOLOGICAL SOURCE: *The Mabinogi—Math, Son of Mathonwy*

The goddess Arianrhod is the Lady of the Silver Wheel, and She Who Wears the Northern Crown. From Her starry fortress, Arianrhod oversees the turning of the Great Cycle and maintains the balance of the universe. She is the Mother of our unfolding and the Lesson Bringer who presents challenges that help us to reveal our inherent Divinity. Hers is not the cruel hand of fate, rather She is the Great Teacher who offers us the opportunity to repay our soul debt and bring our essence back into balance.

Beholden to no man and completely Sovereign within Herself, Arianrhod is the Virgin Mother, bearing sons of sea and sun—of the shadow and the self. Dylan of the Waters is born complete, and returns to the depths of the sea. He is the sense of Divinity immersed in the unconscious of us all. Her other son is not yet fully formed, signifying our need to develop the consciousness of our Divinity which, once complete, will make our souls shine like the sun. To aid in this growth, Arianrhod places three *geas*, or taboos, upon this second son, who would come to be known as *Lleu Llaw Gyffes*, that he must surmount in order to come fully into his Godhood.

In the same way, Arianrhod turns us on Her wheel and spins us into wholeness. The trials She lays before us help us to birth ourselves—inspiring us to move past our limitations to achieve inner Sovereignty. At times, this testing may seem cruel, but it is the universe providing us with an opportunity to manifest our true selves. Through Arianrhod, we pass through the triple rite of passage wherein we gain our names—by answering the call to authenticity; our arms—by overcoming the fears that keep us from being who we are; and a partner not of this earth—by establishing a strong relationship with our higher selves and with the Divine.

We must take up the challenges of Arianrhod if we want to fulfill our highest potential, for no one can change us but ourselves. She is the spark that impels our self re-creation, but only we can bring ourselves to our destinies.

Invocation to Arianrhod

Holy Arianrhod, Lady of the Heavens, fill me with your strength of purpose and ability to catalyze change. Silver Wheel, teach me to honor the ebb and flow of my personal process and become able to recognize the gifts that lie at the heart of life's most difficult lessons. Northern Crown, help me weave the tapestry of my soul anew, filled with the spark of Awen that conquers all shadow, as I walk the cyclic labyrinth leading me to Your sacred Presence.

Branwen

AVALONIAN LANDSCAPE: The Island of Avalon

AVALONIAN CYCLE OF HEALING: Station of Integration

SACRED TIMES

Cycle of the Sun: The now

Cycle of the Moon: The Blue Moon (second full moon in a sun sign)

Cycle of the Stars: The Pole Star

MYTHOLOGICAL SOURCE: *The Mabinogi—Branwen, Daughter of Llyr*

Branwen is the embodiment of Sovereignty and the Soul of the Land. As such, She sits at the Heart of the Avalonian Tradition. She is the Sacred Center found where the Worlds overlap and all realms of being can be accessed. Lady of Two Islands, Branwen is the voice of the unconscious as well as the response of the conscious self. When the two are working in harmony we obtain the torc of Sovereignty, for we are living in partnership with the self.

Metaphorically, Branwen and Her brother Bran are two parts of the same whole, the white raven and the black—the spiritual and the physical. He is the King of the Island of the Mighty; She is King-Maker, bestowing Sovereignty to the King of Ireland. Her very being is a unifying force, bringing peace through marriage to both island nations. When Her husband mistreats and imprisons Her, Branwen trains a starling to make Her brother aware of Her plight, and He, Her other self, responds to Her needs, leading a party to rescue Her.

At the end of Her tale, Branwen dies of a broken heart caused by the carnage resulting from Her rescue. Yet, Hers is the Cauldron of Rebirth, bringing together the individual parts in the struggle to forge a new perspective of self, shining in its wholeness. Merging with the Unconscious once more, She returns to her silent guardianship of the Land. As we move through each turn of the Cycle, our battle for wholeness further opens our heart, thereby allowing a greater revelation of the actualized Center.

Branwen has chosen to reveal Herself through myth not as the fully actualized Center, but as an example to all women needing to walk down their personal paths to empowerment. Immensely compassionate, Branwen understands the reality of women's struggles—the sorrow and joy, the heartbreak and triumph, the bondage and freedom. It is through these trials that we come to find the seat of our souls, and claim the throne of Sovereignty that is our birthright. When we have at last mastered the self, and come fully into our power, we too shall sit in the still, quiet center of our queenship.

INVOCATION TO BRANWEN

Holy Branwen, Lady of Two Islands, fill me with your steadfast grace and radiating beauty. White Raven, teach me to listen to the voice within, that I may move through my challenges and bridge the divide between sorrow and healing—between pain and wholeness. Sovereign Queen, may every heartbeat fill me with the unshakable knowledge that You are within me, and I within You; I need but listen within the depths of all silences to hear the starling's call—and awaken.

13

CONNECTING WITH
THE LADY OF THE LAND

The three foundations of Spirituality: Hearth as altar, work as worship, and service as sacrament.

CELTIC TRIAD

IN THE SAME WAY WE ride the Wheel of the Year, the Cycle reveals itself to us monthly through the moon's phases. Harnessing this energy every month is where our inner work originates. We see echoes of the greater cycle reverberating in the smaller one, pushing us through our day-to-day revelations, building up to greater insights that come through the work of the yearly cycle, culminating in the cycle of our lives when our time here is through. Indeed, even as we cycle around the incarnational wheel, the same energies move through and over us until we finally attain ultimate wholeness—union with the Divine.

At the full moon, women of Avalon come together in ritual, seeking the wisdom of the Goddess to aid and guide the inner process. In the light of the moon's fullness, the answers are revealed, and the work of the month is presented. As the lunar energy wanes, we travel deeply into ourselves, seeking information we need and following guidance we received at the full moon. This journey leads us deeper within ourselves, until the moon is fully obscured and the Mysteries guard themselves.

In solitude, we look into the mirror at the dark moon. Just as we harness the full moon's energy to connect with the Goddess in our community of sisters, at the dark moon we find Her deep within ourselves. The power of the moon turns inward at this time, and so too does women's wisdom. From the dark we turn again toward the light and the promise of renewal that is the new moon, that sliver in the sky sprouting new growth from darkness. As she waxes, we too begin to manifest what we have learned from our inner questing, and our changes become apparent as we work to integrate our newfound wisdoms into our lives. We return at the full, bringing what we have learned and accomplished since our last dance beneath her silver light, asking for the next step on our ever-winding journey home.

The cycle of the year, the cycle of the moon, the cycle of our lives, and the cycle of wisdom all weave the same pattern of Descent, Confrontation, Emergence, Resolution, and Integration. As we align ourselves with these natural rhythms, we will find that our work parallels the energies of the present point of cycle. As we begin the process at the third quarter moon or Calan Gaeaf (Samhain), the Station of Descent, we enter into the Dark Half of the Cycle, focusing upon what hinders us and prevents us from being all that we are. The work continues as we come to the dark moon or Gwyl Mair (Imbolc), the Station of Confrontation. At this darkest point of the Cycle, the shadow is revealed.

We take the hard-earned understanding of our pain and the previously unconscious motivations to which it relates, up into the light with us, to the Emergence into the Light Half of the Cycle at Calan Mai (Beltane) or the first quarter moon. Here, we now plant the seeds of light, that wondrous part of ourselves which will take the place of the darkness we toiled to uproot. Resolution at Gwyl Awst (Lughnasadh) and at the full moon sees the seeds come into fruition. Healing has taken place, and a new energy has come from this Transformation—an energy which will support the genuine self. The Cycle repeats itself as we peel away a new layer and work towards the Descent with new insight and new tools at our disposal.

Connecting with the Goddesses of Avalon

In the Avalonian Tradition, we come before the Goddess at the full moon to seek Her guidance in our work and support through our process. At the dark moon, we look into Her mirror to see what lies beyond the limitations of our sight, driven unremittingly to lift the veil of illusion. The Goddess is our soul's greatest resource and most constant advocate, helping us to stay the course on the path to wholeness. Through ritually empowering our Immram work and harnessing the power of the Avalonian Cycle of Healing, we can make real and meaningful contact with the Ladies of Avalon—seeking the wisdom of the Cauldron found both in our souls and in the landscape of the Sacred Isle itself.

The Goddesses of Avalon are honored at specific points in the Cycle and are associated with particular places in the Sacred Landscape. Depending upon where we are in the the Cycle, we can choose to connect with the goddess who oversees the energy of that Station by performing an Immram at a time and to a place on Avalon corresponding with Her energy. For example, it is recommended to begin aligning ourselves with the Cycle of Healing starting at the Station of Descent. Therefore, we could perform an Immram to the Red Spring during the third quarter moon, in order to connect with Rhiannon. Once in Her presence, we can ask for guidance about the parts of our soul process relevant to the energy of the Station of Descent—uncovering outmoded patterns that hold us back, revealing illusions we have accepted as truths about ourselves, and discovering the true the nature of our shadow.

Alternatively, we can choose to align with the energies of the cycle of the sun, working with the goddess that corresponds to the position we currently occupy in the Wheel of the Year. Doing this will aid our merging with the power of the Great Cycle, and we will surely find that in time, our personal energies will come to mirror the unfolding essence of the natural order. The Cycle has no real starting place so it is possible to begin Cycle of Healing work at any point; we can use the self-reflective questions associated with each Station as a guide to determine our work's focus at any position in the Avalonian Cycle of Healing. However we choose to approach the work, the important thing is that we engage in this transformational process and build a relationship with the Lady and the Land.

Connecting with the Goddesses of Avalon in this fashion is a wonderful opportunity for us to learn more about these sacred matrons and about Avalon itself. We can use time spent in Their presence to inquire about the lessons of Their stories and to discover Their symbols, totems, sacred herbs, and the appropriate ways to honor Them. Working with the Ladies of Avalon can also facilitate our ability to delve deeply into the Sacred Landscape, allowing us to learn more about how these holy sites were used by the women of Avalon.

It is important to remember that the unasked question cannot be answered. The more time spent traveling to the Holy Isle and seeking the company of the Divine, the stronger our connection to the goddesses and the archetypal realm of Avalon will become. As with any discipline, it will take time to hone our skills, but in the long run, our efforts will pay off bountifully. This discipline is seen in its highest manifestation by a commitment to connecting with the Goddesses of Avalon through regular ritual.

Solitary Avalonian Ritual

By definition, ritual is the repetition of a series of actions with the intention to obtain a specifically desired result. In many ways, it is like performing a science experiment. Specific ingredients are mixed in proper proportions and subjected to particular actions. The yield is the sought-after result. The ability to reproduce results is the keystone of science; that is, something is considered scientifically true if the results can be empirically measured and repeated. In many ways, therefore, preparing for ritual is as important as performing it.

The ultimate objective of the Avalonian Tradition is to birth the authentic self; to peel away the masks we wear and shed the roles we play born of others' expectations. As a reflection of this, we come before the Goddess in ritual without makeup or fancy adornment, save for those items which hold significance to the work. We choose to garb ourselves in robes and hooded cloaks of dark blue and black, to help us align our energies with the deep magnetic nature of the Divine Feminine, in resonance with the historic descriptions of Celtic Priestesses. Ideally, these cloaks are made of natural fibers such as wool and linen in order to approximate the clothing native Britons would have worn.

Together, these aid in our linking to the Avalonian archetype—the similarity to the dress of the Priestesses of the Holy Isle. Everything about these vestments, from the color to the fabric, is energetically in synchrony with our roles as Sisters of Avalon. The jewelry we choose to wear in ritual should also reflect this energy. Since we work primarily with feminine lunar energies, silver is best. The stones, forms, and images of our adornments should reflect our personal work, represent Avalon and the Goddess, or be another personal power symbol.

Ritual garb is a powerful tool that facilitates a shift in consciousness—of the self and others—from the secular world to sacred space. Enrobing oneself in clothing and jewelry set aside for ritual use makes a powerful energetic statement. With each ritual, the attire we choose becomes more and more empowered with the magickal essence of our workings. In time, the simple act of dressing in ritual clothing will cause a shift in consciousness, reducing the time and energy needed to complete the metamorphosis from the mundane to the magickal.

It is recommended that you not allow other people to touch your ritual objects, clothing, or jewelry so that energy building up and empowering these objects (keyed into your person and your work) are not dissipated or diluted by others' energies. A good way to store your ritual items is to wrap them in silk, a natural energetic insulator. A silk cloth will prevent any charge from fading.

Before beginning this or any working, it is important to prepare your ritual space and to set your intention. Ensure you have all your needed supplies, that you have turned off the telephone, and have asked people living in a shared space to give you some personal time—these steps are crucial to your working's success. If working outdoors, you must be sure that your clothing is appropriate to the weather conditions; nothing can break ritual concentration more than being too hot or too cold, or wearing inappropriate footwear. Once mundane concerns have been addressed, move forward into creating your sacred space.

The Avalonian Altar

The altar is the focus of ritual in many cultures and belief systems around the world. It is a powerful archetype that is universal in its purpose; a place set apart that acts as a connection between profane and sacred. Very often, this symbolic sacred center included a representation of the *axis mundi*—the world axis—often a pole, tree, or central standing stone; it acted as the focus of the village or homestead. Therefore, when constructing an altar, you are creating a center around which your ritual universe revolves.

Setting up a ritual altar is a powerful devotional experience; time and care should be taken to consciously collect or create objects that will occupy symbolic space on your altar. Ultimately, your altar is an expression of your desire to bridge worlds and connect with the Divine; it should reflect your passion, personality, and the fruits of efforts you have made to understand yourself, Avalon, and her goddesses. What follows is an outline of suggested components for your Avalonian altar. As always, your Sovereign self should have the final say on what you include in your sacred space.

1. Representations of the Three Realms

As Celtic cosmology takes a tripartite view of creation, these facets of the whole are represented on our altar:

> THE SILVER BRANCH: an apple branch with nine silver bells hung along its length, it symbolizes the Upper World or the Druidic circle of Ceuguent. The Silver Branch is what calls us to the

quest. It is the desire of the priestess self to actualize its potential and come into complete awareness of the Divine within. The creation of the Silver Branch as a ritual tool should be done with consciousness and clear purpose. It is helpful to craft this tool during the waxing moon, imbuing it with the intention of it opening the self to Avalon's pathways, resonating over the lake of the spirit to part the mists of illusion.

THE TREE OF LIFE: symbolizing the Middle World or the Druidic Circle of Abred, it is the World Tree that bridges the Three Realms. Represented by a woody plant or small tree on indoor altars, or a fully grown tree—preferably apple—outdoors, the Tree of Life allows us to journey to the Upper and Lower Worlds, taking the Otherworldly energies found in the unconscious Lower World and the transpersonal Upper World and bring them into consciousness in the heart of the self. We can use the wisdoms found above and below to aid in effecting soul change and personal transformation in the here and now.

THE CAULDRON OF INSPIRATION: embodying the aspect of the Lower World or the Druidic Circle of Gwynfyd, the cauldron is a hanging or three-legged iron vessel representing the regenerative and creative powers of the Goddess. It is the source of the wisdom that lies deep within the self beneath the inner waters of the unconscious. The cauldron, holding the essence of the power of the Divine Feminine, is the ultimate object of the soul's quest and a potent tool of transformation. Make an infusion or strong tea of the herb vervain (*Verbena officinalis*), an herb of Sight, by adding two tablespoons of vervain to sixteen ounces of water that has sat for five minutes after boiling. After it is cooled and strained, pour the infusion into the cauldron in preparation for use in this solitary ritual. (NOTE: *If you are pregnant, do not use vervain; make an infusion of catnip* [Nepata cataria] *instead.*

Although both vervain and catnip are herbs that are traditionally taken internally, always check with a health care professional before ingesting any herbal product.)

2. The Apple

Sliced horizontially through its center to reveal the five-pointed star within, the apple is an evocative symbol to keep on your altar, recalling the five Goddesses of Avalon and the five Stations of the Avalonian Cycle of Healing. As we have seen, the apple itself is an ancient archetype of women's wisdom and is one of the most vital symbols of Avalon, the Holy Island that bears its name.

3. The Offering Bowl

Made of whatever material or shape you wish, the offering bowl or plate holds a gift which will be left outside after the ritual working in an energy exchange that honors the local spirits, elementals, and ancestors. This offering can take many forms, including: food, libation, herbs, and stones.

4. Incense

Burning incense during a ritual serves a two purposes: it empowers and reinforces the energetic tone you are trying to set through your work, and it acts as an offering to the goddess with whom you are connecting. It is especially effective to create your own incense blends specific to your ritual intention by researching herbs and resins sacred to Avalon and the goddess you wish to honor. Take into consideration the phase of the moon and the energy of the Station you are working through when making your incense. It is always ideal to harvest and dry these herbs yourself, but you can purchase some of them in metaphysical shops or natural food stores. However you obtain the herbs, grind the components with intention using a mortar and pestle and sprinkle the resulting blend over a lit charcoal disk during your ritual working. The lit charcoal should be placed in a ceramic dish filled with sand or in a small iron cauldron kept on your altar just for this purpose. Resources for herbs and incense blends can be found in the appendix.

5. Intention Ribbons

Ranging from coarse homespun to fine linen, scraps of cloth were tied to overhanging tree branches and left as offerings to the spirits and deities of the many sacred wells that dotted the British Isles. These prayer ribbons would carry the prayers, requests, and intentions of pilgrims to the Goddess' ears, empowered by the three Celtic Realms of Land (the tree), Sea (the well), and Sky (the wind). To keep with this humble yet powerful ancient practice, obtain strips of cloth or ribbons to use as a representation of your commitment to the work of the coming lunar cycle as revealed to you during this moon ritual. These ribbons of may be of different colors, reflecting either the tone or energy of the work, or the place in the Cycle it is holding. After working with them, these intention ribbons will be tied to the Tree of Life on your altar. Like those of the pilgrims of the past, they will hang between Worlds, spanning the threshold space, and broadcast our intent by existing in all Three Realms simultaneously.

6. Other

Objects, statuary, tools like a finger labyrinth, or images to connect you to Avalon and the Lady you are working with may also be included on your altar, as simple or elaborate as you wish. The important thing is to ensure that everything you place on your altar serves a purpose and is a reflection of the energy with which you wish to work or connect.

Between the Worlds

After your altar is set up and your ritual intention is clear, you may proceed with this solitary ritual.

1. Entering the Otherworld

Begin your working with nine shakes of the Silver Branch, symbolically embarking upon your journey beyond the Ninth Wave and into the Otherworld. This action marks the transition of consciousness from what is without to the realm of what is within, and from what is mundane to what is sacred.

2. Establishing the Power Breath

Adopt your Power Breath (p. 54) to help move you into ritual stance. Do this for at least three cycles of nine, focusing on the ebb and flow of your inner tides. You should maintain the Power Breath throughout your working.

3. Three Realms Exercise

Perform the Three Realms exercise (beginning on p. 191) in order to cleanse and clear your energy space as well as to expand your consciousness to the Sacred Landscape within and without.

4. Raising the Stones

Establish safe and sacred space around and within you by envisioning yourself surrounded by a circle of nine standing stones. With your breath and intention, will the circle of stones into existence, taking as much time as you need to really feel them solidly around you. It may be helpful to use nine physical stones to mark your circle and use them to tie into the energy of raising the tall standing stones; quartz crystals or Welsh bluestone (the type used to create the inner circle of Stonehenge, and other ancient British megaliths) are particularly good at holding this energy. When you can feel that the stones are strongly around you, use your Silver Branch to trace the circle three times around you in a moonwise (counterclockwise) direction, connecting the tall stones to each other by a web of silvery energy that maintains your space and empowers your working. When the stones are raised, stand in the center and three times chant or speak the following:

THE NINEFOLD BLESSING OF AVALON

Nine times beat the Owl's Wings
Avalon above me
Nine times ride the Shining Mare
Avalon below me
Nine times drink the Cauldron's Brew
Avalon within me
Nine times turn the Silver Wheel
Avalon around me
Nine times sing the Starling's song
Avalon come through me
Nine times spin the Motherline
Avalon behind me
Nine times weave the Priestess Cloak
Avalon before me
Nine times join the Sister's Dance
Avalon beside me
Nine times birth the Blessed Isle
Avalon beyond me

Ninefold blessings surround me
Ninefold Illuminations fill me
Ninefold transformations make me whole

5. Charging the Cauldron

Using the Hermetic principle that like attracts like, lift your arms to the moon—either directly in her light or through the power of visualization—and inhale her feminine energy, filling your aura structure with lunar essence. Envision yourself enrobed in an orb of silvery moonlight—light and sparkling when the moon is full, heavy and magnetic when the moon is dark. When you feel you are completely filled with moon energy, turn your hands down over the cauldron on your altar and discharge all of the energy you have collected into the waiting vessel. Exhale it until you are completely emptied of the moon energy, now condensed into the vervain or catnip infusion. Holding the charged cauldron as you proceed with the ritual Immram to follow will empower your journey and serve as an additional medium of communication with the Lady, as we will see.

6. Chant: Barge of Power

Barge of Power is a powerful chant that helps to open the doorway into the realms of Avalon. It describes the inner journey to the Holy Island and calls upon the energies of the Three Realms—the Power of Land, the Wisdom of Sea, and the Freedom of Sky—to move us through the veil of illusion and across the lake of the Unconscious, until we arrive at last on her shores. Use this chant to help you to pierce the shadowy mists that seek to bar you from recognizing the truth of all that you are, and to help set you on your path to Avalon. Repeat the chant at least three times in your working, and visualize the energies moving through and around you as you move deeper within.

> *Barge of Power, take me to Her shore*
> *Barge of Wisdom, take me to Her shore*
> *Part the mists which blind me*
> *Reclaim the Lake inside me*
> *Barge of Freedom, take me to Her shore*

7. Journeying to Avalon

Holding the charged cauldron to your chest or in your lap, settle into your space and begin the Immram to the Station site aligned with the intention of your work or which is appropriate to honor the goddess at the present point in the yearly cycle.

RED SPRING: Station of Descent, Rhiannon

THE TOR: Station of Confrontation, Ceridwen

WHITE SPRING: Station of Emergence, Blodeuwedd

MODRON'S MOUND: Station of Resolution, Arianrhod

ISLAND OF AVALON: Station of Integration, Branwen

When you reach Avalon on the Barge, call your guide and journey to the part of the island that is your focus for this working, asking to be brought into the Goddess' presence. Arriving at the sacred space, announce yourself, present your request to connect with the Lady, and speak the reason for your journey; make your intentions known. When you feel the time is right, speak the invocation to the goddess with whom you are seeking to connect (found in chapter 13), or better yet—create your own. Spend time in contemplative silence, awaiting Her arrival and keeping yourself focused and open.

When She arrives at the sacred site, acknowledge Her presence with an outward display of honor and respect—a bow, or perhaps a deep curtsey. The Goddess may appear to you in physical form, in the guise of one of Her sacred animals, or in another form entirely, so keep your mind open to any possibilities. Take the time now to ask for Her guidance and for any information that will help you on your journey of unfolding. Remember to ask specific questions and wait for a reply.

You may receive your answers in many ways—you may hear Her voice in your head, see image or symbols play before your eyes, or even feel an awareness or knowing unassociated with any physical sense. As with all things, it may take time for you to build your discernment and sharpen your receptivity to be clear enough to be conscious of information the Goddess has for you. Do not be discouraged if you meet any challenges in obtaining information, for the universe will ensure that you will receive all you need in a perceivable manner, be it in dreams or as a symbol you encounter multiple times throughout the day. Suspend your disbelief and be open.

When your time spent in communion comes to a close, ask the Goddess to bless the waters of the cauldron you are holding and imbue it with Awen, so that by scrying in its depths, you may receive additional information and insight about your work. When She is done and you feel that it is time for your communication to end, thank the Goddess for Her presence and assistance. Once more, make an obvious sign of respect to honor the Divine Lady, and bid Her farewell with the following, or a line of your own creation:

It is with Love that I have called You, and with Love I now release You
May I serve You in all that I do, and may everything I do serve You.

Watch and feel Her energies gently take leave of you and the sacred site before you. Spend some time in silent contemplation of all that you have seen and experienced. When ready, your guide leads you back through the orchard and to the shores of the lake, where the Barge of Avalon awaits you. Turn once more to face the island, and thank the Lady and all the guardians of this sacred space for supporting your work and allowing you to visit. Bid your guide farewell, and climb aboard the Barge to complete your journey to the other side of the lake, bringing with you the memory of all that has come before to the here and the now.

NOTE: *When first performing this solitary ritual, you may wish to skip the next two steps and move directly to partake of the Graal of Wisdom. When you have accumulated experience and can perform this ritual with confidence, add the next two steps to your ritual practice after connecting with the Goddess and returning from Immram.*

8. Scrying in the Cauldron

Use the empowered cauldron to scry for additional information and insights as described on pg. 102, keeping your ritual intention and the experiences from your Immram and communication with the goddess in mind.

9. Cloth of Intention

Take the ribbon that has been waiting on your altar and spend time infusing it with the goal of your work for the coming cycle, guided by the information received from scrying and in Immrama. When it feels strongly charged with your intention, immerse the ribbon in the waters of the cauldron to connect it with your work and the Divine blessings of the Goddess to support you in your process. Tie the wet ribbon on a branch of the Tree of Life. Throughout the coming month, the plant's vital energies will empower your intentions and will serve as a point of connection where that which is above meets that which is below. Keep the ribbon in the tree until your next moon working, when a different ribbon representing the next month's endeavor will replace it.

10. The Graal of Wisdom

Take three sips of the charged and blessed herbal infusion directly from the cauldron, asking that the gifts of Awen and the Triple Illumination of Wisdom be granted you as you embark upon the work of the coming moon cycle. Take the time to feel this sacred liquid enter your body, making note of any energy shifts that may occur. It is indeed a sacrament, recalling the three drops of wisdom culled from the Cauldron of Ceridwen. As it did for Gwion, may it catalyze our own transformation. Pour the remaining liquid as an offering to the plant representing the Tree of Life, asking that it nourish and empower the intentions represented by the focus ribbon tied into its branches.

11. Taking Down the Stones

With intention, ground out the circle by breathing all remaining energies down into the Earth, envisioning as you do the nine standing stones retreating back into the Mother's womb. Visualize the energies rejuvenating the landscape, cleansing and empowering the land. Breathe the circle down until you feel it has been completely grounded and released. Shake the Silver Branch three times to clear any remaining energies, and to mark your return from the ritual journey. In your own words, thank the Goddess, your guide, our Avalonian ancestors, and the energies of the land for their support of your work.

12. Leaving the Offering

Having absorbed the energies and intentions of your ritual, leave your offering dish on your outdoor altar, or bring it outdoors, even if only to place it outside your windowsill. Leave your offering dish overnight or place its contents beneath a tree or bush as a gift of thanks to the local spirits of the land you live on.

13. Journaling

As with all workings, keep a journal of your ritual work, including questions you asked and the answers that came to you. Make note of the kind of information you received, making sure to draw any symbols or describe any images or memories your work brought up. Record the date, time of day, moon phase, weather, where you are in your menstrual cycle, and your emotional state both before and after the ritual. Through journal keeping, patterns will emerge concerning your experience and your personal process. These patterns will provide you with clues that can lead to greater self-understanding and issue resolution, even if the component pieces may not make sense immediately.

It is always inspiring to read through your journal entries every few months to acknowledge your progress and gain new perspective. The ancients adjure us to "Know Thyself." Keeping a journal of your thoughts and insights as you walk the path of your spiritual unfolding is a powerful and empowering way to come into this self-knowledge, and through it, your knowledge of the Goddess and Avalon.

Performing the solitary Avalonian ritual every month at the full and dark moons is a powerful means to connect with the Goddess and receive Her guidance in our work. Acknowledging patterns, gaining insight into the root causes of destructive behaviors, and receiving a plan for manifesting an aspect of the person we wish to become are critical milestones on our journey. However, we can only truly move forward along the path to wholeness by actively participating in our personal process and actively effecting changes in our lives—that is, making choices based on the information we have received, and living in right action.

Establishing a daily discipline of inner work is a powerful support to help you reset the personal energy you have reclaimed and keep the channels of your perceptions clear, so you will begin to see yourself and the world with new eyes. Make a commitment to yourself to spend at least fifteen minutes a day in sacred space, performing the Middle Pillar exercise and the Three Realms working. Practice your Power Breath whenever and wherever you can. Journey to the Island of Avalon at least three times a week, continuing to explore the landscape area associated with the Goddess or Station you are working with, especially through the use of the Avalonian landscape postures. Alternatively, perform Immrama to all the landscape areas each month at their corresponding moon phases, moving around the Cycle from Descent to Integration, to examine the issue you are working on from all sides.

Bring the changes you have made and the further insights you have obtained with you before the Goddess at your next moon ritual. Build the work of the upcoming cycle on the foundation you laid during the last turn of the lunar tide. The more time and energy you put into your soul growth and desire to build a strong relationship with each Lady of the Holy Island, the wider will swing the doorway to the Realms of Avalon. As always, journal everything. It will serve both as a record of your process and progress, and as a way to honor your sacred nature.

Conclusion

AVALON WITHIN

She lives! She lives within us still!
The Holy Well and Spiraled Hill
The Lake, the Barge and mist-hid swans—
Come sing, with joy, of Avalon

—FROM *LAMENT*, JHENAH TELYNDRU

CHOOSING TO VOYAGE ACROSS THE inner lake to the reach the shores of the Island of Avalon is not a decision to be made lightly. Undertaking this Wonder Journey into the heart of the self signals our willingness to cease being a passenger and take our place in the prow of the Barge—parting the mists of illusion and seeking the truth of all that we are.

For there, at the core of our very being, can be found the key to unlocking the treasure of women's wisdom which is both our birthright and our sacred trust. Traveling this inner pathway catalyzes the unfolding of the map that charts our lives' patterns even as we are weaving them, bringing with it the power for us to change our soul's course. The more conscious we become of our inner landscape, the greater becomes our ability to steer the ship of our soul to a place of empowered Sovereignty.

As above, so below. As within, so without. That which we discover on our quest for the Holy Island is intimately entwined with the process of our own souls. There is much to learn about the sacred nature of Avalon and the path of her priestesses in service to the Goddess. Yet, the higher purpose of the journey is to discover the essence of the Lady Within, and come to an initiation into the heart into the Mysteries of Avalon, dwelling only in the souls of those who seek Her. In understanding the one, we gain understanding of the All.

Beyond all our strivings, Immrama, and quests, the true nature of Avalon reveals itself as the Island of Glass—the universal mirror reflecting the truth of our soul's potential and unveiling the beauty of the blossoming forth of the priestess within—our Sovereignty attained and our wholeness in the Goddess realized.

Appendix 1

AWAKENING THE
INNER LANDSCAPE

IN THE SAME WAY THAT the sacred landscape of Avalon holds a vibratory resonance to the transformations of Ceridwen's Cauldron
and the inner process represented by the Avalonian Cycle of Healing,
our personal energy reflects an innate correspondence to this powerful archetypal system. Making positive use of the potential for growth
inherent in these interrelated paradigms empowers our ability to effect
lasting change in our lives, as well as to form an enduring connection to
the Otherworldly realm of Avalon.

Each landscape feature of the Island of Apples has an associated
energy center. Western tradition uses a system of five energy centers
in the body, rather than the seven-chakra system favored by Eastern
spiritual pathways. This pentatonic structure derives from Hermetic
science and Kabalistic philosophy and is reflected in the five-element
system that lies at the foundation of Western thought.

While three and nine are numbers of prime importance in any Celtic pathway, the number five holds great significance in the Avalonian
Tradition as well. We see it manifest in the Five Seeds at the heart of

the Apple of Wisdom, the five goddesses honored on Avalon, the five transformations of Ceridwen's Cauldron, and in the five Stations of the Avalonian Cycle of Healing. We honor the pattern as it reveals itself, both in the landscape without and in that which lies within.

As we work through the Holy Sites of Cycle made manifest in the landscape of Avalon, we will also consider their corresponding elemental energies as they exist within us. Accompanying the description of each of the five energy centers is a list of constructive and destructive expressions of personality traits and attributes related to their elemental qualities. Identifying areas of imbalance can provide important clues that will assist us in understanding where we are in our process, and will guide us in determining where to focus our Immram work in order to bring these energy centers back into balance.

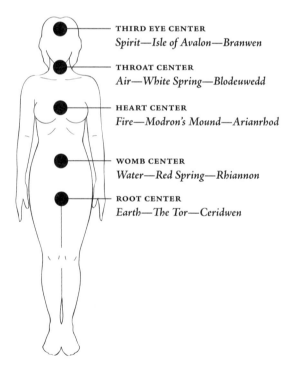

THIRD EYE CENTER
Spirit—Isle of Avalon—Branwen

THROAT CENTER
Air—White Spring—Blodeuwedd

HEART CENTER
Fire—Modron's Mound—Arianrhod

WOMB CENTER
Water—Red Spring—Rhiannon

ROOT CENTER
Earth—The Tor—Ceridwen

Five Energy Centers

Root Center

LANDSCAPE CORRESPONDENCE: The Tor

AVALONIAN CYCLE OF HEALING: Station of Confrontation

The Root Center, located at the base of the spine, is the fertile garden of our souls and keeps us anchored to the physical plane. It is the vehicle of our bodies, and the stable foundation from which all things manifest. Source of abundance and the primal instincts that connect us to this planet and all its living things, the Root Center provides us with the means for survival and the basis for our growth.

Elementally, the Root Center is aligned with the energy of Earth, and corresponds with the sephirah Malkuth on the Kabalistic Tree of Life. It is symbolized in the Western tattwas system by a green square, and holds the vibration of the number ten. The Root Center is ruled by Terra, and in the Avalonian Tradition is seen as the gateway to Physical Manifestation.

Earth-Aligned Aspects of Personality

- *Balanced Earth Attributes*: Grounded, dedicated, loyal, steadfast, persevering, practical, abundant, methodical, dependable, stable, focused, secure, deliberate, patient
- *Imbalanced Earth Attributes*: Stubborn, immovable, materialistic, possessive, envious, greedy, miserly, stuck, limited, literal, shortsighted, narrow-minded, critical

Womb Center

LANDSCAPE CORRESPONDENCE: The Red Spring

AVALONIAN CYCLE OF HEALING: Station of Descent

The Womb Center is the seat of emotion and the portal into the Otherworldly realms. It is the deep well of our memories and the font of our inner wisdom. Ripples of intuition radiate out from this center, a receptive pool that is highly sensitive to even the subtlest energetic shifts, all the while reflecting that which is just below the surface of the Unconscious.

Energetically, the Womb Center is aligned with the element of water, and corresponds with the sephirah Yesod on the Kabalistic Tree of Life. It is symbolized in the Western tattwas system by a blue crescent with its points facing up, and holds the vibration of the number nine. The Womb Center is ruled by the moon, and in the Avalonian Tradition is seen as the Gateway to Women's Mysteries.

Water-Aligned Aspects of Personality

- *Balanced Water Attributes*: Empathetic, intuitive, sensitive, healing, nurturing, protective, emotional, compassionate, receptive, immersive, adaptable, flowing
- *Imbalanced Water Attributes*: Co-dependent, caretaking, overprotective, needy, insecure, hypersensitive, overemotional, irresolute, frequently overwhelmed, martyred, fearful, disorderly, dishonest, secretive, covert

Heart Center

LANDSCAPE CORRESPONDENCE: Modron's Mound
AVALONIAN CYCLE OF HEALING: Station of Resolution

The Heart Center is the seat of the will and its inner flame radiates vital energies. The illuminating hearth fire of Divine inspiration, the Heart Center empowers growth and catalyzes change. The transformational essence of this center grants the courage to enter into the unknown, and bestows the determination to see the process of creation through to its conclusion.

Energetically, the Heart Center is aligned with the element of fire, and corresponds with the sephirah Tiphereth on the Kabalistic Tree of Life. It is symbolized in the Western tattwas system by a red equilateral triangle with its point facing up, and holds the vibration of the number six. The Heart Center is ruled by the sun, and in the Avalonian Tradition is seen as the gateway to the Illuminated Self.

Fire-Aligned Aspects of Personality

- *Balanced Fire Attributes:* Assertive, self-confident, passionate, inspired, determined, vital, energetic, driven, courageous, creative, individualistic, spontaneous, catalytic
- *Imbalanced Fire Attributes:* Willful, reckless, impatient, aggressive, destructive, controlling, egotistical, obsessive, addictive, fanatical, pushy, uncontrollable

Throat Center

LANDSCAPE CORRESPONDENCE: The White Spring
AVALONIAN CYCLE OF HEALING: Station of Emergence

The Throat Center is the seat of intellect and is the portal into the perceptions of the mind. It holds our highest ideals, and is the ultimate source of knowledge. The mechanisms of logic are at work in this center—generating an objective clarity with which to assess all experiences with discernment. The Throat Center holds our awakened consciousness and is dedicated to uncovering the truth wherever it is to be found.

Energetically, the Throat Center is aligned with the element of air, and corresponds with the position of the sephirah Daath on the Kabalistic Tree of Life. It is symbolized in the Western tattwas system by a yellow circle. The Throat Center is ruled by Uranus, and in the Avalonian Tradition is seen as the gateway to the Authentic Self.

Air-Aligned Aspects of Personality

- *Balanced Air Attributes:* Logical, intellectual, idealistic, rational, objective, communicative, social, outgoing, clever, inquisitive, adaptable
- *Imbalanced Air Attributes:* Detached, unaffected, scattered, impractical, verbose, inconsistent, superficial, overly analytical

Third Eye Center

LANDSCAPE CORRESPONDENCE: The Island of Avalon

AVALONIAN CYCLE OF HEALING: Station of Integration

The Third Eye Center is our point of connection with the All. Through this center, we are crowned with the blessings of the Goddess and strive to become fully conscious through the gifts of Her unconditional love. The Third Eye allows us to see through the veil of illusion, bringing into focus the sacred image of our fully actualized self.

Energetically, the Third Eye Center is aligned with the fifth element of Spirit or Aether, and corresponds with the sephirah Kether on the Kabalistic Tree of Life. It is symbolized in the Western tattwas system by a purple oval, and holds the vibration of the number one. The Third Eye Center is ruled by the universe, and in the Avalonian Tradition is seen as the gateway to Connection with the Divine.

Spirit-Aligned Aspects of Personality

- *Balanced Spirit Attributes:* Personal Sovereignty, inner peace, fulfillment, contentment, fully actualized, centered, present, conscious
- *Imbalanced Spirit Attributes:* Disempowered, restless, frustrated, longing, unrealized potential, outwardly focused, distracted, unaware

The Middle Pillar Exercise

The Middle Pillar exercise, a powerful ritual working based upon Kabalistic principles, is an important tool in our quest for self-understanding. The consistent use of this exercise will clear the personal energy field, align and connect our five energy centers, and encourage a sense of inner balance, wholeness, and clarity. The exercise as it is presented here has been adapted from its original form as developed by Israel Regardie; it includes an Avalonian-based focus for the exercise to better tie it into our Avalonian archetypal perspective.

A truly empowering exercise, the Middle Pillar is a cornerstone for our daily devotional work and can be performed anytime there is a need to become centered and connected with our priestess self. It may seem long and complicated at first, but with time and practice, it will become second nature; its cumulative effects on our clarity and perspective will more than convince you of its value in your work. Performing the Middle Pillar exercise before undertaking any ritual or inner work will assist in obtaining a place of centered openness and connection to Divinity.

1. To begin, find your Power Breath. Stand comfortably with your legs hip-distance apart, hands at your sides, palms facing forward.

2. Feel yourself standing in a ray of pure white light, the positive universal energy of the All. Feel a connection between the top of your head and the Source of this light, almost as if it is the only thing that holds you up and keeps you standing.

3. With your breath, begin to pull this energy down through the top of your head as you inhale. Feel it stop at the Third Eye Center, and exhale it through this energy center. Using your breath to pull it down and breathe it out, visualize with each exhalation, your Third Eye getting larger, clearer and more open. Use the symbols, colors, and element associated with this energy center to help you make it as open and active as you can.

4. When you have cycled the energy enough times to sufficiently activate this center as much as you can, take three more breaths through the top of your head into your Third Eye and, as you inhale, bring the energy down into your Throat Center.

5. Exhale the energy you have pulled from your crown and through the Third Eye into your Throat, and exhale the energy out through this center. Continue bringing the energy down and exhaling it out of the Throat until you have fully expanded, cleared and activated this energy center, again using the colors, symbols and element associated with which it is associated. It is important that your visualization include the energetic connection from the universe (the top of your head), through the Third Eye, and down to the Throat. This will serve not only to activate each energy center, but also to clear channels and reinforce communication between them.

6. When you feel your Throat Center is as open and active as possible, take three more breaths through the top of your head, though the Third Eye, to the Throat and then pull the universal energy down as you exhale into your Heart Center.

7. Repeat this process of activating each energy center with your breath and visualization until you have opened and connected all five energy centers (Third Eye, Throat, Heart, Womb, and Root). Don't forget to use the energetic correspondences for each center as you work; when you have become practiced at this exercise, include the Avalonian Middle Pillar Focus for these centers as well. Pay attention to this process. Are some energy centers easier to activate than others? Are there places where pulling the energy down from the centers above feel restricted or blocked? Be sure to journal what goes on during this exercise each time you perform it. These experiences can provide valuable clues for your process work. Perhaps feeling a

block in your Womb Center is related to the issue you are presently working through. Perhaps bringing more water energy into your environment, or addressing the issue in Immrama to the corresponding landscape area can help you both clear the block and resolve the issue. Everything is connected.

8. When you have pulled the energy down from the top of your head through each energy center and have activated them, take some time to breathe the universal energy up and down through your body—down from the top of your head to Root as you inhale … up from Root to the top of your head as you exhale. Do this several times until you feel that the pathway of energy is clear and unobstructed.

9. Inhale now from deep within your center, down the line from the top of your head to your Root, connecting all your energy centers. Exhale this energy to fountain out from each of your energy centers to the farthest reaches of your aura structure. With each exhale, feel the energies you have aligned and opened expand to fill your entire energy field, and as it does so, feel your sphere of perception expand along with it. This is called "fluffing" your aura. Do this as many times as it takes to expand your energy field as far as possible.

10. Starting now from your left foot, breathe your energy up one side of your body to the top of your head as you inhale, then exhale it down the other side of your body to the opposite foot. Do this at least three times, more if it feels appropriate, and switch the direction of the energy flow, starting from your right foot and ending at your left.

11. Repeat the process starting from your toes up over the front of your body to the top of your head, then exhaling down your back to return to your heels. Again, do this at least three times before switching the direction of the energy from back to front.

12. Repeat the process diagonally across your body this time, breathing up from the toes of your left foot to the top of your head, then down your back to the ankle of the right foot. Reverse the process after having done this at least three times.

13. Finally, as you inhale, visualize energy spiraling up your body starting from your feet to the top of your head, and then exhile the spiral down to your feet again. Reverse the process after having done this at least three times.

14. Fluff your aura out again, feeling yourself connected, open, and expanded. Take some time in this space and note the differences in your mental, emotional, and spiritual state before and after performing this exercise. Be sure to journal your insights. Take a moment to thank the Universe. You are now ready to get to work or face the day at your optimal connection with self and the universe. You can now tap into your center with greater ease and your perspective on circumstances or information will be less colored by shadow-based fears and instincts. As with all things, the more you do this work, the easier it will become to connect and the more well laid the path to the All will be.

Avalonian Middle Pillar

Using this visualization while activating each of your energy centers will help connect you to the Avalonian archetype and reinforce the energetic correspondences between the inner and outer landscapes.

THIRD EYE CENTER   *I am the Soul of Avalon*
Divine Healer, Sovereign Lady
Eternal Goddess, birthing All
I am the Source of all Creation
The Soul of Avalon

THROAT CENTER	I am the Winds of Avalon
	Whispering secrets past the white flow
	Touching harp strings, bearing song
	I am the Breath of Inspiration
	The Winds of Avalon

HEART CENTER	I am the Heart of Avalon
	Igniting spirits, dancing circles
	Rounded hilltop's glowing beacon
	I am the Flame of Transformation
	The Heart of Avalon

WOMB CENTER	I am the Well of Avalon
	Souls' reflections, mystic symbols
	Silver mirror of the Moon
	I am the Womb of Generation
	The Well of Avalon

ROOT CENTER	I am the Tor of Avalon
	Suckling Daughters, ever sturdy
	From the Lady's sacred body
	I am the Root of life's Foundation
	The Tor of Avalon

Appendix 2

AVALONIAN RESOURCES

The Sacred Landscape

Chalice Well and Gardens

Here you will find a place of beauty, peace, and healing. Spiritual Pilgrims of all kinds have come to this special place from time immemorial. A quiet visit to the Well is essential for all who come to explore the mysteries and ancient lore of the Isle of Avalon. Come, find calm, and sit beside the waters of peace.

THE CHALICE WELL
Chilkwell Street
Glastonbury, Somerset
BA6 8DD United Kingdom
Tel: 01458 831154
Fax: 01458 835528
Website: www.chalicewell.org.uk

From overseas
Tel: +44 1458 831154
Fax: +44 1458 835528

Glastonbury Tor

www.glastonburytor.org.uk

The Glastonbury Tor site offers a wide range of relevant information about this mysterious and energetic hill, a world energy-centre on the ancient Isle of Avalon.

The White Spring

The Companions of the White Spring have transformed the Victorian stone reservoir through which the White Spring waters run, into the Water Temple of Avalon. Containing many shrines, it is an emerging masterwork of love and devotion, open to pilgrims and visitors alike.

THE WHITE SPRING
Well House Lane
Glastonbury, Somerset
BA6 8BL United Kingdom
Website: www.whitespring.org.uk

Friends of Bride's Mound

Founded in November 1995 and committed to its stated aims: "to preserve, protect, and manage the land and environment known as Bride's Mound."

FRIENDS OF BRIDE'S MOUND
c/o Glastonbury Opportunities
7 Abbey Mews
56-58 High Street
Glastonbury, Somerset
BA6 9DU United Kingdom
Website: http://www.friendsofbridesmound.com

Glastonbury Abbey

A comprehensive website detailing the history, myths and legends, and present-day offerings of Glastonbury Abbey—traditionally, the oldest above-ground church in the world.

GLASTONBURY ABBEY
The Abbey Gatehouse
Magdalene Street
Glastonbury, Somerset
BA6 9EL, United Kingdom
Website: www.glastonburyabbey.com

The Isle of Avalon

www.isleofavalon.co.uk
An excellent guide to the legends, sites, and atmosphere of Glastonbury.

Organizations and Events

The Sisterhood of Avalon

The Sisterhood of Avalon is a fully incorporated, nonprofit international Celtic Women's Mysteries Organization which seeks to balance intuitive wisdom with scholastic achievement. The SOA sponsors the Avalonian Thealogical Seminary; facilitates international training intensives; hosts Spiritual Pilgrimages to Wales, Glastonbury, and other Celtic sacred sites; publishes *The Tor Stone: A Quarterly Journal for Women's Mysteries* e-zine as well as a series of Goddess devotionals and other books through their publishing arm Ninth Wave Press; and provides a variety of learning opportunities for wisdoms shared and insights gained.

SISTERHOOD OF AVALON, INC.
P.O. Box 22
Seneca Falls, New York 13148 USA
Website: www.sisterhoodofavalon.org

Glastonbury Goddess Temple

Per the website: "Our vision is to create and maintain a permanent contemporary Goddess Temple openly dedicated to the Goddess in Glastonbury and its Otherworldly counterpart, the Isle of Avalon. The Goddess Temple is a sacred space open to all, which is specially set aside for the exploration and celebration of the Divine Feminine. It is a holy place where we can worship and honour Her in ways that are old and new and where all our love for Her is welcome."

GLASTONBURY GODDESS TEMPLE
The Glastonbury Experience
2-4 High Street
Glastonbury, Somerset
BA6 9DU United Kingdom
Website: www.goddesstemple.co.uk

The Goddess Conference

www.goddessconference.com

A popular festival held annually in Glastonbury and open to all women and men who love the Goddess.

Study

Avalonian Thealogical Seminary

The Avalonian Thealogical Seminary presents a rigorous training program designed to awaken the innate wisdom in every woman. The course work requires students to push through their perceived limitations and to expand their boundaries on mental, emotional, and spiritual levels. Less a course of study than a guide to effect lasting inner change, deeper understanding and connection to the Divine Feminine, the Avalonian Thealogical Seminary serves as a Midwife to consciously assist in the birth of the empowered woman within.

ATS

c/o Sisterhood of Avalon, Inc.

P.O. Box 22

Seneca Falls, New York 13148 USA

Website: www.avalonseminary.org

Ynys Afallon

www.ynysafallon.com

The homepage of Jhenah Telyndru featuring resources to facilitate the quest for Avalon, including: a calendar of Avalonian workshops and pilgrimages; chant and Immrama CDs; articles, music, and poetry inspired by the Avalonian Tradition—as well as updates on Jhenah's forthcoming books and projects.

The Isle of Avalon Foundation

www.isleofavalonfoundation.com

Based in the heart of the wonderful Somerset town of Glastonbury, this site offers a range of talks, courses of training, and workshops based on all aspects of life with an emphasis on the magic and spiritual nature of experience. With some of the most experienced tutors in their respective fields, the Foundation is a leading educational centre, with an international reputation, that enables its students to work with the unique transformational energies of Glastonbury—the original Isle of Avalon. Courses are available in a broad range of spiritual, metaphysical, healing, and personal-growth subjects.

In the Heart of the Goddess

www.kathyjones.co.uk

Kathy Jones is a healer, writer, ritual dramatist, teacher, priestess, initiatrix, and ceremonialist. She lives and works in Glastonbury and is co-founder of the Isle of Avalon Foundation, the Library of Avalon, the Bridget Healing Centre, the Goddess Conference, the Sanctuary at Glastonbury, and the Glastonbury Goddess Temple.

Labyrinth Resources

The Labyrinth Society

www.labyrinthsociety.org

The mission of the Labyrinth Society is to support all those who create, maintain, and use labyrinths, and to serve the global community by providing education, networking, and opportunities to experience transformation. Their website is a rich compendium of all things labyrinth, including a local labyrinth finder and resources for building or purchasing one for yourself.

Labyrinthos—The Labyrinth Resource Centre, Photo Library and Archive.

www.labyrinthos.net

Provides an information resource for those working with labyrinths and mazes, with extensive photographic and illustration libraries and professional consultation services for owners, designers, publishers, and producers. Labyrinthos publishes and stocks a wide range of maze and labyrinth related books, publications, and products from around the world and also provides lectures, slideshows, events, and tour services for enthusiasts and pilgrims on the labyrinthine path. They are publishers of *Caerdroia—the Journal of Mazes and Labyrinths*, a forum for all those interested in the history, development, and potential of labyrinths and mazes. It is the premier source of information for research, news, views, and theories.

Mid-Atlantic Geomancy

www.geomancy.org/labyrinths

An online resource that explores Earth Mysteries and the Geomantic Tradition. Features an amazing section about labyrinths, and includes a section about Glastonbury Tor.

Art of Awen

www.etsy.com/shop/artofawen

Among her Avalonian-themed offerings, ceramic artist Jocelyn Russell creates beautiful three-dimensional finger labyrinths based on the seven-circuit pattern as it manifests on Glastonbury Tor.

Art and Artisans

Lost Stones—The Preseli Bluestone People

www.loststones.co.uk

Legal suppliers of all types of Preseli Bluestone, the artisans of Lost Stones live and craft the stones in the Preseli Hills of Wales. They create beautiful jewelry, wands, and pendulums, and craft special sets of Nine Bluestones, of particular interest to practitioners of the Avalonian Tradition.

Emily Brunner

www.emilybrunner.com

Emily Brunner is an emerging artist and designer based in Cincinnati, Ohio. A Sister in the Avalonian Tradition, she counts among her inspirations the myths and legends of the ancient Celts. Among other artworks, she is co-creating the Avalonian Oracle with Jhenah Telyndru.

Alice Istanbul Designs

www.istanbuldesigns.com/

Alice Istanbul, a Canadian living in the United States, is a talented artisan whose inspired works feature Avalonian and Druidic designs.

Annabella and Company Creativity Collective

www.annabellaandcompany.com

Avalonian Alicia Grosso creates bath and body products, beadwork, and decorative objects that carry the energy of Avalon.

Brigid Ashwood

www.brigidashwood.com

Brigid Ashwood is one of the Internet's most popular fantasy artists. Influenced by Celtic myth, fairy legends, spirituality, and nature, she creates powerful images of women in their many guises. Her website offers beautiful altar pieces and inspired jewelry that tie into the Welsh Celtic tradition.

Publications

The Tor Stone

www.torstone.org

A quarterly journal charting the female path of personal growth and empowerment through the Mysteries of Avalon and with the guidance of the Goddess. Published at each of the four Celtic Holy Days by the Sisterhood of Avalon, each issue of *The Tor Stone* reflects the prominent energy of each portal and the ways in which our processes of healing and growth as women mirror this endless Cycle.

Online Source Materials

Mabinogi Translations

www.mabinogi.net

The Four Branches online. A new translation with annotations by Will Parker.

The Internet Sacred Text Archive

www.sacred-texts.com/neu/celt

An amazing online resource of hard-to-find and out-of-print public domain books and texts. Features a comprehensive section of Celtic materials.

BIBLIOGRAPHY

Aldhouse-Green, Miranda. *Celtic Goddesses*. London: British Museum Press, 1995.

———. *Celtic World*. Hampshire, UK: Routledge, 1995.

Aldhouse-Green, Miranda, and Ray Howell. *Celtic Wales*. Cardiff: University of Wales Press, 2000

Ashe, Geoffrey. *Avalonian Quest*. London: Metheun, 1982.

Barber, Chris, and David Pykitt. *Journey to Avalon: The Final Discovery of King Arthur*. Newburyport, MA: Weiser Books, 1997.

Bardon, Franz. *Initiation into Hermetics*. Blue Ridge Summit, PA: Brotherhood of Life, 1993.

Benham, Patrick. *The Avalonians*. Somerset, UK: Gothic Image Publications, 1993.

Blake, Steve and Scott Lloyd. *The Keys to Avalon*. Rockport, MA: Element Books, 2000.

Bord, Janet, and Colin Bord. *Guide to Ancient Sites in Britain*. Chicago: Academy Chicago, 1981.

Brennan, J. H. *Astral Doorways*. Newburyport, PA: Weiser Books, 1972.

Bromwich, Rachel, ed. *Trioedd Ynys Prydein—The Welsh Triads*. Cardiff: University of Wales Press, 1961.

Chalice Well Trust. *The Chalice Well, Glastonbury*, Information Booklet, (n.d.).

Coles, John, and Stephen Minnitt. *Industrious and Fairly Civilized: The Glastonbury Lake Village*. Somerset Levels Project and Somerset County Council Museums Service, 1995.

Cunliffe, Barry. *Iron Age Communities in Britain: An Account of England, Scotland and Wales from the Seventh Century BC until the Roman Conquest*. Hampshire, UK: Routledge, 1974.

Ford, Patrick K. *The Mabinogi, and Other Medieval Welsh Tales*. Berkeley: University of California Press, 1977.

Fortune, Dion. *Glastonbury: Avalon of the Heart*. Newburyport, PA: Weiser Books, 2000.

———. *Mystical Qabalah*. Newburyport, PA: Weiser Books, 2000.

Geoffrey of Monmouth. *The History of the Kings of Britain*. Translated by Lewis Thorpe. Chicago: Penguin, 1983 (1966).

———. "The Life of Merlin." Translated by John Jay Parry, in *University of Illinois Studies in Language and Literature, vol. X, no. 3*, The University of Illinois, Urbana, IL., 1925 Retrieved from: http://www.sacred-texts.com/neu/eng/vm/

Gibbs, Ray. *The Legendary Twelve Hides of Glastonbury*. Somerset, UK: Llanerch Enterprises, 1988.

Goodman, Felicitas. *Ecstatic Trance: New Ritual Body Postures*. Haarlem, Netherlands: Binkey Kok Publications, 2003.

Graves, Robert. *The White Goddess: A Historical Grammar of Poetic Myth*. London: Octagon Books, 1972.

Grieve, Maud. *A Modern Herbal, Volume 2*. New York: Dover Publications, 1971.

Harding, Derek William. *The Iron Age in Lowland Britain*. Hampshire, UK: Routledge, 1974.

Hawkins, Desmond. *Avalon and Sedgemoor*. Cornwall, UK: Tabb House, 1989.

Jones, Kathy. *In the Nature of Avalon*. Somerset, UK: Ariadne Publications, 2000.

Keightley, Thomas. *The Fairy Mythology, Illustrative of the Romance and Superstition of Various Countries*. London: H. G. Bohn, 1870.

Kondratiev, Alexei. *The Apple Branch: A Path to Celtic Ritual*. New York: Kensington Books, 2003.

Lonegren, Sig. *Mid-Atlantic Geomancy—Labyrinths* (n.d.). Retrieved from http://www.geomancy.org/labyrinths/index.html

Malory, Thomas. *Le Morte D'Arthur*. New York: Modern Library, 1999.

Mann, Nicholas. *Glastonbury Tor: A Guide to the History and Legends*. London: Annenterprise, 1985.

———. *The Isle of Avalon Sacred Mysteries of Arthur and Glastonbury*. Somerset, UK: Green Magic, 2001.

Markale, Jean. *Women of the Celts*. Rochester, VT: Inner Traditions, 1986.

Matthews, Caitlin. *The Celtic Tradition*. Rockport, MA: Element Books, 1996.

Matthews, John. *Tales of the Celtic Otherworld*. London: Blandford, 1998.

McHardy, Stuart. *The Quest for the Nine Maidens*. Edinburgh, UK: Luath Press, 2003.

Michell, John. *New Light on the Ancient Mystery of Glastonbury*. Somerset, UK: Gothic Image Publications, 1990.

Plants for a Future. "Isatis tinctoria." Retrieved from http://www.pfaf.org/database/plants.php?Isatis+tinctoria, 2000.

Possehl, Gregory. *The Indus Civilization: A Contemporary Perspective*. Lanham, MD: AltaMira Press, 2003.

Rahtz, Philip. *Glastonbury: Myth and Archaeology*. London: Trafalgar Square, 2003.

Reade, W. Winwood. *The Veil of Isis, or, Mysteries of the Druids*. Newcastle, CA: Newcastle Publishing Company, Inc., 1992.

Regardie, Israel, et al. *The Middle Pillar: The Balance Between Mind and Magic*. St. Paul, MN: Llewellyn Publications, 1998.

Roberts, Anthony. *Glastonbury: Ancient Avalon, New Jerusalem*. London: Rider & Company, 1978.

Rolleston, T. W. *Celtic Myths and Legends*. Dover Publications, 1990.

Rolleston, Thomas. *Myths and Legends of the Celtic Race*. London: G. G. Harrap & Company, 1911. Retrieved from http://www.sacred-texts.com/neu/celt/mlcr/index.htm

Skene, William F. *The Four Ancient Books of Wales*. London: Edmonston and Douglas, 1868. Retrieved from http://www.sacred-texts.com/neu/celt/fab/index.htm

Spence, Lewis. *The Mysteries of Britain: Secret Rites and Traditions of Ancient Britain*. London: Senate, 1994.

Tennyson, Alfred. *Idylls of the King*. Chicago: Penguin Books, 1989.

Three Initiates. *Kybalion: A Study of the Hermetic Philosophy of Ancient Egypt and Greece*. Batavia, IL: Yoga Publication Society, 1908.

West, Melissa Gayle. *Exploring the Labyrinth: A Guide for Healing and Spiritual Growth*. New York: Broadway, 2000.

Wilde, Lyn. *Celtic Women: In Legend, Myth and History*. Poole, UK: Blandford, 1997.

Williams, Mary, ed. *Glastonbury and Britain: A Study in Patterns*. East Sussex, UK: Research Into Lost Knowledge Organization (RILKO) Books, 1990.

Wright, John F. *A Compilation of Triads: The Traditional Laws, Customs, and Wisdoms of The Pre-Christian Celtic People Of What Is Now Known As Scotland, Wales, And Ireland*, 1995. Retrieved from http://www.featherlessbiped.com/rowanhold/3things.htm

INDEX

Wearyall Hill, 44, 47, 160, 178–180, 182

White Spring, 18–19, 61–62, 133–138, 140, 142, 186, 206, 208, 245, 264, 274, 277

Salmon /Otter, 92

Salmon of Llyn Llyw, 157

Samhain. *See* Calan Gaeaf

Scilly Islands, 178

Scrying, 100–104, 147, 265–266

Sea Within, 189, 191–193

Self, 4–5, 10, 12–16, 22, 25–32, 35–36, 46–47, 53, 55, 62–65, 88–90, 94, 96, 99, 105, 108–110, 113, 115, 118–120, 123, 126, 130–131, 136, 140–142, 144, 150–153, 156–157, 163, 165–169, 172–175, 183, 188–190, 193, 215–218, 221–224, 226–229, 238, 240, 243–244, 246–250, 253, 255–258, 271, 277–279, 282

Shadow, 2–3, 11–12, 14–15, 26–31, 34–35, 61–64, 66, 87, 90, 94, 98, 105, 108–110, 114, 119–120, 131, 133, 136, 150–151, 154, 156, 158, 167, 172–173, 177, 183, 189–191, 201, 216–219, 221–222, 225, 227–228, 235, 244, 246–248, 253–254

Shape-shifting, 29

Sight, 3–4, 12, 15, 33, 52, 56–57, 59, 65–66, 72, 90, 94, 98, 100–103, 105, 114, 116–117, 119, 134, 144, 152, 170, 172, 176, 183, 246, 253, 258

Silver Branch, 56, 242, 257–258, 261–262, 267

Sisterhood of Avalon, 46, 93, 121

Sky Within, 189, 192–194

Somerset, 16–17, 41, 50, 111, 176–177, 182

Somerset Levels, 17, 176–177

Sovereignty, 6, 12–13, 15, 22, 26, 34–35, 42, 44, 47, 63, 65, 85, 136, 139, 141, 150, 153, 156, 158, 166–168, 170, 175, 187, 198, 232, 236, 239, 241–243, 246, 248–250, 271–272, 278

Spirit, 6, 18–19, 30, 32, 39, 43, 48, 61, 72, 113, 162, 164, 175, 183, 185–187, 190, 195, 197–198, 212, 216, 235, 241, 258, 274, 278

Spoils of Annwn. *See* Preiddeu Annwn

St. Brigid, 180

St. Michael's Tower, 114

Stag of Redynvre, 156

Stonehenge, 177, 179, 261

Symbols, 9, 22, 33, 39, 49, 96, 103, 125, 142–143, 145–146, 190, 222–225, 228, 236, 255, 259, 264, 267, 279–280, 283

Taliesin, 24–25, 27, 32–33, 120–121, 175, 235, 244

Third Eye Center, 186, 274, 278–279, 282

Third Quarter, 91, 253–254

Three Rays, 29, 70, 163, 244

Three Realms
  Realm of Land, 156, 188, 191
  Realm of Sea, 157, 188, 192
  Realm of Sky, 157, 189, 193

Three Realms Working
  Land Within, 189–192
  Sea Within, 189, 191–193
  Sky Within, 189, 192–194

Throat Center, 186, 192, 274, 277, 280, 283

Tiphereth, 277

Tor Valley
  Modron's Mound (Chalice Hill), 18, 62, 208

Womb Center, 191, 274–276, 281, 283
Women of Avalon, 10, 22, 25, 35, 46, 61, 100–101, 121, 167, 252, 255
Wounded King, 11, 22, 34, 42, 93, 154
Wounded Queen, 163
Wren/Hawk, 133

Y Tarddell Rudd, 200, 203–204
Y Tarddell Wen, 200, 206–207

Y Twrr, 200, 205
Yesod, 276
Ynis Witrin, 176, 183
Ynys Afallon (Island of Avalon), 4, 8, 46, 175, 200, 209, 232
Ynys Mon (Anglesey), 46, 47, 166
Ynys Prydein, 113, 233

GET MORE AT LLEWELLYN.COM

Visit us online to browse hundreds of our books and decks, plus sign up to receive our e-newsletters and exclusive online offers.

- Free tarot readings • Spell-a-Day • Moon phases
- Recipes, spells, and tips • Blogs • Encyclopedia
- Author interviews, articles, and upcoming events

GET SOCIAL WITH LLEWELLYN

Find us on **Facebook**

www.Facebook.com/LlewellynBooks

Follow us on

www.Twitter.com/Llewellynbooks

GET BOOKS AT LLEWELLYN

LLEWELLYN ORDERING INFORMATION

Druid Magic
The Practice of Celtic Wisdom
Maya Magee Sutton, Ph.D., and Nicholas R. Mann

Enter into the adventure of awakening the Druid within. If you want to explore the Druid mysteries, this book will help you roll up your mystical sleeves. For those who want to know who the Celts and the Druids really were, this book presents the Celtic myths, Greek and Roman writings, and archaeological evidence that allows the ancient Druid tradition to speak for itself. If you want to learn the primary tenets of Druidry, or visit the Celtic Otherworlds and lie in the "streambed of Druidic inspiration," this book will take you on that journey.

978-1-56718-481-5
368 pp., 7 $^1/_2$ x 9 $^1/_8$ $17.95

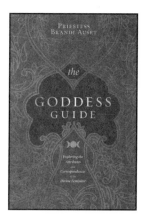

The Goddess Guide

Exploring the Attributes and Correspondences of the Divine Feminine

Priestess Brandi Auset

Which goddess will help me invite love into my life? Is there an Indian goddess who presides over wealth? Does Kuan Yin represent compassion or truth?

For anyone who's ever wondered which form of the Divine Feminine to invoke for a particular ritual, blessing, prayer, or meditation, *The Goddess Guide* is a goddess-send! As the first and only book of its kind on the market today, this invaluable at-a-glance cross-reference offers instant info on more than 400 goddesses from diverse cultures around the world—simply look up the keyword that best matches your intention.

The goddesses are organized according to their names, attributes, colors, elements, sabbats, light and dark feminine aspects (maidens, mothers, and crones), and geographical regions. Get to know all aspects of the goddesses who bring about healing, heightened passion, success, weight loss, and much more. This reference book deserves a spot on every serious practitioner's bookshelf.

978-0-7387-1551-3
336 pp., 6 x 9 $16.95

TO ORDER, CALL 1-877-NEW-WRLD
Prices subject to change without notice
Order at Llewellyn.com 24 hours a day, 7 days a week!

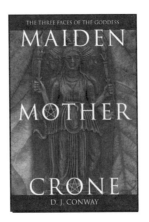

MAIDEN, MOTHER, CRONE
The Three Faces of the Goddess
D. J. CONWAY

The Triple Goddess is with every one of us each day of our lives. In our inner journeys toward spiritual evolution, each woman and man goes through the stages of Maiden (infant to puberty), Mother (adult and parent), and Crone (aging elder).

Maiden, Mother, Crone is a guide to the myths and interpretations of the Great Goddess archetype and her three faces—so that we may better understand and gracefully accept the cycle of birth and death.

978-0-87542-171-1
240 pp., 6 x 9 $15.95

THE DRUID ISLE
ELLEN EVERT HOPMAN

The Druid Isle takes you into the world of Ethne, a Druid healer, and her warrior partner, Ruad. When their beautiful daughter Aife undertakes training on a Druid island, she falls in love with Lucius, a handsome young man who has traded his priestly studies at a Christian monastery for the Druid life. But their love—and their beliefs—are threatened in the face of a lustful king and relentless Roman monks.

Set on a third-century island off the coast of Scotland, this instructional Celtic tale delves deeper into the spiritual mystery of the Druids and offers a fascinating look at the Romans, Gauls, and Britons.

978-0-7387-1956-6
288 pp., 6 x 9 $18.95

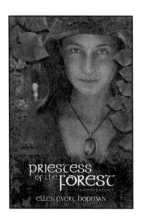

PRIESTESS OF THE FOREST
A Druid Journey
ELLEN EVERT HOPMAN

In the tradition of Marion Zimmer Bradley's Mists of Avalon, Ellen Evert Hopman weaves Druid history and spirituality into an engaging love story. This Bardic teaching tale is set in a fictional third-century Ireland when Christianity is sweeping across the Celtic Isles. During this time of crisis, love blooms between Ethne, a Druid healer, and her patient, a Fennid warrior. Their passionate affair suffers a tragic blow when Ethne is called upon to become the high queen.

Told from the Druid perspective, Hopman recreates the daily life, magical practices, politics, and spiritual lives of the ancient Celts during this historic turning point. Druid holy days, rites, rituals, herbal lore, and more are brought to life in this Celtic fantasy—illuminating Druidic teachings and cultural wisdom.

978-0-7387-1262-8
360 pp., 6 x 9 $18.95